LITERARY LIFELINES

Produced by The Diagram Group

Editorial Director: *Nicola Chalton*
Editorial: *Margaret Doyle, Theodore Rowland Entwistle, Bridget Giles, Moira Johnston, Reet Nelis, John Latimer Smith, Jamie Stokes*

Art Director: *Darren Bennett*
Art and Design: *Chris Allcott, Brian Hewson, Jane Johnson, Kyri Kyriacou, Kathy McDougall, Philip Patenall, Graham Rosewarne*

Production Director: *Richard Hummerstone*
Production: *Mark Carry, Lee Lawrence, Eitetsu Nozawa, Philip Richardson*

Research Director: *Patricia Robertson*
Research: *Carole Dease, Peter Dease, Jamie Joseph, Ruth Joseph, Laura Mahoney, Ed Morris, Susannah Sayler, Matt Smout, Darrell Spencer*

Contributors: *Nancy Bailey, Annelie Beaton, Jeanne Brady, Nicola Chalton, Deedee Cuddihy, Chris von Dehsen, Margaret Doyle, Theodore Rowland Entwistle, Bridget Giles, Brian Glancey, Alice Goldie, Paula Hammond, Elaine Henderson, Jonathan Hilton, Jane Horwood, Dr. Saul Kelly, Ann Kramer, David Lambert, Min Lee, Howard Loxton, Fiona Moore, Christopher Pick, Maureen Rissik, Jamie Stokes, John Williams, Dr. Robert Youngson*

Published 1998 by
Grolier Educational
Danbury, Connecticut 06816

Published by arrangement with
Diagram Visual Information Limited
195 Kentish Town Road
London
NW5 2JU

Art and picture credits listed on page 256.

Literary lifelines
     p. cm.
   Includes bibliographical references and index.
   ISBN 0–7172–9211–8 (set)
   1. Literature—Bio–bibliography—Juvenile literature. 2. Authors–
 –Biography—Juvenile literature.
PN451.L57   1998
809
[B]—DC21   97–49180
                                                      CIP
                                                       AC

Cataloging information to be obtained directly from Grolier Educational
First Edition
Printed in the United States of America

LITERARY LIFELINES

McC-Pat

VOLUME 7

**THE
DIAGRAM
GROUP**

GROLIER EDUCATIONAL
Sherman Turnpike, Danbury, Connecticut 06816

CONTENTS

INTRODUCTION

The ten volumes of *Literary Lifelines* contain concise biographies of 1,000 leading figures in the history of world literature. Alongside each biography is a chronology of the major world events that took place during each author's lifetime. This core reference set of writers from all over the world represents nearly 3,000 years of creative writing – from works of the ancient Greeks, through the recognized classics of world literature, and up to the famous blockbusters of today. Novelists, poets, playwrights, and short-story writers are included, and all literary forms are covered – from children's stories and fantasy to science fiction and thrillers.

Each author in *Literary Lifelines* gets two pages (an example is shown opposite). On the left-hand page there is a **biography**, a list of the **author's works**, a portrait of the author, and an image of a book cover for one of the author's books or some other object or scene relevant to the author's life. On the right-hand page there is a list of **other writers** who are similar to the author in some way (they were writing in the same period, come from the same region, or were writing the same type of literature). For example, for Petrarch there is a list of other medieval writers, for Leo Tolstoy there is a list of other Russian writers, and for J.R.R. Tolkien there is a list of other fantasy writers. Below this list is an illustrated chronology of **world events** that took place around the time the author was alive.

The **biography** (left-hand page) on each author includes an outline of the author's life and an introduction to the author's works. It is designed to give a clear and concise statement of what the author is best known for and to help the reader understand some of the influences that shaped the author's writing. For instance, it might be interesting to learn that Cervantes, the author of *Don Quixote*, was captured by pirates and spent five years as a slave, and that when the crime writer James Ellroy was ten years old his mother was brutally murdered by a killer who was never found. Literary terms and historical events that are in bold in the biography are explained in the **glossary**, which appears at the end of each volume (beginning on page 208). Names of other authors mentioned in the biography who have an entry of their own in *Literary Lifelines* are set in small capitals (for example, CHARLES DICKENS).

The **author's works** (left-hand page) are listed in date order. The dates given are of first publication or, in the case of plays, of first performance. Titles of books, long poems, and other works published on their own are in italics (for example, *Bleak House*); short poems, short stories, and other works not published on their own are in quotes (for example, "O Captain! My Captain!").

The list of **other writers** (right-hand page) is intended to help readers make connections between authors. For instance, from this list the reader can discover at a glance that Virgil and Horace wrote in the same period, that Raymond Chandler and

Jim Thompson wrote similar types of books, and that Anton Chekhov and Ivan Turgenev were both Russian writers. These links between authors will encourage readers to find out about other writers.

The chronology of **world events** (right-hand page) gives the reader an idea of the historical context in which the author lived and wrote. It can be seen from this chart, for instance, that during the American Civil War of 1861–65 Leo Tolstoy was in his 20s; referring back to the left-hand page, the list of works shows that this is the time at which he began writing *War and Peace*. Those who explore further will find that in the same period Lewis Carroll published *Alice's Adventures in Wonderland*, Victor Hugo published *Les Misérables*, and Charles Dickens produced *Great Expectations*.

The 1,000 authors of *Literary Lifelines* are arranged alphabetically through the ten volumes. The **contents** page at the front of each volume lists the authors contained in that volume. All 1,000 authors are indexed at the back of each volume. In the **index** (which begins on page 216) authors are listed by name, by region, and by literary genre. Thus, for example, the writer Hans Christian Andersen can be found by looking for him under "A" for Andersen, or under "S" for "Scandinavian writers," or under "C" for "children's writers"; similarly, George Eliot can be found under "E" for Eliot, "B" for "British and Irish writers," "W" for "women writers," or "N" for "novelists." Likewise, Alice Walker can be found under "W" for Walker, "A" for "American writers," "A" for "African-American writers," "W" for "women writers," or "N" for "novelists." The index also includes some of the most famous works mentioned in *Literary Lifelines*, as well as some of literature's most enduring characters. So readers who have heard of *The Color Purple*, for example, can find it in the index and discover who wrote it, and those who love Peter Pan or the superspy James Bond can find out who created them.

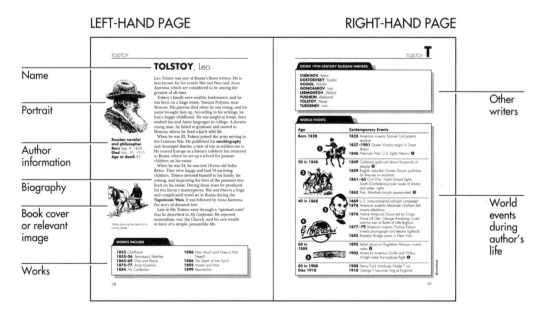

McCARTHY, Mary

Politics and the social pretenses of liberal intellectuals are at the heart of Mary McCarthy's work, which includes seven novels, many short stories, and essays.

McCarthy was born in Seattle. Her parents both died of flu when she was six, and she was raised by relatives in a strict Catholic environment. This upbringing is the subject of one of her novels, the **autobiographical** *Memories of a Catholic Girlhood*. After attending private school she went to Vassar College, where she met the poets ELIZABETH BISHOP and MURIEL RUKEYSER.

McCarthy graduated with honors at age 21, and soon afterward she married the first of her four husbands and moved to New York City. There she mixed with writers and other intellectuals, and in 1942, at age 30, she published her first novel. *The Company She Keeps* is a **satire** about New York intellectuals. She often used her friends, and even herself, as models for her characters. *The Group*, her bestselling novel, focuses on a group of graduates and their experiences after college. It is a comic exploration of the values and lifestyles of college-educated, middle-class women, following the group of friends through first sexual experiences, marriage, and domestic duties. The book was made into a movie in 1966.

In later works McCarthy explored political themes, including the **Vietnam War**, the Watergate scandal (in *The Mask of State*), and terrorism (in *Cannibals and Missionaries*). Most of her work, both fiction and nonfiction, is about the response of intellectuals to political and moral problems.

American novelist and short-story writer
Born Jun. 21, 1912
Died Oct. 25, 1989
Age at death 77

Book cover for one of McCarthy's novels

WORKS INCLUDE

1942 *The Company She Keeps*
1949 *The Oasis*
1955 *A Charmed Life*
1957 *Memories of a Catholic Girlhood*
1961 *On the Contrary*

1963 *The Group*
1971 *Birds of America*
1974 *The Mask of State*
1979 *Cannibals and Missionaries*
1987 *How I Grew*

OTHER POST-1940 NOVELISTS

BALDWIN, James
BELLOW, Saul
CAMUS, Albert
GARCÍA MÁRQUEZ, Gabriel
GOLDING, William
HELLER, Joseph
IRVING, John
LESSING, Doris

MORRISON, Toni
SALINGER, J.D.
SINGER, Isaac Bashevis
SOLZHENITSYN, Aleksandr
UPDIKE, John
VIDAL, Gore
WALKER, Alice

SEE INDEX FOR FULL LIST

WORLD EVENTS

Age	Contemporary Events
Born 1912	**1914–18** World War I
	1917 Russian Revolution establishes Communist government ❶
	1926 British scientist John Logie Baird demonstrates television
	1927 Joseph Stalin becomes dictator of Russia
	1931 Empire State Building in New York City completed
20 in 1932	**1933** Nazi Party, led by Adolf Hitler, gains control in Germany
	1939–45 World War II: allies, led by U.S. and Great Britain, fight axis powers, led by Germany and Japan
	1945 U.S. drops first atomic bombs on Japan ❷
	1950–53 Korean War: North Korea and China fight South Korea, the U.S., and United Nations troops
40 in 1952	**1957** Eisenhower sends troops to Little Rock, Arkansas, to ensure school desegregation
	1960 John F. Kennedy elected president ❸
	1964–75 Vietnam War: war between communist North Vietnam and U.S. forces supporting South Vietnam ❹
	1967 Arabs and Israelis fight in Six Day War
	1969 American astronaut walks on Moon ❺
60 in 1972	**1980** Ronald Reagan elected president
	1981 U.S. launches first space shuttle
Dies 1989	**1989** Communist regimes fall throughout Eastern Europe

© DIAGRAM

McCULLERS, Carson

American novelist
Born Feb. 19, 1917
Died Sep. 29, 1967
Age at death 50

Carson McCullers was one of the greatest novelists of the American South. Her best-known novels were completed by the time she was 34. She wrote about feelings that are common to a lot of us; about people who think they're different and don't fit in and who feel sad and lonely as a result.

McCullers was born Lula Carson Smith in Columbus, Georgia, and like her characters she didn't fit in too well when she was growing up. Encouraged by her mother, she spent a lot of time on her own, playing the piano and writing plays. At the age of 17 she moved to New York City, where she took a series of odd jobs and studied writing part time. At 20 she married Reeves McCullers, eventually divorcing and remarrying him.

McCullers's first novel, *The Heart Is a Lonely Hunter*, was published when she was only 23. It tells the story of a deaf-mute man and the troubled people who confide in him. Critics praised the book and were astounded that it had been written by someone so young. Six years later her most successful novel, *The Member of the Wedding*, was published. Like McCullers's first book, it is set in the American South and centers on a group of characters troubled by feelings of loneliness and inner turmoil. One critic called it the work of "a genius." She later adapted the novel as a successful play.

A short novel, *The Ballad of the Sad Cafe*, and a collection of stories followed. Only a few years later McCullers, who had been sick on and off since childhood, was struck down by a series of terrible illnesses from which she never fully recovered.

Scene from a performance of *The Member of the Wedding*

WORKS INCLUDE

1940 *The Heart Is a Lonely Hunter*
1941 *Reflections in a Golden Eye*
1946 *The Member of the Wedding*
1951 *The Ballad of the Sad Cafe*
1958 *The Square Root of Wonderful*

1961 *Clock without Hands*
1964 *Sweet as a Pickle and Clean as a Pig*
1971 *The Mortgaged Heart* (published after she died)

OTHER POST-1940 NOVELISTS

BALDWIN, James
BELLOW, Saul
CAMUS, Albert
GARCÍA MÁRQUEZ, Gabriel
GOLDING, William
HELLER, Joseph
IRVING, John
LESSING, Doris

MORRISON, Toni
SALINGER, J.D.
SINGER, Isaac Bashevis
SOLZHENITSYN, Aleksandr
UPDIKE, John
VIDAL, Gore
WALKER, Alice

SEE INDEX FOR FULL LIST

WORLD EVENTS

Age	Contemporary Events
Born 1917 	**1917** Russian Revolution establishes Communist government **1926** British scientist John Logie Baird demonstrates television **1927** Joseph Stalin becomes dictator of Russia ❶ **1929** Stock Market crash ushers in Great Depression ❷ **1931** Empire State Building in New York City completed **1933** Nazi Party, led by Adolf Hitler, gains control in Germany
20 in 1937 	**1939–45** World War II: allies, led by U.S. and Great Britain, fight axis powers, led by Germany and Japan **1945** U.S. drops first atomic bombs on Japan **1945** United Nations (UN), organization working for betterment of humanity, founded **1950–53** Korean War: North Korea and China fight South Korea, the U.S., and United Nations troops ❸
40 in 1957   **Dies 1967**	**1957** Eisenhower sends troops to Little Rock, Arkansas, to ensure school desegregation **1960** John F. Kennedy elected president **1963** Led by Rev. Martin Luther King, Jr., thousands march on Washington DC to press for civil rights for African Americans ❹ **1964–75** Vietnam War: war between communist North Vietnam and U.S. forces supporting South Vietnam ❺ **1967** Arabs and Israelis fight in Six Day War

McEWAN, Ian

English novelist, short-story writer, and screenwriter
Born Jun. 21, 1948

Some critics think that Ian McEwan could become one of the greatest British writers of his generation. Others find his work deliberately shocking, with little literary merit. Most do agree, however, that he writes elegantly and carefully in an icy-clear and at times unnervingly funny style. McEwan has been dubbed "Ian Macabre" for his fascination with vice, child abuse, and violence.

McEwan was born in the army town of Aldershot, southern England. His father was in the army, and McEwan grew up in distant parts of what was then the British Empire, including Singapore and North Africa. After attending more than seven different schools, McEwan was sent to a boarding school in England, which he hated. He then studied English at the universities of Sussex and East Anglia.

McEwan's first publication was a collection of short stories called *First Love, Last Rites*, which he wrote for his course at East Anglia. Although written by a 27-year-old college student, the book won a major British award and was widely reviewed in the U.S. and Britain. The stories deal with a variety of sexual fantasies and perversions, and McEwan has since said the collection was like an outpouring after years of repression that stemmed from his childhood.

The Cement Garden, McEwan's first novel, also created a stir. Four children attempt to conceal the deaths of their parents, and the elder two take to playing "Mummy and Daddy" too seriously. Three of his novels (*The Innocent*, *The Comfort of Strangers*, and *The Cement Garden*) have been made into films, and McEwan has also written screenplays and plays.

McEwan's acclaimed and controversial first novel

WORKS INCLUDE

1975 First Love, Last Rites	**1981** The Comfort of Strangers
1978 The Cement Garden	**1987** The Child in Time
1978 In Between the Sheets and Other Stories	**1990** The Innocent
	1992 Black Dogs
1981 The Imitation Game	**1997** Enduring Love

OTHER POST-1940 NOVELISTS

BALDWIN, James
BELLOW, Saul
CAMUS, Albert
GARCÍA MÁRQUEZ, Gabriel
GOLDING, William
HELLER, Joseph
IRVING, John
LESSING, Doris

MORRISON, Toni
SALINGER, J.D.
SINGER, Isaac Bashevis
SOLZHENITSYN, Aleksandr
UPDIKE, John
VIDAL, Gore
WALKER, Alice

SEE INDEX FOR FULL LIST

WORLD EVENTS

Age	Contemporary Events
Born 1948	**1950–53** Korean War: North Korea and China fight South Korea, the U.S., and United Nations troops **1957** Eisenhower sends troops to Little Rock, Arkansas, to ensure school desegregation
10 in 1958 	**1960** John F. Kennedy elected president ❶ **1963** Led by Rev. Martin Luther King, Jr., thousands march on Washington DC to press for civil rights for African Americans ❷ **1964–75** Vietnam War: war between communist North Vietnam and U.S. forces supporting South Vietnam
20 in 1968 	**1969** American astronaut walks on Moon ❸ **1975–79** Communist forces murder hundreds of thousands in Cambodia ❹
30 in 1978 	**1981** U.S. launches first space shuttle **1987** Gorbachev begins reforms in USSR: perestroika (restructuring) and glasnost (openness)
40 in 1988 	**1989** Communist regimes fall throughout Eastern Europe **1991** Gulf War: UN forces, led by U.S., defeat Iraq and free Kuwait **1992** Bill Clinton elected president **1994** First multiracial elections in South Africa end years of white minority rule. They are won by Nelson Mandela, African National Congress leader ❺

© DIAGRAM

McGINLEY, Phyllis

American poet and children's writer
Born Mar. 21, 1905
Died Feb. 22, 1978
Age at death 72

Times — — Three

Poems by
Phyllis McGinley

A collection of McGinley's award-winning poetry

Phyllis McGinley's humorous poetry commenting on the details of middle-class lives was widely popular in her time and earned her a **Pulitzer Prize**. She has been called the best American woman writer of light verse.

McGinley was born in Ontario, Oregon, where she grew up in a Roman Catholic family. As a child she began writing poetry. After graduating from college (she had attended the University of Southern California and the University of Utah), she continued to write and to publish poems in literary magazines while supporting herself by teaching and doing odd jobs. She eventually settled in New York City, where she began to publish in the *New Yorker* magazine.

McGinley published her first collection of poems, *On the Contrary*, when she was 29. Over the next decades she published a number of collections, including *Love Letters*, which earned her the EDNA ST. VINCENT MILLAY Memorial Award. Her collection *Times Three* won the Pulitzer Prize in 1961, the first book of light verse to do so. It contained an introduction by the great English poet W.H. AUDEN, who praised her work highly.

McGinley wrote about relationships and domestic life, including many funny observations of children and marriage. These themes are reflected in some of her book titles, for example, *Husbands Are Difficult*. She was a skillful **satirist**, poking fun at the attitudes and lifestyles of the middle class, her primary audience. McGinley also wrote 17 children's books and a book on saints.

WORKS INCLUDE

1934 *On the Contrary*
1937 *One More Manhattan*
1940 *A Pocketful of Wry*
1941 *Husbands Are Difficult*
1954 *Love Letters*

1959 *Province of the Heart*
1960 *Times Three*
1962 *Boys Are Awful*
1964 *Sixpence in Her Shoe*
1969 *Saint-Watching*

OTHER POST-1940 POETS

ANGELOU, Maya
BISHOP, Elizabeth
BRODSKY, Joseph
DUNCAN, Robert
GINSBERG, Allen
HAYDEN, Robert
HEANEY, Seamus
HUGHES, Ted

LOWELL, Robert
PAZ, Octavio
PLATH, Sylvia
SEXTON, Anne
THOMAS, Dylan
WALCOTT, Derek
YEVTUSHENKO, Yevgeny

SEE INDEX FOR FULL LIST

WORLD EVENTS

Age	Contemporary Events
Born 1905	**1908** Henry Ford introduces Model T car **1914–18** World War I **1917** Russian Revolution establishes Communist government ❶
20 in 1925	**1926** British scientist John Logie Baird demonstrates television **1927** Joseph Stalin becomes dictator of Russia **1931** Empire State Building in New York City completed **1933** Nazi Party, led by Adolf Hitler, gains control in Germany **1939–45** World War II: allies, led by U.S. and Great Britain, fight axis powers, led by Germany and Japan
40 in 1945	**1945** U.S. drops first atomic bombs on Japan ❷ **1950–53** Korean War: North Korea and China fight South Korea, the U.S., and United Nations troops **1957** Eisenhower sends troops to Little Rock, Arkansas, to ensure school desegregation **1960** John F. Kennedy elected president **1961** East Germans build Berlin Wall ❸ **1964–75** Vietnam War: war between communist North Vietnam and U.S. forces supporting South Vietnam ❹
60 in 1965 **Dies 1978**	**1967** Arabs and Israelis fight in Six Day War **1969** American astronaut walks on Moon **1975–79** Communist forces murder hundreds of thousands in Cambodia ❺

© DIAGRAM

McGONAGALL, William

William McGonagall was a 19th-century Scottish writer who is often described as the worst poet in the world.

McGonagall was born in Scotland, the son of an immigrant Irish cloth weaver. After spending some time in the remote Scottish islands, the McGonagall family settled in the city of Dundee. William learned his father's trade and became a weaver.

McGonagall married when he was 16. He lived a quiet life, occasionally acting in plays at the theater in Dundee. His literary career was slow to begin; his first book of verse, *Poetic Gems*, was published when he was 52. Soon he had a dedicated group of fans who found his work funny and refreshingly simple.

After his first poems began to appear in newspapers and magazines, McGonagall made a series of tours in Scotland and gave public readings of his verses. In the city of Edinburgh crowds of college students turned up to hear him read. His fame quickly spread. In 1880 he visited London and in 1887 gave readings in New York City.

Most people did not think that McGonagall's poetry was good, but many people found it extremely funny. McGonagall himself did not intend his poems to be comic. He wrote about Scotland, people he met, and events in the news. One of his most famous poems, "The Tay Bridge Disaster," describes the destruction of a bridge and the train on it by a violent storm.

Scottish poet
Born 1830
Died 1902
Age at death c. 72

Scene from the film *The Great McGonagall*

WORKS INCLUDE

1890 *Poetic Gems*

OTHER 19TH-CENTURY POETS

BROWNING, Elizabeth Barrett
BROWNING, Robert
BRYANT, William Cullen
BYRON, Lord
COLERIDGE, Samuel Taylor
DICKINSON, Emily
DUNBAR, Paul Laurence
HOUSMAN, A.E.

KEATS, John
LONGFELLOW, Henry Wadsworth
SHELLEY, Percy Bysshe
SWINBURNE, Algernon Charles
TENNYSON, Alfred
WHITMAN, Walt
WORDSWORTH, William

SEE INDEX FOR FULL LIST

WORLD EVENTS

Age	Contemporary Events
Born 1830 	**1834** American inventor Cyrus McCormick patents reaper, machine used to harvest grain **1835** American inventor Samuel Colt patents revolver **1846** Mexican War: U.S. fights Mexico **1849** California gold rush draws thousands of people ❶
20 in 1850 	**1859** English naturalist Charles Darwin publishes his theories on evolution **1861–65** Civil War: North (Union) fights South (Confederacy) over issues of slavery and states' rights **1865** Pres. Abraham Lincoln assassinated ❷ **1869** U.S. transcontinental railroad completed
40 in 1870 	**1876** American scientist Alexander Graham Bell invents telephone **1876** Native American Sioux led by Crazy Horse kill Gen. George Armstrong Custer and his men at Battle of Little Bighorn ❸ **1877–79** American inventor Thomas Edison invents phonograph and electric lightbulb **1883** Brooklyn Bridge opens in New York
60 in 1890  **Dies 1902**	**1890** Last major battle of the Indian Wars is fought at Wounded Knee, South Dakota **1895** Italian physicist Guglielmo Marconi invents radio ❹ **1896** First modern Olympic Games held in Athens, Greece

© DIAGRAM

McKAY, Claude

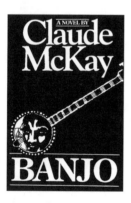

Jamaican-born American poet and novelist
Born Sep. 15, 1889
Died May 22, 1948
Age at death 58

Book cover for a novel by McKay

Claude McKay was a leading figure of the **Harlem Renaissance** – an explosion of African-American literary and artistic talent in 1920s New York.

McKay, the youngest of 11 children, was born in Jamaica, then a British colony. An older brother, a schoolteacher, introduced him to literature, science, and politics, encouraging him to question authority and think for himself. McKay's first poetry book, *Constab Ballads*, was published when he was 23, and it won a literary prize. He used the prize money to travel to America, where he settled in New York City.

McKay had been taught to be proud of his heritage, so he was shocked to encounter racism for the first time in America. At age 30 he published his best-known poem, "If We Must Die." It expresses both McKay's love for America and his hatred of racism and was written in response to the racial violence that erupted in America in 1919. Aged 33, McKay published *Harlem Shadows*, his most famous collection. These are angry poems based on McKay's experience of the constant degradation endured by the African-American community. Scholars have described the book as the inspiration for the Harlem Renaissance. After the publication of *Harlem Shadows* McKay went to Marseilles, in France, where he lived for ten years, and where he wrote *Home to Harlem*, his most highly regarded novel.

McKay had a major influence on black America's search for identity. His books were widely read at the height of the **civil rights movement** in the 1960s. He remained dedicated throughout his life to the fight against racism and injustice.

WORKS INCLUDE

1912 *Constab Ballads*
1919 *"If We Must Die"*
1922 *Harlem Shadows*
1928 *Home to Harlem*
1929 *Banjo*

1933 *Banana Bottom*
1937 *A Long Way from Home*
1940 *Harlem: Negro Metropolis*
1953 *Selected Poems* (published after he died)

OTHER POETS 1900–40

AKHMATOVA, Anna
AUDEN, W.H.
DOOLITTLE, Hilda
ELIOT, T.S.
FROST, Robert
GRAVES, Robert
HUGHES, Langston
LOWELL, Amy

MASEFIELD, John
MILLAY, Edna St. Vincent
MOORE, Marianne
POUND, Ezra
SASSOON, Siegfried
TAGORE, Rabindranath
YEATS, W.B.

SEE INDEX FOR FULL LIST

WORLD EVENTS

Age	Contemporary Events
Born 1889	**1895** Italian physicist Guglielmo Marconi invents radio ❶
	1896 First modern Olympic Games held in Athens, Greece
	1903 American inventors Orville and Wilbur Wright make first airplane flight
	1908 Henry Ford introduces Model T car
20 in 1909	**1914–18** World War I
	1917 Russian Revolution establishes Communist government
	1917 U.S. enters World War I ❷
	1919 Prohibition introduced in U.S. ❸
	1926 British scientist John Logie Baird demonstrates television
	1927 American aviator Charles A. Lindbergh makes first solo flight across Atlantic
	1927 Joseph Stalin becomes dictator of Russia
40 in 1929	**1931** Empire State Building in New York City completed
	1933 Nazi Party, led by Adolf Hitler, gains control in Germany
	1936–39 Spanish Civil War: conservative forces overthrow government
	1939–45 World War II: allies, led by U.S. and Great Britain, fight axis powers, led by Germany and Japan ❹
	1941 Germany invades USSR
	1945 U.S. drops first atomic bombs on Japan
Dies 1948	**1945** United Nations (UN), organization working for betterment of humanity, founded ❺

© DIAGRAM

McMILLAN, Terry

American novelist
Born Oct. 18, 1951

WAITING
TO
E·X·H·A·L·E

Terry McMillan

Book cover for McMillan's most
popular novel

With her novel *Waiting to Exhale* novelist Terry McMillan shot to fame and became the voice of young, professional African-American women.

McMillan was born in Port Huron, Michigan, where she and her sisters and brothers were raised by their mother; Terry's father died when she was 16. In 1979 she graduated from the University of California in Berkeley, then studied film and earned a master's degree at Columbia University in New York. She worked at word processing to support herself and her son while she wrote.

McMillan's big break came when she was 32 and was accepted at a writers' colony where she began *Mama*, her first novel. When it was published, her publishers wanted to market it to a white audience, believing that black readers do not buy books. McMillan promoted the book herself, and she found hundreds of fans, many of them black. Her second novel, *Disappearing Acts*, is about star-crossed lovers, and her third, *Waiting to Exhale*, became a *New York Times* bestseller. In it McMillan focuses on the problem of male–female relationships among African-American professional women who are both cynical and romantic. She created characters that young black women could identify with, and her fresh voice and humor made her popular with both white and black readers. McMillan also wrote the screenplay for *Waiting to Exhale*, which was made into a movie starring Whitney Houston.

In 1996 McMillan published her fourth novel, *How Stella Got Her Groove Back*. She is also an academic and has received a number of grants and honors.

WORKS INCLUDE

1987 *Mama*
1989 *Disappearing Acts*
1990 *Breaking Ice: An Anthology of Contemporary African-American Fiction* (editor)

1992 *Waiting to Exhale*
1996 *How Stella Got Her Groove Back*

OTHER POST-1940 NOVELISTS

BALDWIN, James
BELLOW, Saul
CAMUS, Albert
GARCÍA MÁRQUEZ, Gabriel
GOLDING, William
HELLER, Joseph
IRVING, John
LESSING, Doris

MORRISON, Toni
SALINGER, J.D.
SINGER, Isaac Bashevis
SOLZHENITSYN, Aleksandr
UPDIKE, John
VIDAL, Gore
WALKER, Alice

SEE INDEX FOR FULL LIST

WORLD EVENTS

Age	Contemporary Events
Born 1951 	**1957** Eisenhower sends troops to Little Rock, Arkansas, to ensure school desegregation **1960** John F. Kennedy elected president **❶**
10 in 1961 	**1961** East Germans build Berlin Wall **❷** **1963** Led by Rev. Martin Luther King, Jr., thousands march on Washington DC to press for civil rights for African Americans **❸** **1964–75** Vietnam War: war between communist North Vietnam and U.S. forces supporting South Vietnam **1969** American astronaut walks on Moon
20 in 1971	**1974** Pres. Richard M. Nixon resigns presidency **❹** **1975–79** Communist forces murder hundreds of thousands in Cambodia **❺** **1980** Ronald Reagan elected president
30 in 1981 	**1981** U.S. launches first space shuttle **1987** Gorbachev begins reforms in USSR: perestroika (restructuring) and glasnost (openness) **❻** **1989** Communist regimes fall throughout Eastern Europe
40 in 1991	**1991** Gulf War: UN forces, led by U.S., defeat Iraq and free Kuwait **❼** **1992** Bill Clinton elected president **1994** First multiracial elections in South Africa end years of white minority rule. They are won by Nelson Mandela, African National Congress leader

McMURTRY, Larry

American novelist
Born Jun. 3, 1936

Larry McMurtry is a novelist who was born, raised, and educated in Texas; his work is closely identified with the scenery and people there.

Born in Wichita Falls, Texas, McMurtry graduated from North Texas State University and earned a further degree from Rice. After being "starved for books" on his family's ranch, he started writing at college and produced a critically acclaimed first novel, *Horseman, Pass By*, at age 25. This was made into the film *Hud*, starring Paul Newman, and deals with life as seen through the eyes of a 17-year-old boy whose grandfather is forced to slaughter his diseased cattle herd.

McMurtry's next two novels, including the well-known *The Last Picture Show*, are also set in Texas and describe the frustrations of small-town life there. McMurtry then explored the way people cope with the move from country to city life in *Moving On* and *Terms of Endearment*. In these and other works ordinary characters seem to drift aimlessly around scenes of old-style Texas. McMurtry also likes to write about the way that reality does not always live up to people's expectations. Many of his novels, including *Terms of Endearment* and *The Last Picture Show*, have been made into successful Hollywood films.

Perhaps McMurtry's most famous work is *Lonesome Dove*, which won the **Pulitzer Prize** in 1986. It is about Texas rangers on their last trail drive. This was made into a hugely popular TV miniseries first shown in 1988.

These days McMurtry runs rare bookstores in Dallas and Washington, D.C., and continues to write.

Book cover for one of McMurtry's novels

WORKS INCLUDE

1961 *Horseman, Pass By*	**1983** *The Desert Rose*
1966 *The Last Picture Show*	**1985** *Lonesome Dove*
1970 *Moving On*	**1988** *Anything for Billy*
1975 *Terms of Endearment*	**1992** *Evening Star*
1982 *Cadillac Jack*	**1993** *Streets of Laredo*

OTHER POST-1940 NOVELISTS

BALDWIN, James
BELLOW, Saul
CAMUS, Albert
GARCÍA MÁRQUEZ, Gabriel
GOLDING, William
HELLER, Joseph
IRVING, John
LESSING, Doris

MORRISON, Toni
SALINGER, J.D.
SINGER, Isaac Bashevis
SOLZHENITSYN, Aleksandr
UPDIKE, John
VIDAL, Gore
WALKER, Alice

SEE INDEX FOR FULL LIST

WORLD EVENTS

Age	Contemporary Events
Born 1936 	**1939–45** World War II: allies, led by U.S. and Great Britain, fight axis powers, led by Germany and Japan **1945** U.S. drops first atomic bombs on Japan **1950–53** Korean War: North Korea and China fight South Korea, the U.S., and United Nations troops ❶
20 in 1956 	**1957** Eisenhower sends troops to Little Rock, Arkansas, to ensure school desegregation **1960** John F. Kennedy elected president ❷ **1964–75** Vietnam War: war between communist North Vietnam and U.S. forces supporting South Vietnam ❸ **1967** Arabs and Israelis fight in Six Day War **1969** American astronaut walks on Moon ❹ **1974** Pres. Richard M. Nixon resigns presidency ❺ **1975–79** Communist forces murder hundreds of thousands in Cambodia ❻
40 in 1976 	**1980** Ronald Reagan elected president **1981** U.S. launches first space shuttle **1989** Communist regimes fall throughout Eastern Europe **1991** Gulf War: UN forces, led by U.S., defeat Iraq and free Kuwait **1994** First multiracial elections in South Africa end years of white minority rule. They are won by Nelson Mandela, African National Congress leader
60 in 1996	

© DIAGRAM

McPHERSON, James Alan

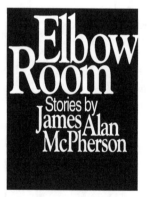

American short-story writer and novelist
Born Sep. 16, 1943

Book cover for McPherson's award-winning short stories

James Alan McPherson is a gifted writer of short stories and novels, whose second book, *Elbow Room*, won him the 1978 **Pulitzer Prize**.

McPherson was born in Savannah, Georgia, and grew up at the height of the **civil rights movement**. He attended a segregated school but also experienced the end of segregation in schools, housing, and public places. A federal loan enabled him to attend Morris Brown College in Atlanta, Georgia, from which he graduated aged 22. In the same year his short story "Gold Coast" was awarded first prize by *Atlantic Monthly*, and McPherson was offered a place at Harvard Law School. He received his law degree in 1968.

Atlantic Monthly continued to publish McPherson's work and helped fund the publication of his first collection of short stories, *Hue and Cry*, when he was 26. He was appointed contributing editor to the magazine in 1969.

McPherson's ideas are different from those of many other black writers of the 1960s. He believes all cultures are connected and, in an advertisement for *Hue and Cry*, stated that he hoped his stories would be read by all kinds of people: the old, the young, the lonely, the confused, and the wronged. He does not write about people because of their race and tries to keep the question of color in the background. His sympathies lie with every person who is trying to make their way in the vastness of America and who suffers injustice.

WORKS INCLUDE

1965 "Gold Coast"
1969 *Hue and Cry*
1977 *Elbow Room*
1987 *A World Unsuspected*
1988 *The Prevailing South*

OTHER POST-1940 WRITERS

BALDWIN, James
BELLOW, Saul
CAMUS, Albert
GARCÍA MÁRQUEZ, Gabriel
GOLDING, William
HELLER, Joseph
IRVING, John
LESSING, Doris

MORRISON, Toni
SALINGER, J.D.
SINGER, Isaac Bashevis
SOLZHENITSYN, Aleksandr
UPDIKE, John
VIDAL, Gore
WALKER, Alice

SEE INDEX FOR FULL LIST

WORLD EVENTS

Age	Contemporary Events
Born 1943	**1945** U.S. drops first atomic bombs on Japan
	1945 Cold War begins between USSR and U.S.
	1950–53 Korean War: North Korea and China fight South Korea, the U.S., and United Nations troops ❶
	1953 New Zealand explorer Edmund Hillary climbs Mount Everest
	1957 Eisenhower sends troops to Little Rock, Arkansas, to ensure school desegregation
	1960 John F. Kennedy elected president ❷
20 in 1963	**1963** Led by Rev. Martin Luther King, Jr., thousands march on Washington DC to press for civil rights for African Americans
	1964–75 Vietnam War: war between communist North Vietnam and U.S. forces supporting South Vietnam ❸
	1967 Arabs and Israelis fight in Six Day War
	1969 American astronaut walks on Moon ❹
	1980 Ronald Reagan elected president ❺
	1981 U.S. launches first space shuttle ❻
40 in 1983	**1989** Communist regimes fall throughout Eastern Europe
	1991 Gulf War: UN forces, led by U.S., defeat Iraq and free Kuwait
	1992 Bill Clinton elected president
	1994 First multiracial elections in South Africa end years of white minority rule. They are won by Nelson Mandela, African National Congress leader

© DIAGRAM

MELVILLE, Herman

American novelist
Born Aug. 1, 1819
Died Sep. 28, 1891
Age at death 72

Herman Melville is one of the most important figures in American literature. His reputation is based largely on one classic novel, *Moby-Dick*.

Melville, the son of a wealthy merchant, was born in New York City. His father died when Melville was 13, leaving the family in poverty. He left school to support his family, working at various jobs until he was 22, when he became a seaman on a whaling ship bound for the Pacific. Melville deserted the ship on the Marquesas Islands and lived with the islanders until another ship rescued him and took him to Tahiti. He eventually landed in what is now Hawaii and enlisted in the U.S. Navy.

After he left the navy at age 25, Melville wrote novels based on his experiences. The books made him extremely popular. He soon gained a reputation as an author of exotic adventure stories. At age 31 Melville moved to Pittsfield, Massachusetts, where he became a close friend of NATHANIEL HAWTHORNE. Melville had almost completed *Moby-Dick* when Hawthorne encouraged him to change it from a simple book about whaling to an **allegorical** and **philosophical** novel. On one level *Moby-Dick* is the story of Captain Ahab's search for the fierce white whale known as Moby-Dick. It is full of details about whaling and a whaler's life. On another level it is a story of a man's search for meaning in his life and a tale of good versus evil.

Moby-Dick, published when Melville was 32, was not a popular success. It was only recognized as a masterpiece 30 years after Melville's death.

The whaling ship Melville went to sea on when he was 22

WORKS INCLUDE

1846 *Typee: A Peep at Polynesian Life*
1847 *Omoo: A Narrative of Adventures in the South Seas*
1849 *Mardi*
1851 *Moby-Dick*

1856 *The Piazza Tales*
1857 *The Confidence-Man*
1924 *Billy Budd* (published after he died)

OTHER 19TH-CENTURY NOVELISTS

AUSTEN, Jane
BRONTË, Charlotte, Emily, and Anne
COOPER, James Fenimore
DICKENS, Charles
ELIOT, George
HARDY, Thomas
HAWTHORNE, Nathaniel
HUGO, Victor

JAMES, Henry
SCOTT, Sir Walter
STEVENSON, Robert Louis
STOWE, Harriet Beecher
TOLSTOY, Leo
ZOLA, Émile

SEE INDEX FOR FULL LIST

WORLD EVENTS

Age	Contemporary Events
Born 1819 	**1834** American inventor Cyrus McCormick patents reaper, machine used to harvest grain ❶ **1837–1901** Queen Victoria reigns in Great Britain
20 in 1839	**1846** Mexican War: U.S. fights Mexico ❷ **1849** California gold rush draws thousands of people **1854** Admiral Matthew Perry forces Japanese to sign trade treaty with U.S.
40 in 1859  	**1859** English naturalist Charles Darwin publishes his theories on evolution **1860** Pony Express, American mail delivery service, established ❸ **1861–65** Civil War: North (Union) fights South (Confederacy) over issues of slavery and states' rights ❹ **1865** Pres. Abraham Lincoln assassinated ❺ **1869** U.S. transcontinental railroad completed **1876** American scientist Alexander Graham Bell invents telephone **1876** Native American Sioux led by Crazy Horse kill Gen. George Armstrong Custer and his men at Battle of Little Bighorn **1877–79** American inventor Thomas Edison invents phonograph and electric lightbulb ❻
60 in 1879 **Dies 1891**	**1883** Brooklyn Bridge opens in New York **1888** George Eastman perfects "Kodak" box camera

© DIAGRAM

27

MENANDER

Greek playwright
Born c. 342 BC
Died c. 292 BC
Age at death c. 50

Carving of Menander holding an actor's mask

Menander was an **ancient Greek** writer of comedy drama. He was born in the city of Athens into a wealthy family. Scholars think that his father was a general and a prominent politician. Menander probably got his enthusiasm for the theater from his uncle Alexis, who was a friend of several playwrights and may have been a writer himself.

Not much is known about Menander's life, and very little of his writing has survived. He is remembered because other writers, particularly the Roman comic playwrights TERENCE and Plautus, based many of their plays on his. For centuries after his death Menander was the most popular of ancient Greek writers.

Drama had been an important part of Greek society for hundreds of years before Menander was born. Regular competitions were held to find the best play, and almost everybody attended drama festivals to see the entrants. The earliest dramas were **tragedies**. Later, comedy became more popular, and writers such as ARISTOPHANES wrote plays in a style known as Old Attic Comedy ("Attic" because they came from a region of Greece called Attica). Menander became the leading representative of a more sophisticated style known as New Attic Comedy.

Although he wrote over 100 plays, Menander won the drama prize only 8 times. His comedy was much more subtle and clever than audiences were used to, and he was never very popular with the ordinary public. Through the work of later imitators, however, Menander became the inspiration for a style of European drama called **comedy of manners**, which has been popular since the 17th century.

WORKS INCLUDE

Only one of Menander's plays survives in a complete form: *The Bad-Tempered Man*, performed about 317 BC. The date it was written is not known. Fragments of other plays have been found. Their titles include *Anger, Afraid of Noises, The Unpopular Man*, and *The Girl with Her Hair Cut Short*.

OTHER ANCIENT GREEK WRITERS

AESCHYLUS	**SOPHOCLES**
AESOP	
ARISTOPHANES	
EURIPIDES	
HESIOD	
HOMER	
PINDAR	
SAPPHO	

WORLD EVENTS

Before his birth

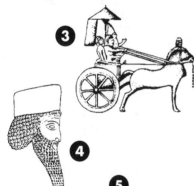

BC 2000–1501 Egyptian civilization at height of its power and achievements

2000–1200 Beginning of Greek civilization on Peloponnesus (modern mainland Greece) ❶

c. 1250 Trojan War: Greeks destroy city of Troy in Asia Minor (modern Turkey) ❷

1000 King David forms Kingdom of Israel and establishes Jerusalem as the capital city

776 Greeks hold first Olympic Games

722 Assyrians conquer Kingdom of Israel ❸

605–562 Nebuchadnezzar rules Babylon

580 Greek philosopher and mathematician Pythagoras born

551 Chinese philosopher Confucius born

521 Jews rebuild Temple, their major site of worship, in Jerusalem

486 Xerxes becomes king of Persia ❹

469 Greek philosopher Socrates born

461 Athens, Greek city-state, becomes a democracy ❺

447 Athenians begin building the Parthenon, a temple to goddess Athena

431–404 Peloponnesian War: Athens fights military city-state of Sparta

399 Socrates condemned to death for his beliefs

384 Greek philosopher Aristotle born

During his life

338–323 Alexander the Great conquers Greece, Asia Minor, Persia, and Egypt ❻

After his death

281 Alexander the Great's empire divided into three kingdoms

© DIAGRAM

MEREDITH, George

English novelist and poet
Born Feb. 12, 1828
Died May 18, 1909
Age at death 81

MODERN LOVE

AND

POEMS OF THE
ENGLISH ROADSIDE,

WITH

Poems and Ballads.

BY

GEORGE MEREDITH,

LONDON:
1862.

Title page for a collection of Meredith's poems

A poetic style of writing gives the novels of George Meredith a character all of their own. Most of them are romantic comedies, full of wit.

Meredith was born in Portsmouth, in southern England. He was the son of a tailor and claimed to be descended from Welsh princes. His mother's family had set aside money to pay for his education. For part of the time he was at a school in Germany run by the Moravian Church, a Protestant group.

Meredith began his career as an apprentice to a lawyer but soon gave up law to write poems and articles. His first published prose, the short work *The Shaving of Shagpat*, came out when he was 27. It is a fantastic tale in imitation of *The Arabian Nights*. His first full-length novel was *The Ordeal of Richard Feverel*, a romantic comedy with a sad ending. Its treatment of sex made it controversial, and for a time it was banned. About this time his first wife left him. He wrote about the breakdown of his marriage in *Modern Love*, a book of **sonnets**.

Meredith could not make enough money from his novels and poems, so he took a job as a reader of manuscripts for a book publisher. For a time he also wrote for a small local newspaper. In his late 30s he served briefly as a war correspondent in a conflict between Prussia (now northern Germany) and Austria. He finally achieved success and financial independence in the 1870s with several novels that sold well. *The Egoist*, considered by many to be his masterpiece, explores every aspect of self-centeredness, the part of human nature Meredith believed to be the most evil.

WORKS INCLUDE

1855 *The Shaving of Shagpat*
1859 *The Ordeal of Richard Feverel*
1862 *Modern Love*
1871 *The Adventures of Harry Richmond*

1876 *Beauchamp's Career*
1879 *The Egoist*
1885 *Diana of the Crossways*
1890 *One of Our Conquerors*
1895 *The Amazing Marriage*

OTHER 19TH-CENTURY NOVELISTS

AUSTEN, Jane
BRONTË, Charlotte, Emily, and Anne
COOPER, James Fenimore
DICKENS, Charles
ELIOT, George
HARDY, Thomas
HAWTHORNE, Nathaniel
HUGO, Victor

JAMES, Henry
MELVILLE, Herman
SCOTT, Sir Walter
STEVENSON, Robert Louis
STOWE, Harriet Beecher
TOLSTOY, Leo
ZOLA, Émile

SEE INDEX FOR FULL LIST

WORLD EVENTS

Age	Contemporary Events
Born 1828 	**1828** Andrew Jackson elected president **1837–1901** Queen Victoria reigns in Great Britain **1846** Mexican War: U.S. fights Mexico ❶
20 in 1848 	**1849** California gold rush draws thousands of people **1859** English naturalist Charles Darwin publishes his theories on evolution **1861** Italy unified ❷ **1861–65** Civil War: North (Union) fights South (Confederacy) over issues of slavery and states' rights ❸ **1865** Pres. Abraham Lincoln assassinated
40 in 1868 	**1869** U.S. transcontinental railroad completed **1876** American scientist Alexander Graham Bell invents telephone **1876** Native American Sioux led by Crazy Horse kill Gen. George Armstrong Custer and his men at Battle of Little Bighorn **1877–79** American inventor Thomas Edison invents phonograph and electric lightbulb ❹
60 in 1888 ❺ *G Marconi*	**1888** George Eastman perfects "Kodak" box camera **1895** Italian physicist Guglielmo Marconi invents radio ❺ **1903** American inventors Orville and Wilbur Wright make first airplane flight
80 in 1908 Dies 1909	**1908** Henry Ford introduces Model T car

© DIAGRAM

MEREDITH, William

American poet
Born Jan. 9, 1919

William Meredith is most famous for the war poems contained in his first volume of poetry, *Love Letter from an Impossible Land*.

Meredith was born in New York City and received his degree from Princeton University in 1940. He was to keep up his relationship with the university for some years after his graduation; during the late 1940s and mid-1960s he served three terms as a teacher of creative writing there.

During **World War II** Meredith served in the U.S. Army Air Force and in the U.S. Navy – much of his earlier poetry reflects what he experienced during this time. In common with many other poets and writers, he was both horrified and fascinated by the world conflict. The 12 war poems in *Love Letter from an Impossible Land*, published when he was 25, describe how he felt as a young man: on the brink of a promising life but facing the possibility of death.

Ships and Other Figures, Meredith's second collection, and *The Wreck of the Thresher*, about the loss of an American submarine, were based on his experiences in the navy. Some critics say that Meredith's later poems are not as intense and do not move the reader as much as his war poems. He is, however, a clever, positive, and honest poet whose work has earned him much praise. *Love Letter from an Impossible Land* won the Yale Series of Younger Poets competition in 1944, and *Partial Accounts: New and Selected Poems* won the 1988 **Pulitzer Prize** for poetry.

As well as writing his own poetry, Meredith has translated some of the work of the French **surrealist** poet GUILLAUME APOLLINAIRE.

WILLIAM MEREDITH

LOVE LETTER FROM AN IMPOSSIBLE LAND

Poems of World War II experiences

Book cover for a collection of poems about World War II

WORKS INCLUDE

1944 *Love Letter from an Impossible Land*
1948 *Ships and Other Figures*
1964 *The Wreck of the Thresher and Other Poems*

1970 *Earth Walk: New and Selected Poems*
1975 *Hazard, the Painter*
1987 *Partial Accounts: New and Selected Poems*

OTHER POST-1940 POETS

ANGELOU, Maya
BISHOP, Elizabeth
BRODSKY, Joseph
DUNCAN, Robert
GINSBERG, Allen
HAYDEN, Robert
HEANEY, Seamus
HUGHES, Ted

LOWELL, Robert
PAZ, Octavio
PLATH, Sylvia
SEXTON, Anne
THOMAS, Dylan
WALCOTT, Derek
YEVTUSHENKO, Yevgeny

SEE INDEX FOR FULL LIST

WORLD EVENTS

Age	Contemporary Events
Born 1919	**1927** Joseph Stalin becomes dictator of Russia
	1931 Empire State Building in New York City completed
	1933 Nazi Party, led by Adolf Hitler, gains control in Germany ❶
20 in 1939	**1939–45** World War II: allies, led by U.S. and Great Britain, fight axis powers, led by Germany and Japan
	1945 U.S. drops first atomic bombs on Japan
	1950–53 Korean War: North Korea and China fight South Korea, the U.S., and United Nations troops
	1957 Eisenhower sends troops to Little Rock, Arkansas, to ensure school desegregation ❷
40 in 1959	**1960** John F. Kennedy elected president ❸
	1964–75 Vietnam War: war between communist North Vietnam and U.S. forces supporting South Vietnam
	1967 Arabs and Israelis fight in Six Day War
	1969 American astronaut walks on Moon ❹
60 in 1979	**1980** Ronald Reagan elected president ❺
	1981 U.S. launches first space shuttle ❻
	1991 Gulf War: UN forces, led by U.S., defeat Iraq and free Kuwait
	1992 Bill Clinton elected president
	1994 First multiracial elections in South Africa end years of white minority rule. They are won by Nelson Mandela, African National Congress leader

MERRILL, James

American poet
Born Mar. 3, 1926
Died Feb. 7, 1995
Age at death 68

Book cover for a collection of
Merrill's poetry

James Merrill is one of the most highly regarded American poets of the late 20th century. Among the many awards he has received, he was given the **Pulitzer Prize** in 1977 for his poetry collection *Divine Comedies.*

Merrill was born in New York City to extremely wealthy parents. He was educated at home by private tutors until the age of 12, when his parents divorced, and he was sent to Lawrenceville School. When he was 16 and in his senior year, his father privately printed his first collection of poems, *Jim's Book.* Army service during **World War II** interrupted his studies at Amherst College, but he returned after the war had ended and graduated in 1947.

Recognized from the first as a master of poetic form, Merrill at first wrote poems that reflected his traditional upbringing. Later collections, such as *Nights and Days*, deal in a more mature way with personal themes. *Nights and Days* won Merrill the first National Book Award and gave him a reputation as a writer of moving love poetry.

The Pulitzer Prize-winning *Divine Comedies* is a mystical poem featuring a ghost called Ephraim who instructs the poet with messages from beyond the grave. Two more books, *Mirabell's Books of Number* and *Scripts for the Pageant*, also feature the ghostly Ephraim. Later, all three were put together into a 560-page **epic** poem called *The Changing Light at Sandover.* This is considered to be Merrill's finest work and has been compared to the work of the great Irish poet W.B. YEATS.

WORKS INCLUDE

1942 *Jim's Book*
1959 *The Country of a Thousand Years of Peace*
1966 *Nights and Days*
1977 *Divine Comedies*

1978 *Mirabell's Books of Number*
1980 *Scripts for the Pageant*
1982 *The Changing Light at Sandover*
1988 *The Inner Room*
1995 *A Scattering of Salts*

OTHER POST-1940 POETS

ANGELOU, Maya
BISHOP, Elizabeth
BRODSKY, Joseph
DUNCAN, Robert
GINSBERG, Allen
HAYDEN, Robert
HEANEY, Seamus
HUGHES, Ted

LOWELL, Robert
PAZ, Octavio
PLATH, Sylvia
SEXTON, Anne
THOMAS, Dylan
WALCOTT, Derek
YEVTUSHENKO, Yevgeny

SEE INDEX FOR FULL LIST

WORLD EVENTS

Age	Contemporary Events
Born 1926 	**1927** Joseph Stalin becomes dictator of Russia **1933** Nazi Party, led by Adolf Hitler, gains control in Germany **1939–45** World War II: allies, led by U.S. and Great Britain, fight axis powers, led by Germany and Japan ❶ **1945** U.S. drops first atomic bombs on Japan
20 in 1946 	**1950–53** Korean War: North Korea and China fight South Korea, the U.S., and United Nations troops ❷ **1957** Eisenhower sends troops to Little Rock, Arkansas, to ensure school desegregation **1960** John F. Kennedy elected president ❸ **1964–75** Vietnam War: war between communist North Vietnam and U.S. forces supporting South Vietnam
40 in 1966	**1967** Arabs and Israelis fight in Six Day War **1969** American astronaut walks on Moon **1980** Ronald Reagan elected president ❹ **1981** U.S. launches first space shuttle
60 in 1986  **Dies 1995**	**1989** Communist regimes fall throughout Eastern Europe **1991** Gulf War: UN forces, led by U.S., defeat Iraq and free Kuwait **1992** Bill Clinton elected president **1994** First multiracial elections in South Africa end years of white minority rule. They are won by Nelson Mandela, African National Congress leader ❺

© DIAGRAM

MERWIN, W.S.

**American poet
and translator
Born** Sep. 30, 1927

W.S. Merwin is a major American poet and translator. He has won many prizes and awards, including the **Pulitzer Prize** in 1971 for his collection *The Carrier of Ladders.*

William Stanley Merwin was born in New York City and grew up in Union City, New Jersey, and Scranton, Pennsylvania. He studied English at Princeton University, followed by one year of graduate study in modern languages. From 1949 to 1956 he was in Europe, working first as a tutor, at one time for the son of the English poet ROBERT GRAVES, and then translating classic Spanish and French plays for the British Broadcasting Corporation (BBC) in London.

Merwin's first book, published when he was 25, was *A Mask for Janus.* One of the major themes in his poetry is the idea that words give order to life and help us relate to the natural world about us – he feels strongly that we are abusing the environment because we have lost touch with it. Critics have described Merwin as a kind of negative WALT WHITMAN. While Whitman glorified humanity's connection to nature in the 19th century, Merwin talks about the tragedy of having lost that connection in the 20th century. This is the depressing message of *The Carrier of Ladders.*

Merwin has also published essays, partly **autobiographical** prose works, and translations of important writers such as the South American poet PABLO NERUDA and the Russian poet OSIP MANDELSTAM. His other translations range from **ancient Greek** to **medieval** Spanish plays and are highly acclaimed.

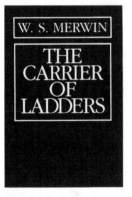

Book cover for Merwin's award-winning poetry collection

WORKS INCLUDE

1952 *A Mask for Janus*
1954 *The Dancing Bears*
1956 *Green with Beasts*
1960 *The Drunk in the Furnace*
1967 *The Lice*

1970 *The Carrier of Ladders*
1977 *The Compass Flower*
1983 *Opening the Hand*
1993 *The Second Four Books of Poems*

OTHER POST-1940 POETS

ANGELOU, Maya
BISHOP, Elizabeth
BRODSKY, Joseph
DUNCAN, Robert
GINSBERG, Allen
HAYDEN, Robert
HEANEY, Seamus
HUGHES, Ted

LOWELL, Robert
PAZ, Octavio
PLATH, Sylvia
SEXTON, Anne
THOMAS, Dylan
WALCOTT, Derek
YEVTUSHENKO, Yevgeny

SEE INDEX FOR FULL LIST

WORLD EVENTS

Age	Contemporary Events
Born 1927 	**1927** Joseph Stalin becomes dictator of Russia **1933** Nazi Party, led by Adolf Hitler, gains control in Germany **1939–45** World War II: allies, led by U.S. and Great Britain, fight axis powers, led by Germany and Japan **1945** U.S. drops first atomic bombs on Japan ❶
20 in 1947  	**1950–53** Korean War: North Korea and China fight South Korea, the U.S., and United Nations troops ❷ **1957** Eisenhower sends troops to Little Rock, Arkansas, to ensure school desegregation **1960** John F. Kennedy elected president **1964–75** Vietnam War: war between communist North Vietnam and U.S. forces supporting South Vietnam
40 in 1967	**1967** Arabs and Israelis fight in Six Day War **1969** American astronaut walks on Moon ❸ **1980** Ronald Reagan elected president **1981** U.S. launches first space shuttle ❹
60 in 1987	**1989** Communist regimes fall throughout Eastern Europe **1991** Gulf War: UN forces, led by U.S., defeat Iraq and free Kuwait **1992** Bill Clinton elected president **1994** First multiracial elections in South Africa end years of white minority rule. They are won by Nelson Mandela, African National Congress leader ❺

© DIAGRAM

MICHENER, James A.

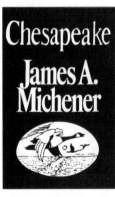

American novelist and short-story writer
Born Feb. 3, 1907
Died Oct. 16, 1997
Age at death 90

Book cover for one of Michener's epic novels

James A. Michener was a bestselling author known for his long, complex historical novels that cover huge periods of time.

James Albert Michener was raised in Bucks County, Pennsylvania, and graduated from Swarthmore College when he was 22. He worked as a teacher and college professor until he was 35, after which he became an editor in New York City.

During **World War II** Michener served in the U.S. Navy and was stationed in the South Pacific. His wartime experiences provided him with material for his first novel, *Tales of the South Pacific*, which won the **Pulitzer Prize** when he was 41. It was made into a musical, *South Pacific*, in 1949 and a movie in 1958. These successes provided Michener with the freedom to write full time.

Michener's **epic** novels are characterized by broad time spans and carefully researched historical detail. *Hawaii*, for example, begins with the actual formation of the islands millions of years ago and ends in 1959, the year Hawaii became a U.S. state. Michener interweaves the plot with information on physical geography, culture, and history.

Michener's other novels are equally detailed. For example, in *The Source* he tells the 12,000-year story of Palestine against the backdrop of an archeological dig. In *Centennial* he traces the history of Colorado. Similarly, he follows 500 years of South African history in *The Covenant*. Michener also published several nonfiction works, including *Literary Reflections* and *The World Is My Home*, his **autobiography**.

WORKS INCLUDE

1947 *Tales of the South Pacific*
1953 *The Bridges at Toko-Ri*
1954 *Sayonara*
1959 *Hawaii*
1965 *The Source*

1974 *Centennial*
1978 *Chesapeake*
1980 *The Covenant*
1992 *The World Is My Home*
1993 *Literary Reflections*

OTHER POST-1940 NOVELISTS

BALDWIN, James
BELLOW, Saul
CAMUS, Albert
GARCÍA MÁRQUEZ, Gabriel
GOLDING, William
HELLER, Joseph
IRVING, John
LESSING, Doris

MORRISON, Toni
SALINGER, J.D.
SINGER, Isaac Bashevis
SOLZHENITSYN, Aleksandr
UPDIKE, John
VIDAL, Gore
WALKER, Alice

SEE INDEX FOR FULL LIST

WORLD EVENTS

Age	Contemporary Events
Born 1907	**1914–18** World War I **1917** Russian Revolution establishes Communist government
20 in 1927 	**1927** Joseph Stalin becomes dictator of Russia ❶ **1933** Nazi Party, led by Adolf Hitler, gains control in Germany **1939–45** World War II: allies, led by U.S. and Great Britain, fight axis powers, led by Germany and Japan **1945** U.S. drops first atomic bombs on Japan ❷
40 in 1947 	**1950–53** Korean War: North Korea and China fight South Korea, the U.S., and United Nations troops **1960** John F. Kennedy elected president ❸ **1964–75** Vietnam War: war between communist North Vietnam and U.S. forces supporting South Vietnam
60 in 1967	**1967** Arabs and Israelis fight in Six Day War **1969** American astronaut walks on Moon ❹ **1981** U.S. launches first space shuttle
80 in 1987  **Dies 1997**	**1989** Communist regimes fall throughout Eastern Europe **1993** African nation of Eritrea declares independence from Ethiopia **1994** First multiracial elections in South Africa end years of white minority rule. They are won by Nelson Mandela, African National Congress leader ❺

© DIAGRAM

39

MILLAY, Edna St. Vincent

American poet and playwright
Born Feb. 22, 1892
Died Oct. 19, 1950
Age at death 58

E D N A
ST. VINCENT
M I L L A Y
A F E W
FIGS FROM
THISTLES

Book cover for an early collection of Millay's poetry

Poet Edna St. Vincent Millay (who also wrote under the pen name Nancy Boyd) used traditional forms of poetry writing – **ballads** and **sonnets** – but in her youth she lived a very unconventional life as a well-known Greenwich Village "bohemian" and **feminist**.

Millay was born in Rockland, Maine. She and her two sisters were raised by their divorced mother, a nurse. While studying at Vassar College, Millay published her first poem. After graduating, she moved to New York City, where she joined the artists and intellectuals who had gathered in Greenwich Village, then a center of creative activity.

At age 25 Millay published her first volume of poetry, *Renascence and Other Poems*. This was followed three years later by *A Few Figs from Thistles*, which captures the intensity of her life then. It contains the famous poem that begins "My candle burns at both ends; / It shall not last the night." This volume was expanded and published in 1922 as *The Harp-Weaver and Other Poems*, for which Millay received the **Pulitzer Prize** in 1923.

Although many of Millay's poems describe her active love life, she was also politically active. In the 1920s she demonstrated against the death sentence given to Sacco and Vanzetti, two **anarchists** who were widely believed to have been wrongly convicted of murder and who were executed in 1927. She was also concerned about the rise of **fascism** in Europe. These issues are the subjects of some of her poems, but Millay is mostly remembered for her earlier work, which celebrates the pleasures to be had in life and love.

WORKS INCLUDE

1917 *Renascence and Other Poems*
1920 *A Few Figs from Thistles*
1921 *The Lamp and the Bell*
1922 *The Harp-Weaver and Other Poems*
1928 *The Buck in the Snow*
1931 *The Fatal Interview*
1939 *Huntsman, What Quarry?*
1940 *Make Bright the Arrows: 1940 Notebook*

SEE INDEX FOR FULL LIST

OTHER POETS 1900–40

AKHMATOVA, Anna
AUDEN, W.H.
DOOLITTLE, Hilda
ELIOT, T.S.
FROST, Robert
GRAVES, Robert
HUGHES, Langston
LOWELL, Amy

MASEFIELD, John
MOORE, Marianne
POUND, Ezra
SASSOON, Siegfried
TAGORE, Rabindranath
YEATS, W.B.

WORLD EVENTS

Age	Contemporary Events
Born 1892  ❶	**1895** Italian physicist Guglielmo Marconi invents radio **1903** American inventors Orville and Wilbur Wright make first airplane flight ❶ **1908** Henry Ford introduces Model T car
20 in 1912  ❷ ❸	**1912** Luxury liner *Titanic* sinks **1914–18** World War I **1917** Russian Revolution establishes Communist government **1917** U.S. enters World War I **1919** Prohibition introduced in U.S. ❷ **1926** British scientist John Logie Baird demonstrates television **1927** Joseph Stalin becomes dictator of Russia **1929** Stock Market crash ushers in Great Depression **1931** Empire State Building in New York City completed ❸
40 in 1932  ❹ ❺ **Dies 1950**	**1933** Nazi Party, led by Adolf Hitler, gains control in Germany **1939–45** World War II: allies, led by U.S. and Great Britain, fight axis powers, led by Germany and Japan **1945** U.S. drops first atomic bombs on Japan ❹ **1945** United Nations (UN), organization working for betterment of humanity, founded ❺ **1945** Cold War begins between USSR and U.S. **1950–53** Korean War: North Korea and China fight South Korea, the U.S., and United Nations troops

MILLER, Arthur

American playwright and screenwriter
Born Oct. 17, 1915

Arthur Miller is one of America's leading playwrights. He has written some of the most important and famous plays of the 20th century.

Miller was born in New York City. Just before the **Great Depression** his father's business closed, and the family was reduced to near poverty. This sudden change in fortune had a strong influence on Miller – in many of his plays families are destroyed because they live by the rules of a society that says money is the most important thing.

At school Miller was more interested in sports than literature, but all that changed when he read *The Brothers Karamazov* by the Russian novelist FYODOR DOSTOEVSKY. Miller decided to become a writer and enrolled at the University of Michigan to study journalism.

Miller's first successful play, *All My Sons*, was performed when he was 32. About a factory owner who sells faulty aircraft parts during **World War II**, the play clearly shows Miller's belief that the desire for money in American society encourages people to act immorally. Two years later *Death of a Salesman*, probably Miller's greatest play, was produced. It is about a man who kills himself when he realizes he will never be considered a success. The play won Miller a **Pulitzer Prize** in 1949.

Miller's 1953 play, *The Crucible*, is based on the 17th-century Salem witch trials, but it is really an attack on the anti**communist** trials held during the **McCarthy Era**. From 1956 to 1961 Miller was married to the famous actress Marilyn Monroe. He wrote the screenplay for her last movie, *The Misfits*.

One of Miller's popular and highly regarded plays

WORKS INCLUDE

1947 *All My Sons*	**1964** *After the Fall*
1949 *Death of a Salesman*	**1980** *The American Clock*
1953 *The Crucible*	**1990** *The Last Yankee*
1955 *A View from the Bridge*	**1994** *Broken Glass*
1964 *Incident at Vichy*	**1995** *Plain Girl*

OTHER POST-1940 PLAYWRIGHTS

ALBEE, Edward
BECKETT, Samuel
BRECHT, Bertolt
FUGARD, Athol
GENET, Jean
KUSHNER, Tony
MAMET, David
NORMAN, Marsha

OSBORNE, John
PINTER, Harold
SHEPARD, Sam
SIMON, Neil
SOYINKA, Wole
WILLIAMS, Tennessee

SEE INDEX FOR FULL LIST

WORLD EVENTS

Age	Contemporary Events
Born 1915	**1917** Russian Revolution establishes Communist government
	1927 Joseph Stalin becomes dictator of Russia
	1933 Nazi Party, led by Adolf Hitler, gains control in Germany ❶
20 in 1935	**1939–45** World War II: allies, led by U.S. and Great Britain, fight axis powers, led by Germany and Japan ❷
	1945 U.S. drops first atomic bombs on Japan
	1950–53 Korean War: North Korea and China fight South Korea, the U.S., and United Nations troops
40 in 1955	**1960** John F. Kennedy elected president ❸
	1964–75 Vietnam War: war between communist North Vietnam and U.S. forces supporting South Vietnam
	1969 American astronaut walks on Moon
60 in 1975	**1981** U.S. launches first space shuttle ❹
	1989 Communist regimes fall throughout Eastern Europe
	1991 Gulf War: UN forces, led by U.S., defeat Iraq and free Kuwait ❺
	1994 First multiracial elections in South Africa end years of white minority rule. They are won by Nelson Mandela, African National Congress leader
80 in 1995	**1995** Federal building blown up in Oklahoma City, Oklahoma

© DIAGRAM

MILLER, Caroline

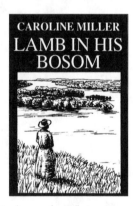

American novelist and short-story writer
Born Aug. 26, 1903
Died Jul. 12, 1992
Age at death 88

CAROLINE MILLER
LAMB IN HIS BOSOM

Book cover for Miller's acclaimed first novel

Caroline Miller won a **Pulitzer Prize** in 1934 for her first novel, *Lamb in His Bosom.*

Miller was born Caroline Pafford in Waycross, Georgia. Right after graduating from high school she married her former English teacher when she was just 17, and became Caroline Miller. In the happy early years of her marriage she spent time walking the Georgia countryside, meeting the swamp dwellers who later appeared in her first work.

While raising three sons, she took up writing to add to the family's finances. Her first attempts were short stories, but she could not get any published. One developed into a novel, *Lamb in His Bosom,* and with the help of Pulitzer Prize-winner JULIA PETERKIN it was published when Miller was 30. Set in Georgia in the 1840s, when the countryside was still frontier land, the book focuses on the life of Cean Carver and her journey of self-discovery. It is written in an unsentimental style and combines historical fact and fiction. *Lamb in His Bosom* also relates the stories of the whole Carver family. One of the central male characters is based on Miller's own great-grandfather, a minister who had settled in Waycross during the frontier period. Miller was praised for her realistic portrayal of frontier life, the detailing of daily life, and her descriptions of the Georgia countryside.

After Miller had divorced her first husband and remarried, she wrote *Lebanon,* 11 years after her first novel. Again it is set in frontier Georgia, but this novel is a romance and was not as well received.

WORKS INCLUDE

1933 *Lamb in His Bosom*
1944 *Lebanon*

OTHER NOVELISTS 1900–40

CONRAD, Joseph
FAULKNER, William
FITZGERALD, F. Scott
FORSTER, E.M.
HEMINGWAY, Ernest
JOYCE, James
KAFKA, Franz
LAWRENCE, D.H.

LONDON, Jack
MANN, Thomas
ORWELL, George
PROUST, Marcel
STEINBECK, John
WHARTON, Edith
WOOLF, Virginia

SEE INDEX FOR FULL LIST

WORLD EVENTS

Age	Contemporary Events
Born 1903  ❶	**1903** American inventors Orville and Wilbur Wright make first airplane flight **1914–18** World War I ❶ **1917** Russian Revolution establishes Communist government
20 in 1923  ❷	**1927** Joseph Stalin becomes dictator of Russia **1933** Nazi Party, led by Adolf Hitler, gains control in Germany **1939–45** World War II: allies, led by U.S. and Great Britain, fight axis powers, led by Germany and Japan ❷
40 in 1943  ❸	**1945** U.S. drops first atomic bombs on Japan **1950–53** Korean War: North Korea and China fight South Korea, the U.S., and United Nations troops **1960** John F. Kennedy elected president ❸
60 in 1963  ❹	**1964–75** Vietnam War: war between communist North Vietnam and U.S. forces supporting South Vietnam **1967** Arabs and Israelis fight in Six Day War **1969** American astronaut walks on Moon **1981** U.S. launches first space shuttle ❹
80 in 1983  ❺ **Dies 1992**	**1987** Gorbachev begins reforms in USSR: perestroika (restructuring) and glasnost (openness) **1991** Gulf War: UN forces, led by U.S., defeat Iraq and free Kuwait ❺ **1992** Bill Clinton elected president

© DIAGRAM

MILLER, Henry

American novelist
Born Dec. 26, 1891
Died Jun. 7, 1980
Age at death 88

One of Henry Miller's popular novels

Henry Miller is famous for the novels that chronicle his life in Paris, France, between 1930 and 1940. Well known for describing sex with frankness, the novels focus on a penniless artist who struggles to survive in Paris as a creative "free spirit."

Miller was born in New York City, the only child of German-American working-class parents. His difficult relationship with his mother is reflected in his life (he married five times) and in his novels' characters. After high school he drifted through various jobs in the U.S. and Europe, settling in Paris, where he wrote and painted. At 40 he found his "writing voice"; after many drafts *Tropic of Cancer* was published in Paris in 1934, and it received praise from T.S. ELIOT.

Encouraged by ANAÏS NIN, he wrote *Black Spring* and *Tropic of Capricorn*. These novels alternate between his Brooklyn childhood and his vagabond life in Paris. He wrote a study of the poet ARTHUR RIMBAUD, identifying with Rimbaud as a rebellious figure and a sexual adventurer. For Miller the human sexual drive was part of creative expression, and he made no moral judgments about sexuality. He used dream, symbols, fantasy, humor, and personal experience in his writings.

After a brief time in Greece, depicted in *The Colossus of Maroussi*, he settled in California in the 1940s and continued to write. He became a hero of the **beat generation**. In 1961 *Tropic of Cancer* was banned in the U.S. as obscene. Only after a long court battle during which he was publicly supported by many writers was the ban lifted. The novel became a bestseller.

WORKS INCLUDE

1934 *Tropic of Cancer*
1936 *Black Spring*
1939 *Tropic of Capricorn*
1941 *The Colossus of Maroussi*
1949 *Sexus*

1953 *Plexus*
1956 *Quiet Days in Clichy*
1956 *The Time of the Assassins: A Study of Rimbaud*
1960 *Nexus*

OTHER NOVELISTS 1900–40

CONRAD, Joseph
FAULKNER, William
FITZGERALD, F. Scott
FORSTER, E.M.
HEMINGWAY, Ernest
JOYCE, James
KAFKA, Franz
LAWRENCE, D.H.

LONDON, Jack
MANN, Thomas
ORWELL, George
PROUST, Marcel
STEINBECK, John
WHARTON, Edith
WOOLF, Virginia

SEE INDEX FOR FULL LIST

WORLD EVENTS

Age	Contemporary Events
Born 1891 	**1895** Italian physicist Guglielmo Marconi invents radio **1903** American inventors Orville and Wilbur Wright make first airplane flight **1908** Henry Ford introduces Model T car ❶
20 in 1911 	**1912** Woodrow Wilson elected president **1914–18** World War I ❷ **1917** Russian Revolution establishes Communist government **1927** Joseph Stalin becomes dictator of Russia
40 in 1931 	**1931** Empire State Building in New York City completed **1933** Nazi Party, led by Adolf Hitler, gains control in Germany ❸ **1939–45** World War II: allies, led by U.S. and Great Britain, fight axis powers, led by Germany and Japan **1945** U.S. drops first atomic bombs on Japan **1950–53** Korean War: North Korea and China fight South Korea, the U.S., and United Nations troops ❹
60 in 1951 	**1960** John F. Kennedy elected president ❺ **1964–75** Vietnam War: war between communist North Vietnam and U.S. forces supporting South Vietnam ❻ **1967** Arabs and Israelis fight in Six Day War **1969** American astronaut walks on Moon
80 in 1971 Dies 1980	

© DIAGRAM

MILLER, Jason

American playwright
Born Apr. 22, 1939

Jason Miller's fame as a playwright rests solely on *That Championship Season*, the second of his two full-length plays.

Miller was born in Long Island, New York, but brought up in Scranton, Pennsylvania. He attended St. Patrick's High School, where he was encouraged by one of his teachers to study elocution because of his deep, strong voice. He went on to study theater and playwriting at the University of Scranton and then drama at the Catholic University of America in Washington, D.C.

Miller's first full-length play, *Nobody Hears a Broken Drum*, was produced when he was 31; it was not, however, a success. For the next two years, while writing his second play, he took jobs as a bit-part actor, truck driver, messenger, and waiter. *That Championship Season*, produced when he was 33, was to make him famous. The play is about the 20th annual reunion of four members of a high school championship basketball team and their coach. The surprising part is that the men, now middle-aged, have not changed much. As young men they won the championship game by cheating, and as adults they are still selfish and dishonest. Although they claim to be friends, they do not hesitate to betray each other. To them, winning is still everything.

The play won the New York Drama Critics' Circle Award in 1972 and the Tony Award for best play as well as the **Pulitzer Prize** in 1973. Since *That Championship Season* Miller has concentrated on his acting career. He was nominated for an Academy Award in 1974 for his role as the priest in *The Exorcist*.

Miller's famous play about a basketball team reunion

WORKS INCLUDE

1967 *It's a Sin to Tell a Lie*	**1970** *Lou Gehrig Did Not Die of Cancer*
1967 *Circus Lady*	
1967 *Perfect Son*	**1970** *Nobody Hears a Broken Drum*
1968 *Stone Step*	**1972** *That Championship Season*

OTHER POST-1940 PLAYWRIGHTS

ALBEE, Edward
BECKETT, Samuel
BRECHT, Bertolt
FUGARD, Athol
GENET, Jean
KUSHNER, Tony
MAMET, David
MILLER, Arthur

NORMAN, Marsha
OSBORNE, John
PINTER, Harold
SHEPARD, Sam
SIMON, Neil
SOYINKA, Wole
WILLIAMS, Tennessee

SEE INDEX FOR FULL LIST

WORLD EVENTS

Age	Contemporary Events
Born 1939 	**1939–45** World War II: allies, led by U.S. and Great Britain, fight axis powers, led by Germany and Japan **1945** U.S. drops first atomic bombs on Japan **1950–53** Korean War: North Korea and China fight South Korea, the U.S., and United Nations troops ❶ **1957** Eisenhower sends troops to Little Rock, Arkansas, to ensure school desegregation
20 in 1959 	**1960** John F. Kennedy elected president ❷ **1964–75** Vietnam War: war between communist North Vietnam and U.S. forces supporting South Vietnam **1967** Arabs and Israelis fight in Six Day War **1969** American astronaut walks on Moon ❸ **1974** Pres. Richard M. Nixon resigns presidency
40 in 1979 	**1980** Ronald Reagan elected president **1981** U.S. launches first space shuttle **1987** Gorbachev begins reforms in USSR: perestroika (restructuring) and glasnost (openness) ❹ **1989** Communist regimes fall throughout Eastern Europe ❺ **1991** Gulf War: UN forces, led by U.S., defeat Iraq and free Kuwait **1992** Bill Clinton elected president **1994** First multiracial elections in South Africa end years of white minority rule. They are won by Nelson Mandela, African National Congress leader

© DIAGRAM

MILNE, A.A.

English children's writer and playwright
Born Jan. 18, 1882
Died Jan. 31, 1956
Age at death 74

Piglet, Christopher Robin, and Pooh Bear

A.A. Milne was a popular and productive English writer. Although he wrote many different kinds of books, he will always be remembered as the author of the children's classic *Winnie-the-Pooh*.

Alan Alexander Milne was born in London, England. At school one of his teachers was the science fiction writer H.G. WELLS. Milne studied math at Cambridge University and then, aged 24, went to work for a well-known **satirical** magazine called *Punch*.

In 1914 **World War I** broke out and Milne joined the army. The horrors he witnessed on the battlefields left him with a lifelong disgust of war and a longing for the innocence of childhood. In the army Milne wrote plays to amuse his comrades, and when the war was over, he began a career as a comic playwright. He also began to write poetry for children.

Milne became famous when he was 42 with the publication of *When We Were Very Young*, a collection of poetry for children. He followed this two years later with *Winnie-the-Pooh*, which is based on stories he told to his own son Christopher Robin, which is also the name of the little boy whose animal friends are the main characters in the book.

Although Milne continued to write books for adults, it was always his work for children that brought him recognition. His second volume of poems for children, *Now We Are Six*, was just as popular as his first, and *The House at Pooh Corner*, which relates the further adventures of Pooh Bear and friends, was an instant success. Milne also wrote a popular stage version of the classic children's novel *The Wind in the Willows* by KENNETH GRAHAME.

WORKS INCLUDE

1919 *Mr. Pim Passes By*	**1926** *Winnie-the-Pooh*
1921 *The Red House Mystery*	**1927** *Now We Are Six*
1921 *The Truth about Blayds*	**1928** *The House at Pooh Corner*
1922 *The Dover Road*	**1932** *The Perfect Alibi*
1924 *When We Were Very Young*	**1939** *It's Too Late Now*

OTHER CHILDREN'S WRITERS

ADAMS, Harriet Stratemeyer
ALCOTT, Louisa May
ANDERSEN, Hans Christian
BARRIE, J.M.
BLYTON, Enid
CARLE, Eric
CARROLL, Lewis
DAHL, Roald

KIPLING, Rudyard
LEAR, Edward
POTTER, Beatrix
REID BANKS, Lynne
SENDAK, Maurice
TWAIN, Mark

SEE INDEX FOR FULL LIST

WORLD EVENTS

Age	Contemporary Events
Born 1882 	**1883** Brooklyn Bridge opens in New York **1888** George Eastman perfects "Kodak" box camera **1895** Italian physicist Guglielmo Marconi invents radio ❶
20 in 1902 	**1903** American inventors Orville and Wilbur Wright make first airplane flight **1908** Henry Ford introduces Model T car **1912** Luxury liner *Titanic* sinks ❷ **1914–18** World War I **1917** Russian Revolution establishes Communist government
40 in 1922	**1926** British scientist John Logie Baird demonstrates television **1927** Joseph Stalin becomes dictator of Russia **1929** Stock Market crash ushers in Great Depression ❸ **1931** Empire State Building in New York City completed **1933** Nazi Party, led by Adolf Hitler, gains control in Germany ❹ **1935** Italy invades Abyssinia (Ethiopia) **1939–45** World War II: allies, led by U.S. and Great Britain, fight axis powers, led by Germany and Japan
60 in 1942 **Dies 1956**	**1945** U.S. drops first atomic bombs on Japan ❺ **1950–53** Korean War: North Korea and China fight South Korea, the U.S., and United Nations troops

© DIAGRAM

51

MILOSZ, Czeslaw

Polish-American poet, novelist, and essayist
Born Jun. 30, 1911

Czeslaw Milosz is one of Poland's leading modern poets. In 1980 he was awarded the **Nobel Prize** for literature.

Born in Vilnius, Lithuania, which was then part of Poland, Milosz published his first book of poetry, *Poem of the Frozen Time*, when he was just 22.

Milosz studied at the University of Vilnius. There he became a socialist and headed up a group of poets who predicted an upcoming disaster. The disaster came in 1939 when Germany invaded Poland and **World War II** broke out. Milosz was an active member of the resistance movement in Warsaw.

At age 34, when the war ended, Milosz published a book of verse entitled *Salvage*, which so impressed the new **communist** rulers of Poland that they made him a junior diplomat. His first appointment was in Washington, D.C. After a time in Paris Milosz returned to the United States, where he took a teaching post at the University of California, Berkeley. Ten years later he became a U.S. citizen.

Milosz continued to write in Polish, his native language, but published many works in English, some of which he translated himself.

One of Milosz's most famous works is the essay collection *The Captive Mind*, which deals with the effects of communism on Polish writers. He later returned to this theme in an **autobiographical** novel, *The Seizure of Power*. This story about life in Warsaw after a change in power begins with the Russian occupation of the city at the end of World War II.

Czeslaw Milosz **The Seizure of power**

Milosz's powerful novel about communism in Poland

WORKS INCLUDE

1933 *Poem of the Frozen Time*
1945 *Salvage*
1953 *The Captive Mind*
1955 *The Seizure of Power*
1959 *Native Realm*

1988 *Collected Poems: 1931–87*
1991 *Provinces: Poems 1987–91*
1992 *Beginning with My Streets*
1994 *The Year of the Hunter*
1995 *Facing the River*

OTHER EASTERN EUROPEAN WRITERS

ANDRIC, Ivo
CANETTI, Elias
CAPEK, Karel
ELYTIS, Odysseus
HASEK, Jaroslav
HAVEL, Vaclav
KAFKA, Franz
KAZANTZAKIS, Nikos

KUNDERA, Milan
LEM, Stanislaw
REYMONT, Wladyslaw S.
SEFERIS, George
SEIFERT, Jaroslav
SIENKIEWICZ, Henryk

WORLD EVENTS

Age	Contemporary Events
Born 1911 	**1914–18** World War I ❶ **1917** Russian Revolution establishes Communist government **1927** Joseph Stalin becomes dictator of Russia
20 in 1931	**1933** Nazi Party, led by Adolf Hitler, gains control in Germany **1939–45** World War II: allies, led by U.S. and Great Britain, fight axis powers, led by Germany and Japan **1945** U.S. drops first atomic bombs on Japan ❷ **1950–53** Korean War: North Korea and China fight South Korea, the U.S., and United Nations troops
40 in 1951	**1960** John F. Kennedy elected president **1964–75** Vietnam War: war between communist North Vietnam and U.S. forces supporting South Vietnam ❸ **1967** Arabs and Israelis fight in Six Day War **1969** American astronaut walks on Moon ❹
60 in 1971	**1981** U.S. launches first space shuttle **1989** Communist regimes fall throughout Eastern Europe
80 in 1991  	**1991** Gulf War: UN forces, led by U.S., defeat Iraq and free Kuwait ❺ **1994** First multiracial elections in South Africa end years of white minority rule. They are won by Nelson Mandela, African National Congress leader

© DIAGRAM

MILTON, John

John Milton was one of the greatest English poets. He was born in London and educated at Cambridge University. His father was a successful lawyer and composer who was wealthy enough to afford a second house in the country. Milton spent six years in private study there after finishing college in 1632. He had given up his original ambition to become a priest and decided to devote his life to God as a poet instead.

Milton began to write poetry while he was at college. He completed one of his first major works, *Lycidas,* perhaps the finest short poem in English, at age 29. Five years later in 1642 the **English Civil War** divided the country as Oliver Cromwell fought to overthrow the king. At the outbreak of war Milton stopped composing poetry and threw himself into writing political essays supporting Cromwell's aims. In the same period Milton also became aware that he was slowly going blind.

In 1660 the monarchy was restored, and Milton retired to devote himself to poetry. His ambition had always been to compose an **epic** poem to rival the works of ancient writers such as HOMER and VIRGIL. By then completely blind, he began dictating his great poem, *Paradise Lost,* to his wife and daughters. The work, published when he was 55, was immediately recognized as an outstanding achievement. It tells the story of how Satan was thrown out of Heaven and how he came to Earth to corrupt Adam and Eve. The themes of war and religious conflict it explores constantly remind the reader of the troubled times Milton lived through.

English poet and essayist
Born Dec. 9, 1608
Died Nov. 8, 1674
Age at death 65

Title page of a political essay by Milton

WORKS INCLUDE

1629 "On the Morning of Christ's Nativity"	**1645** *Poems*
c. 1631 "L'Allegro"	**1667** *Paradise Lost*
c. 1631 "Il Penseroso"	**1671** *Paradise Regained*
1634 *Comus*	**1671** *Samson Agonistes*
1637 *Lycidas*	

OTHER 17TH-CENTURY WRITERS

BEHN, Aphra
BRADSTREET, Anne
BUNYAN, John
CERVANTES, Miguel de
CONGREVE, William
CYRANO de BERGERAC
DONNE, John
DRYDEN, John

JONSON, Ben
La FONTAINE, Jean de
LOPE de VEGA
MOLIÈRE
PEPYS, Samuel
RACINE, Jean

SEE INDEX FOR FULL LIST

WORLD EVENTS

Age	Contemporary Events
Born 1608 	**1611** King James Bible published **1614** Indian princess Pocahontas marries Virginia settler John Rolfe **1618–48** Thirty Years' War: Catholic and Protestant powers fight in Europe **1619** First group of Black Africans in North America sold as indentured servants at Jamestown **1620** Pilgrims, aboard the *Mayflower*, land in Plymouth, Massachusetts ❶
20 in 1628 	**1628** English scientist William Harvey publishes his discovery of circulation of blood ❷ **1629** English Puritans (dissenters from established church) establish colony of Massachusetts Bay **1642–51** English Civil War: conflict between king and his followers (Royalists or Cavaliers) and parliamentary supporters (Roundheads) **1643–1715** Louis XIV reigns in France
40 in 1648 	**1649** King Charles I of England beheaded; England becomes republic ❸ **1653–58** England ruled by Oliver Cromwell **1660** Charles II restored to English throne (Restoration) **1665** British physicist Isaac Newton proposes theory of gravity ❹
60 in 1668 **Dies 1674**	**1668** Newton builds first reflecting telescope

© DIAGRAM

MISHIMA Yukio

Japanese novelist and playwright
Born Jan. 14, 1925
Died Nov. 25, 1970
Age at death 45

Mishima Yukio was one of Japan's leading modern writers. He wrote about Japanese society and the changes it has gone through in the 20th century.

Mishima was born in Tokyo and attended Tokyo University, where he studied law. During **World War II** he was rejected by the army because of his poor health. He later felt guilty that he had survived the war when so many others had been killed.

In 1948, when Mishima was 23, his first novel, *Confessions of a Mask*, was published. It was strongly based on Mishima's own life and shows how society forced him to hide his homosexuality behind a mask of "normality." This was the first time a Japanese writer had talked about homosexuality. It was translated into English and widely praised.

Another of Mishima's early novels, *The Temple of the Golden Pavilion*, was also highly praised. It is based on the true story of a young Buddhist monk who, angered at his own physical ugliness, comes to hate the beauty of the temple where he studies and destroys it. Mishima went on to write popular modern versions of traditional Japanese No plays.

All his life Mishima was fascinated by the traditions of the samurai warriors. He came to feel that Japan had become weak after its defeat in World War II and needed new leadership. In 1970 Mishima publicly committed ritual suicide in an attempt to bring about an angry uprising against the government. On the day of his death he finished writing the fourth and final part of his greatest novel, *The Sea of Fertility* – a critical study of Japanese society in the 20th century.

Mishima posing as a samurai warrior

WORKS INCLUDE

1949 *Confessions of a Mask*
1950 *Thirst for Love*
1954 *The Sound of Waves*
1956 *The Temple of the Golden Pavilion*

1960 *After the Banquet*
1963 *The Sailor Who Fell from Grace with the Sea*
1969–71 *The Sea of Fertility* (4 vols. – fourth volume published after he died)

OTHER ASIAN AND MIDDLE EASTERN WRITERS

BASHO, Matsuo
DESAI, Anita
DING LING
DU FU
HAYASHI Fumiko
KALIDASA
KAWABATA Yasunari
MURASAKI Shikibu

NARAYAN, R.K.
OZ, Amos
SHIMAZAKI Toson
TAGORE, Rabindranath
TANIZAKI Junichiro
WU CHENGEN

SEE INDEX FOR FULL LIST

WORLD EVENTS

Age	Contemporary Events
Born 1925 	**1926** British scientist John Logie Baird demonstrates television **1927** Joseph Stalin becomes dictator of Russia ❶ **1931** Empire State Building in New York City completed **1933** Nazi Party, led by Adolf Hitler, gains control in Germany ❷
10 in 1935  	**1935** Italy invades Abyssinia (Ethiopia) **1939–45** World War II: allies, led by U.S. and Great Britain, fight axis powers, led by Germany and Japan ❸ **1944** Allies stage D-Day invasion at Normandy, France, and begin to retake Europe
20 in 1945	**1945** U.S. drops first atomic bombs on Japan **1945** United Nations (UN), organization working for betterment of humanity, founded ❹ **1945** Cold War begins between USSR and U.S. **1950–53** Korean War: North Korea and China fight South Korea, the U.S., and United Nations troops
30 in 1955 	**1957** Eisenhower sends troops to Little Rock, Arkansas, to ensure school desegregation **1960** John F. Kennedy elected president **1964–75** Vietnam War: war between communist North Vietnam and U.S. forces supporting South Vietnam ❺
40 in 1965 **Dies 1970** 	**1967** Arabs and Israelis fight in Six Day War **1969** American astronaut walks on Moon ❻

© DIAGRAM

MISTRAL, Gabriela

Gabriela Mistral combined a busy life – first as a teacher and then as a diplomat – with a gift for poetry that brought her the **Nobel Prize** for literature in 1945. She was the first South American writer to win the prize.

Born in Vicuña, Chile, Mistral's real name was Lucila Godoy Alcayaga. She used the pen name Gabriela Mistral only for her poetry. A gifted teacher, she became an important figure in Chile's education system. She traveled in Mexico, the United States, and Europe to study teaching methods and became a visiting professor at several colleges, including the University of Puerto Rico.

Later in life Mistral became a diplomat, working in the world's capitals during some of the most turbulent years of the 20th century, including **World War II** and the beginning of the **Cold War** in Europe.

In contrast to the horrors of war, Mistral's poetry is personal, full of warmth and emotion. Her main themes are childhood, death, love, motherhood, and religion. She began writing poetry in her 20s after the suicide of her fiancé. Her "Sonnets on Death" won a writing contest in Chile in 1914. In addition, Mistral wrote verses for children and fantasy stories.

Mistral wrote in her native tongue, Spanish. She became one of the most translated of all South American writers: her work has appeared in English, French, German, Italian, and Swedish. American poet LANGSTON HUGHES translated a selection of her verses that was published just after she died. Mistral never married but adopted a child who later died.

Chilean poet
Born Apr. 7, 1889
Died Jan. 10, 1957
Age at death 67

GABRIELA
MISTRAL'S
ANTHOLOGY

Book cover for a collection of Mistral's poetry

WORKS INCLUDE

1922 Desolation	Published after she died
1924 Tenderness	**1957** Selected Poems of Gabriela Mistral
1936 Poems	**1967** Gabriela Mistral's Anthology
1938 Felling	**1972** Crickets and Frogs
	1974 The Elephant and His Secret

OTHER LATIN AMERICAN WRITERS

ALEGRÍA, Claribel
ALLENDE, Isabel
ASTURIAS, Miguel Angel
BENEDETTI, Mario
BORGES, Jorge Luis
CABRERA INFANTE, Guillermo
FUENTES, Carlos
GARCÍA MÁRQUEZ, Gabriel

MACHADO de ASSIS, Joaquim Maria
NERUDA, Pablo
ONETTI, Juan Carlos
PAZ, Octavio
ROA BASTOS, Augusto
RULFO, Juan
VARGAS LLOSA, Mario

SEE INDEX FOR FULL LIST

WORLD EVENTS

Age	Contemporary Events
Born 1889 	**1895** Italian physicist Guglielmo Marconi invents radio **1903** American inventors Orville and Wilbur Wright make first airplane flight **1908** Henry Ford introduces Model T car ❶
20 in 1909 	**1914–18** World War I ❷ **1917** Russian Revolution establishes Communist government **1926** British scientist John Logie Baird demonstrates television **1927** Joseph Stalin becomes dictator of Russia
40 in 1929  	**1931** Empire State Building in New York City completed **1933** Nazi Party, led by Adolf Hitler, gains control in Germany **1939–45** World War II: allies, led by U.S. and Great Britain, fight axis powers, led by Germany and Japan ❸ **1941** Germany invades USSR **1945** U.S. drops first atomic bombs on Japan **1945** United Nations (UN), organization working for betterment of humanity, founded ❹
60 in 1949 **Dies 1957**	**1950–53** Korean War: North Korea and China fight South Korea, the U.S., and United Nations troops **1955** African-Americans protest segregation in Montgomery Bus Boycott **1956** Soviets suppress anti-Communist uprising in Hungary ❺

© DIAGRAM

MITCHELL, Margaret

American novelist
Born Nov. 8, 1900
Died Aug. 16, 1949
Age at death 48

Poster for the famous film version
of Mitchell's novel

Margaret Mitchell was the author of one of the most famous novels ever written, *Gone with the Wind*.

Mitchell was born in Atlanta, Georgia. Her father was president of the local historical society, and Mitchell grew up listening to stories about old Atlanta and the battles the Confederate Army had fought there during the **American Civil War**. Later, she used these tales as inspiration for *Gone with the Wind*.

At age 22 Mitchell began a career as a journalist, but an ankle injury forced her to retire. By that time she had married and started work on her novel, which took ten years to complete. When a traveling book editor visited Atlanta in search of new material, she reluctantly let him have a look at her manuscript. The novel was published when Mitchell was 36.

Gone with the Wind is the vividly drawn tale of Southern life during and after the Civil War told through the lives of two families, their slaves, friends, and relatives, centering on Scarlett O'Hara and Rhett Butler. It has been praised as the first novel to tell the story of the Civil War from a Southern woman's point of view but criticized for glorifying a society that practiced slavery. A romantic **epic**, it is full of stirring events and has created a lasting image of the South for over 60 years. It won the **Pulitzer Prize** in 1937. Worldwide sales are enormous: about 250,000 copies are sold in paperback in the U.S. alone each year, and the book has been translated into some 30 languages. The 1939 film version starring Clark Gable and Vivien Leigh is one of the most popular films ever made.

Mitchell never published another book during her lifetime and died after an automobile accident.

WORKS INCLUDE

1936 *Gone with the Wind*
Published after she died
1976 *Margaret Mitchell's "Gone with the Wind" Letters*

1985 *A Dynamo Going to Waste: Letters to Allen Edee 1919–21*
1996 *Lost Laysen*

OTHER NOVELISTS 1900–40

CONRAD, Joseph
FAULKNER, William
FITZGERALD, F. Scott
FORSTER, E.M.
HEMINGWAY, Ernest
JOYCE, James
KAFKA, Franz
LAWRENCE, D.H.

LONDON, Jack
MANN, Thomas
ORWELL, George
PROUST, Marcel
STEINBECK, John
WHARTON, Edith
WOOLF, Virginia

SEE INDEX FOR FULL LIST

WORLD EVENTS

Age	Contemporary Events
Born 1900	**1903** American inventors Orville and Wilbur Wright make first airplane flight ❶ **1908** Henry Ford introduces Model T car
10 in 1910	**1914–18** World War I **1917** Russian Revolution establishes Communist government **1917** U.S. enters World War I ❷ **1919** Prohibition introduced in U.S. ❸
20 in 1920	**1920** 19th Amendment to U.S. Constitution grants women vote **1926** British scientist John Logie Baird demonstrates television **1927** American aviator Charles A. Lindbergh makes first solo flight across Atlantic **1927** Joseph Stalin becomes dictator of Russia
30 in 1930	**1931** Empire State Building in New York City completed ❹ **1933** Nazi Party, led by Adolf Hitler, gains control in Germany **1936–39** Spanish Civil War: conservative forces overthrow government **1939–45** World War II: allies, led by U.S. and Great Britain, fight axis powers, led by Germany and Japan ❺
40 in 1940 **Dies 1949**	**1941** Germany invades USSR ❻ **1945** U.S. drops first atomic bombs on Japan **1945** United Nations (UN), organization working for betterment of humanity, founded

© DIAGRAM

MITFORD, Nancy

Nancy Mitford became successful for her comic novels about upper-class English society and for her popular **biographies**.

The eldest of seven children of the second Baron Redesdale, an eccentric British nobleman, she and her five sisters were unconventionally raised and educated at home by a series of governesses.

Mitford left home as soon as she could and lived for a time with EVELYN WAUGH and his wife while she began writing for *Harper's Magazine* and *Vogue*. Her first novel, *Highland Fling*, was published when she was 27. Then she made her name with four highly amusing books, beginning with *The Pursuit of Love*. These recount the lively activities and gently irresponsible behavior of a large group of upper-class relatives, based loosely on her own remarkable family. In them her father is **satirized** as "Uncle Matthew."

After an unsuccessful marriage of 15 years, Mitford moved in the 1940s to Paris, France, where she spent the rest of her life. There she wrote the sequels to *The Pursuit of Love* and then turned to writing biographies, including one of France's King Louis XIV.

Mitford was also an essayist, and in 1955 she coined the terms "U" and "non-U" – "U" standing for "upper-class" – to describe words with similar meanings that were or were not sociably acceptable in British aristocratic circles: "writing paper" was "U," "notepaper" was definitely "non-U." These terms show her keen observation of people, which also makes the characters in her novels and their dialogue believable.

English novelist and biographer
Born Nov. 28, 1904
Died Jun. 30, 1973
Age at death 68

Book of essays showing Mitford aged 6 with her parents

WORKS INCLUDE

1931	*Highland Fling*	**1957**	*Voltaire in Love*
1945	*The Pursuit of Love*	**1960**	*Don't Tell Alfred*
1949	*Love in a Cold Climate*	**1962**	*The Water Beetle*
1951	*The Blessing*	**1966**	*The Sun King*
1953	*Madame de Pompadour*	**1970**	*Frederick the Great*

OTHER POST-1940 NOVELISTS

BALDWIN, James
BELLOW, Saul
CAMUS, Albert
GARCÍA MÁRQUEZ, Gabriel
GOLDING, William
HELLER, Joseph
IRVING, John
LESSING, Doris

MORRISON, Toni
SALINGER, J.D.
SINGER, Isaac Bashevis
SOLZHENITSYN, Aleksandr
UPDIKE, John
VIDAL, Gore
WALKER, Alice

SEE INDEX FOR FULL LIST

WORLD EVENTS

Age	Contemporary Events
Born 1904 	**1908** Henry Ford introduces Model T car **1912** Luxury liner *Titanic* sinks **1914–18** World War I ❶ **1917** Russian Revolution establishes Communist government
20 in 1924  	**1926** British scientist John Logie Baird demonstrates television **1927** Joseph Stalin becomes dictator of Russia ❷ **1929** Stock Market crash ushers in Great Depression ❸ **1931** Empire State Building in New York City completed **1933** Nazi Party, led by Adolf Hitler, gains control in Germany ❹ **1939–45** World War II: allies, led by U.S. and Great Britain, fight axis powers, led by Germany and Japan
40 in 1944	**1945** U.S. drops first atomic bombs on Japan **1950–53** Korean War: North Korea and China fight South Korea, the U.S., and United Nations troops **1957** Eisenhower sends troops to Little Rock, Arkansas, to ensure school desegregation **1960** John F. Kennedy elected president
60 in 1964 **Dies 1973**	**1964–75** Vietnam War: war between communist North Vietnam and U.S. forces supporting South Vietnam ❺ **1967** Arabs and Israelis fight in Six Day War **1969** American astronaut walks on Moon ❻

© DIAGRAM

MOFOLO, Thomas

Lesotho novelist
Born Aug. 2, 1875
Died Sep. 8, 1948
Age at death 73

Book cover to Mofolo's
major work

Thomas Mofolo was the first African novelist. He was born in the British colony of Basutoland, now called Lesotho, which was surrounded by white-ruled South Africa. His parents were Christians, and Mofolo attended the local mission school when he could. Despite being very poor, he managed to earn a teacher's certificate when he was 22. He began working for a Christian printing press, but business was interrupted by the **Boer War**, fought between the British and the white South Africans. After the war he studied carpentry and then began teaching, and in 1904 he returned to work at the printing press.

Mofolo was encouraged by his friends to begin writing. His first novel, *The Traveler of the East*, was serialized in a Lesotho newspaper when he was 31 and came out in book form the following year. This was the first novel written by an African and the first in an African language and is more important for historical than literary reasons. It is a very religious book about a Lesotho man's quest for wisdom. Mofolo's masterpiece, *Chaka*, was written around 1911. This story of the famous 19th-century Zulu king Shaka is a moral tale of his rise to power and increasingly cruel behavior. The printing press refused to publish the book until 1925, and by this time Mofolo had written about another great king, Moshoeshoe I – the founder of Lesotho – but had lost the manuscript in a fire. Disheartened, he gave up writing. Mofolo spent the rest of his life in various business ventures that were not always successful, and he died in poverty.

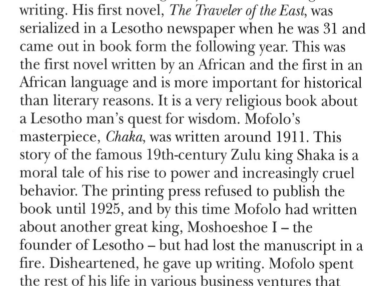

WORKS INCLUDE

1907 *The Traveler of the East*
1910 *Pitseng*
1925 *Chaka*

OTHER AFRICAN WRITERS

ACHEBE, Chinua
CLARK-BEKEDEREMO, John Pepper
COETZEE, J.M.
FUGARD, Athol
GORDIMER, Nadine
HEAD, Bessie
MAHFOUZ, Naguib
NETO, Agostinho

NGUGI wa Thiong'o
NWAPA, Flora
OKRI, Ben
PATON, Alan
ROBERT, Shaaban
SENGHOR, Léopold Sédar
SOYINKA, Wole

SEE INDEX FOR FULL LIST

WORLD EVENTS

Age	Contemporary Events
Born 1875 	**1876** American scientist Alexander Graham Bell invents telephone
	1876 Native American Sioux led by Crazy Horse kill Gen. George Armstrong Custer and his men at Battle of Little Bighorn
	1877–79 American inventor Thomas Edison invents phonograph and electric lightbulb
	1883 Brooklyn Bridge opens in New York
20 in 1895  	**1895** Italian physicist Guglielmo Marconi invents radio ❶
	1903 American inventors Orville and Wilbur Wright make first airplane flight ❷
	1908 Henry Ford introduces Model T car
	1914–18 World War I
40 in 1915 	**1917** Russian Revolution establishes Communist government ❸
	1926 British scientist John Logie Baird demonstrates television
	1927 Joseph Stalin becomes dictator of Russia ❹
	1931 Empire State Building in New York City completed
	1933 Nazi Party, led by Adolf Hitler, gains control in Germany
60 in 1935  **Dies 1948**	**1939–45** World War II: allies, led by U.S. and Great Britain, fight axis powers, led by Germany and Japan ❺
	1945 U.S. drops first atomic bombs on Japan
	1948 Apartheid laws, depriving nonwhite people of rights, introduced in South Africa

MOLIÈRE

French playwright
Born Jan. 15, 1622
Died Feb. 17, 1673
Age at death 51

Original costume design for
The Would-Be Gentleman

Molière was the pen name of Jean-Baptiste Poquelin, one of the greatest French comedy writers. The son of a wealthy upholsterer, Molière was born in Paris and had a strict upbringing at a Jesuit school. Despite qualifying as a lawyer, he never practiced law. His first love was the theater, and at the age of 21 he formed a theater company with a group of friends. They toured France for a number of years before coming to the attention of King Louis XIV, who gave them a permanent theater.

When he was 40, Molière had his first major success as a playwright with *The School for Wives*. The play poked fun at the limited education that was given to daughters of rich families, and it was the first of what are generally regarded as a series of masterpieces.

Molière's comedies range from broad slapstick comedy to subtle **satire**. He nearly always acted in the lead role himself. Molière firmly believed that there was "no comedy without truth, and no truth without comedy." He made fun of anyone he thought was dishonest, and because of this he often found himself in trouble – two of his plays, *The Imposter* and *Don Juan*, were banned.

Later in life Molière concentrated on writing musical comedies. In these plays the drama was interrupted by songs and dance or a combination of both. He was taken ill while performing in *The Imaginary Invalid* and died the same day. After his death the theater group Comédie Française was formed to promote his works. They are still enjoyed by modern theatergoers throughout the world.

WORKS INCLUDE

1662 *The School for Wives*
1664 *The Imposter*
1665 *Don Juan*
1666 *The Misanthrope*
1666 *The Doctor in Spite of Himself*

1668 *The Miser*
1668 *George Dandin*
1670 *The Would-Be Gentleman*
1672 *The Learned Ladies*
1673 *The Imaginary Invalid*

OTHER 17TH-CENTURY WRITERS

BEHN, Aphra
BRADSTREET, Anne
BUNYAN, John
CERVANTES, Miguel de
CONGREVE, William
CYRANO de BERGERAC
DONNE, John
DRYDEN, John

JONSON, Ben
La FONTAINE, Jean de
LOPE de VEGA
MILTON, John
PEPYS, Samuel
RACINE, Jean

SEE INDEX FOR FULL LIST

WORLD EVENTS

Age	Contemporary Events
Born 1622	**1628** English scientist William Harvey publishes his discovery of circulation of blood ❶
	1630 Caribbean island of Tortuga becomes pirate headquarters
	1632 Mogul king builds Taj Mahal as tomb for his wife in Agra, India
	1636 Harvard, first college in American colonies, opens
20 in 1642	**1642–51** English Civil War: conflict between king and his followers (Royalists or Cavaliers) and parliamentary supporters (Roundheads)
	1643 Italian physicist Evangelista Torricelli invents barometer
	1643–1715 Louis XIV reigns in France ❷
	1648 English religious leader George Fox founds Society of Friends (Quakers)
	1649 King Charles I of England beheaded; England becomes republic ❸
	1652 Dutch found colony at Cape of Good Hope, Africa
	1653–58 England ruled by Oliver Cromwell ❹
	1654 French physicist Blaise Pascal invents calculating machine that performs addition and multiplication
	1654 First Jews arrive in New Amsterdam
	1660 Charles II restored to English throne (Restoration)
40 in 1662 **Dies 1673**	**1665** British physicist Isaac Newton proposes theory of gravity ❺

© DIAGRAM

MOMADAY, N. Scott

American poet and novelist
Born Feb. 27, 1934

N. Scott Momaday's writings started a new wave of Native-American literature. His ancestors include Kiowas, Cherokees, and Anglo-Americans, and he writes mostly about his search for cultural identity.

Navarre Scott Momaday was born at the Kiowa Indian Hospital in Lawton, Oklahoma. His family settled at Jemez Pueblo, New Mexico, where his parents were teachers. Though they were accepted by the community, they were not allowed to participate in sacred ceremonies. At 18 he went to the University of New Mexico, then to the University of Virginia, where he was influenced by the work of WILLIAM FAULKNER.

Momaday began by writing poetry: his novel, *House Made of Dawn*, which won the 1969 **Pulitzer Prize**, began as a series of poems. It is about Abel, a Native American, who returns to his reservation after serving in **World War II**. Momaday explores relationships between races and the often complicated, violent encounters between different groups.

With powerful, sharply detailed writings Momaday recreates the lost landscape of his childhood and his people. In *The Way to Rainy Mountain*, which is illustrated by his father, Momaday uses poems, stories, myths, and memoirs to illustrate the development and decline of Kiowa culture. *The Names* is a poetic memoir of his childhood. For Momaday Native-American myths are about another plane of reality: he is very influenced by the bear figure, which is prominent in Kiowa myth and in his own stories and paintings.

a novel by
N. SCOTT MOMADAY
HOUSE
MADE OF
DAWN

Book cover for Momaday's first novel, *House Made of Dawn*

WORKS INCLUDE

1968 House Made of Dawn
1969 The Way to Rainy Mountain
1973 Colorado, Summer/Fall/Winter/Spring
1974 Angle of Geese
1976 The Gourd Dancer

1976 The Names
1989 The Ancient Child
1992 In the Presence of the Sun: Stories and Poems 1961–91

OTHER POST-1940 POETS

ANGELOU, Maya
BISHOP, Elizabeth
BRODSKY, Joseph
DUNCAN, Robert
GINSBERG, Allen
HAYDEN, Robert
HEANEY, Seamus
HUGHES, Ted

LOWELL, Robert
PAZ, Octavio
PLATH, Sylvia
SEXTON, Anne
THOMAS, Dylan
WALCOTT, Derek
YEVTUSHENKO, Yevgeny

SEE INDEX FOR FULL LIST

WORLD EVENTS

Age	Contemporary Events
Born 1934 	**1939–45** World War II: allies, led by U.S. and Great Britain, fight axis powers, led by Germany and Japan **1945** U.S. drops first atomic bombs on Japan ❶ **1945** Cold War begins between USSR and U.S. **1950–53** Korean War: North Korea and China fight South Korea, the U.S., and United Nations troops
20 in 1954 	**1957** Eisenhower sends troops to Little Rock, Arkansas, to ensure school desegregation **1960** John F. Kennedy elected president **1964–75** Vietnam War: war between communist North Vietnam and U.S. forces supporting South Vietnam ❷ **1967** Arabs and Israelis fight in Six Day War **1969** American astronaut walks on Moon ❸
40 in 1974 	**1975–79** Communist forces murder hundreds of thousands in Cambodia ❹ **1980** Ronald Reagan elected president ❺ **1981** U.S. launches first space shuttle **1989** Communist regimes fall throughout Eastern Europe **1991** Gulf War: UN forces, led by U.S., defeat Iraq and free Kuwait **1992** Bill Clinton elected president
60 in 1994	**1994** First multiracial elections in South Africa end years of white minority rule. They are won by Nelson Mandela, African National Congress leader

© DIAGRAM

69

MONTAIGNE,
Michel de

French essayist
Born Feb. 28, 1533
Died Sep. 13, 1592
Age at death 59

Montaigne's family home in southwest France

Michel de Montaigne is famous as the writer who invented the essay – a short piece that discusses the author's personal thoughts about a particular subject.

Born at his family estate in southwest France, Montaigne benefited from his father's advanced views about education that he had formed while serving as a soldier in Italy – then the center of European culture. As a baby he was sent to live with a peasant family so that his earliest memories would be of humble surroundings. His father then hired tutors who brought him up speaking nothing but Latin, the ancient **Roman** language. At school when all the other pupils were struggling to learn Latin, Montaigne spent his time reading the classics of Roman literature.

As a young man Montaigne studied in Paris and at the University of Bordeaux. He then returned to his home region to serve in the legal courts, a job he disliked but carried out with characteristic skill and devotion to duty. Aged 38 he "retired" to his family estate and devoted himself to writing.

Montaigne's first book of collected essays was published when he was 47. It covers a huge range of subjects, reflecting Montaigne's wide interests and learning. In one famous essay, "Of Cannibals," he wrote about the native peoples of the Americas, which were then just beginning to be explored by Europeans. He argued that the beliefs of different cultures should be respected, and he was always interested in new ideas and new discoveries.

WORKS INCLUDE

1569 *Apologia for Raymond Sebond*
1580–88 *Essays*
1774 *Journal of Travels* (published after he died)

OTHER 16TH-CENTURY WRITERS

ARIOSTO, Ludovico
CELLINI, Benvenuto
ERASMUS
KYD, Thomas
MARLOWE, Christopher
RABELAIS, François
SHAKESPEARE, William
SIDNEY, Sir Philip

SPENSER, Edmund
TASSO, Torquato

WORLD EVENTS

Age	Contemporary Events
Born 1533 **❶**	**1533–84** Reign of Ivan IV (the Terrible) in Russia **❶** **1541** John Calvin introduces Reformation (reform of the church) in Geneva, Switzerland **1543** Polish astronomer Nicholas Copernicus publishes his theory that Earth revolves around Sun **❷**
20 in 1553 **❷** **❸**	**1553** Mary I (Bloody Mary) becomes queen of England **1555** Tobacco brought to Europe from America **1558–1603** Elizabeth I rules England **❸** **1564–1642** Life of Galileo Galilei, Italian astronomer and mathematician **1567** Two million South American Indians die of typhoid fever **1569** Flemish (modern day Belgium) geographer Gerhardus Mercator produces first world map using projection that bears his name **1572** 20,000 French Protestants killed in Paris, France, in St. Bartholomew's Day Massacre
40 in 1573 **❹** **❺** **Dies 1592**	**1577–80** English navigator Francis Drake sails around the world **❹** **1588** English navy defeats Spanish Armada (Spanish fleet) **❺** **c. 1590** Dutch eyeglass maker Zacharias Janssen invents microscope **1592–98** Korean Admiral Yi Sung Si invents and uses ironclad warships in war against Japan

© DIAGRAM

MONTALE, Eugenio

Italian poet, critic, and essayist
Born Oct. 12, 1896
Died Sep. 12, 1981
Age at death 84

the Bones of
cuttlefish
EUGENIO MONTALE

Book cover for Montale's first collection of poetry

Eugenio Montale is an important figure in modern Italian literature. He won the **Nobel Prize** for literature in 1975.

Montale was born in the city of Genoa, a large and ancient seaport in northwest Italy, and spent his youth in a small village nearby on the shores of the Ligurian Sea. The harsh, dry landscape and rugged coastline of his homeland seem to have strongly influenced his poetry, which is difficult, private, and full of a sense of loneliness. His first collection of poems, *The Bones of Cuttlefish*, was published when he was 29.

Like many European poets writing in the period after **World War I**, Montale felt there was little hope for the future. His style of writing was influenced by the work of the great poet T.S. ELIOT, whose famous poem *The Waste Land* Montale translated into Italian. He wanted to create a new kind of Italian poetry that could escape from the influence of the great literature of Italy's past. One of the ways he tried to do this was by writing about his own personal experience. Critics called Montale's poetry "hermetic" because, like a hermit, he concentrated only on himself.

When the **fascists** came to power in Italy before **World War II**, Montale opposed them despite the risk of being sent to jail. He became a newspaper editor and was well known for his literary criticism. After the war he continued writing poetry, which gradually became less difficult to understand. *Xenia*, one of his last collections, is a series of moving love poems to his dead wife.

WORKS INCLUDE

1925 *The Bones of Cuttlefish*
1939 *The Occasions*
1956 *The Storm and Other Poems*
1956 *The Butterfly of Dinard*
1963 *Satura: Five Poems*

1965 *Selected Poems*
1970 *Xenia*
1978 *Selected Essays*
1980 *It Depends: A Poet's Notebook*

OTHER ITALIAN WRITERS

ARIOSTO, Ludovico
CALVINO, Italo
CARDUCCI, Giosuè
D'ANNUNZIO, Gabriele
DANTE
ECO, Umberto
FO, Dario
LAMPEDUSA, Giuseppe di

LEVI, Primo
MANZONI, Alessandro
MORAVIA, Alberto
PIRANDELLO, Luigi
QUASIMODO, Salvatore
SVEVO, Italo

SEE INDEX FOR FULL LIST

WORLD EVENTS

Age	Contemporary Events
Born 1896 	**1903** American inventors Orville and Wilbur Wright make first airplane flight **1908** Henry Ford introduces Model T car **1914–18** World War I ❶
20 in 1916 	**1917** Russian Revolution establishes Communist government **1927** Joseph Stalin becomes dictator of Russia ❷ **1931** Empire State Building in New York City completed **1933** Nazi Party, led by Adolf Hitler, gains control in Germany ❸
40 in 1936 	**1939–45** World War II: allies, led by U.S. and Great Britain, fight axis powers, led by Germany and Japan ❹ **1945** U.S. drops first atomic bombs on Japan **1950–53** Korean War: North Korea and China fight South Korea, the U.S., and United Nations troops
60 in 1956	**1957** Eisenhower sends troops to Little Rock, Arkansas, to ensure school desegregation **1960** John F. Kennedy elected president ❺ **1964–75** Vietnam War: war between communist North Vietnam and U.S. forces supporting South Vietnam ❻ **1967** Arabs and Israelis fight in Six Day War **1969** American astronaut walks on Moon
80 in 1976 ❼ **Dies 1981**	**1980** Ronald Reagan elected president ❼ **1981** U.S. launches first space shuttle

© DIAGRAM

73

MONTGOMERY, L.M.

Canadian children's writer
Born Nov. 30, 1874
Died Apr. 24, 1942
Age at death 67

Book cover for Montgomery's popular novel *The Story Girl*

L.M. Montgomery's classic novel *Anne of Green Gables* has become a favorite of young female readers around the world.

Lucy Maud Montgomery was born on Prince Edward Island, Canada. When she was two, her mother died, and her father remarried and moved away, leaving the young Montgomery to be raised by her cruel grandparents. At 15 she published her first poem in the local paper. She became a teacher and a reporter in Halifax, Nova Scotia, then at age 24 she returned to Prince Edward Island to care for her grandmother. There she wrote for magazines and began what was to become her classic.

Montgomery wrote and rewrote *Anne of Green Gables* and received several rejections from publishers before it was finally accepted when she was 34. It tells the story of Anne, a young orphan adopted by an elderly couple who were hoping for a boy. The novel captures the struggles and dreams of childhood and adolescence, and in many ways it reflects Montgomery's own experiences. It was instantly a success and was said to have been admired by MARK TWAIN. In response to its popularity Montgomery wrote seven "Anne" sequels, including *Anne of Avonlea* and *Rilla of Ingleside*, which follow the heroine through teaching, marriage, and raising a family.

In 1911, after the death of her grandmother, Montgomery married a preacher and moved with him to Ontario. While raising a family, she managed to write a book every other year, producing more than 20 novels and short-story collections.

WORKS INCLUDE

1908 *Anne of Green Gables*
1909 *Anne of Avonlea*
1911 *The Story Girl*
1915 *Anne of the Island*
1917 *Anne's House of Dreams*

1919 *Rainbow Valley*
1921 *Rilla of Ingleside*
1923 *Emily of New Moon*
1936 *Anne of Windy Poplars*
1939 *Anne of Ingleside*

OTHER CHILDREN'S WRITERS

ADAMS, Harriet Stratemeyer
ALCOTT, Louisa May
ANDERSEN, Hans Christian
BARRIE, J.M.
BLYTON, Enid
CARLE, Eric
CARROLL, Lewis
DAHL, Roald

KIPLING, Rudyard
LEAR, Edward
MILNE, A.A.
POTTER, Beatrix
REID BANKS, Lynne
SENDAK, Maurice
TWAIN, Mark

SEE INDEX FOR FULL LIST

WORLD EVENTS

Age	Contemporary Events
Born 1874  	**1876** American scientist Alexander Graham Bell invents telephone **1876** Native American Sioux led by Crazy Horse kill Gen. George Armstrong Custer and his men at Battle of Little Bighorn ❶ **1877–79** American inventor Thomas Edison invents phonograph and electric lightbulb **1883** Brooklyn Bridge opens in New York **1888** George Eastman perfects "Kodak" box camera ❷
20 in 1894  	**1895** Italian physicist Guglielmo Marconi invents radio ❸ **1903** American inventors Orville and Wilbur Wright make first airplane flight **1908** Henry Ford introduces Model T car **1912** Luxury liner *Titanic* sinks
40 in 1914	**1914–18** World War I ❹ **1917** Russian Revolution establishes Communist government **1926** British scientist John Logie Baird demonstrates television **1927** Joseph Stalin becomes dictator of Russia ❺ **1931** Empire State Building in New York City completed **1933** Nazi Party, led by Adolf Hitler, gains control in Germany ❻
60 in 1934 **Dies 1942** ❻	**1939–45** World War II: allies, led by U.S. and Great Britain, fight axis powers, led by Germany and Japan

© DIAGRAM

MOORCOCK, Michael

Michael Moorcock is the most important British fantasy author of the 1960s and '70s.

Moorcock was born in London, England. As a child he read and was influenced by EDGAR RICE BURROUGHS. When he left school, he contributed stories to a magazine called *Tarzan Adventures* and then became editor there. He also worked as a blues singer in London nightclubs.

Moorcock's first novel, *Caribbean Crisis*, was written when he was 23, under the pen name Desmond Reid. Two years later he became editor of a science fiction magazine, *New Worlds*, where he began to publish **experimental** fiction by authors like J.G. BALLARD and BRIAN ALDISS. Although *New Worlds* became a very influential magazine, it did not make money. To make a living, Moorcock wrote commercial fantasy novels at great speed, sometimes in a matter of days. In 1971 *New Worlds* stopped publication, and Moorcock, then aged 32, turned to writing more serious fiction. He also continued his musical career, performing with the rock band Hawkwind and his own band, Deep Fix.

Starting with *The Sundered Worlds*, published when he was 26, most of Moorcock's novels form part of a series about the adventures of a central figure, the Eternal Champion. Instead of living in the Universe, the Eternal Champion lives in a "multiverse" where there are different layers of reality. This allows him to become different characters, with names such as Jerry Cornelius, Elric of Melniboné, and Dorian Hawkmoon, who all fight to balance the forces of order and chaos. Moorcock is also respected as a writer of serious modern fiction.

English fantasy/science fiction writer
Born Dec. 18, 1939

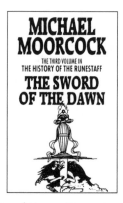

One of Moorcock's complex fantasy novels

WORKS INCLUDE

1962 *Caribbean Crisis*	**1981** *Byzantium Endures*
1965 *The Sundered Worlds*	**1984** *The Laughter of Carthage*
1965 *Stormbringer*	**1988** *Mother London*
1968 *The Sword of the Dawn*	**1992** *Jerusalem Commands*
1972 *The English Assassin*	**1995** *Blood: A Southern Fantasy*

OTHER FANTASY WRITERS

ADAMS, Douglas
BURROUGHS, Edgar Rice
DUNSANY, Lord
HAGGARD, H. Rider
HOWARD, Robert E.
Le GUIN, Ursula K.
LEIBER, Fritz
McCAFFREY, Anne

PRATCHETT, Terry
TOLKIEN, J.R.R.
WHITE, T.H.

WORLD EVENTS

Age	Contemporary Events
Born 1939 	**1939–45** World War II: allies, led by U.S. and Great Britain, fight axis powers, led by Germany and Japan **1945** U.S. drops first atomic bombs on Japan **1950–53** Korean War: North Korea and China fight South Korea, the U.S., and United Nations troops ❶ **1957** Eisenhower sends troops to Little Rock, Arkansas, to ensure school desegregation
20 in 1959	**1960** John F. Kennedy elected president ❷ **1964–75** Vietnam War: war between communist North Vietnam and U.S. forces supporting South Vietnam **1967** Arabs and Israelis fight in Six Day War **1969** American astronaut walks on Moon ❸ **1974** Pres. Richard M. Nixon resigns presidency
40 in 1979 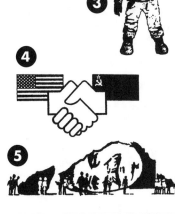	**1980** Ronald Reagan elected president **1981** U.S. launches first space shuttle **1987** Gorbachev begins reforms in USSR: perestroika (restructuring) and glasnost (openness) ❹ **1989** Communist regimes fall throughout Eastern Europe ❺ **1991** Gulf War: UN forces, led by U.S., defeat Iraq and free Kuwait **1992** Bill Clinton elected president **1994** First multiracial elections in South Africa end years of white minority rule. They are won by Nelson Mandela, African National Congress leader

© DIAGRAM

MOORE, Clement Clarke

Clement Clarke Moore was an American scholar who is remembered today for one poem, "A Visit from St. Nicholas," with its famous first line, "T'was the night before Christmas."

The son of a bishop, Moore grew up in an extremely wealthy family in New York City. After graduating from Columbia College, he settled on his family's estate in Manhattan, devoting his time to the study of Hebrew, the language of the Bible, and **ancient Greek**. From 1821 to 1850 Moore was professor of Asian and Greek literature at the Episcopal General Theological Seminary, built on land that he had donated. A political conservative, Moore opposed the expansion of democracy and the abolition of slavery.

When he was 43, Moore wrote the poem "A Visit from St. Nicholas" as a Christmas present to his children. It was published anonymously in the *Troy Sentinel* (N.Y.) in 1823. This popular poem helped shape America's ideas of Christmas. In those days Christmas was a time for crowds of rowdy young men to roam the streets and go from door to door demanding gifts in return for songs; the poem depicted Christmas as a celebration centered on the family and particularly the children. Its vivid descriptions changed the image of St. Nicholas from a dignified bishop of tradition to a plump, jolly old man, the origin of today's Santa Claus.

Moore produced a number of scholarly works, including a Hebrew dictionary and some political addresses. He also published a volume of other poetry and edited two volumes of his father's sermons.

American poet
Born Jul. 15, 1779
Died Jul. 10, 1863
Age at death 83

Illustration for Moore's poem "A Visit from St. Nicholas"

WORKS INCLUDE

1804 *Observations upon Certain Passages in Mr. Jefferson's Notes on Virginia*
1809 *A Compendious Lexicon of the Hebrew Language*

1844 *Poems*
1848 *"A Visit from St. Nicholas"*
1850 *George Castriot, Surnamed Scanderbeg, King of Albania*

OTHER 19TH-CENTURY POETS

BROWNING, Elizabeth Barrett
BROWNING, Robert
BRYANT, William Cullen
BYRON, Lord
COLERIDGE, Samuel Taylor
DICKINSON, Emily
DUNBAR, Paul Laurence
HOUSMAN, A.E.

KEATS, John
LONGFELLOW, Henry Wadsworth
SHELLEY, Percy Bysshe
SWINBURNE, Algernon Charles
TENNYSON, Alfred
WHITMAN, Walt
WORDSWORTH, William

SEE INDEX FOR FULL LIST

WORLD EVENTS

Age	Contemporary Events
Born 1779 	**1789** George Washington elected first president of U.S. **1789–99** French Revolution: French people revolt against monarchy
20 in 1799	**1804** Merriwether Lewis and William Clark begin exploration of Louisiana Territory ❶ **1812–14** War of 1812: U.S. fights Britain **1814** British troops capture Washington, DC ❷ **1815** Napoleon defeated at Waterloo (Belgium)
40 in 1819 ❸ 	**1821–29** Greek War of Independence against Turkey **1834** American inventor Cyrus McCormick patents reaper, machine used to harvest grain ❸ **1837–1901** Queen Victoria reigns in Great Britain
60 in 1939 ❹ 	**1846** Mexican War: U.S. fights Mexico **1849** California gold rush draws thousands of people **1854** Admiral Matthew Perry forces Japanese to sign trade treaty with U.S. ❹
80 in 1859 ❺  **Dies 1863**	**1859** English naturalist Charles Darwin publishes his theories on evolution **1860** Pony Express, American mail delivery service, established ❺ **1861–65** Civil War: North (Union) fights South (Confederacy) over issues of slavery and states' rights

PONY EXPRESS
10 Days to San Francisco!

MOORE, Marianne

American poet
Born Nov. 15, 1887
Died Feb. 5, 1972
Age at death 84

Selected
Poems

....

MARIANNE
MOORE

Book cover for a collection of
Moore's highly praised poems

Marianne Moore was a renowned American poet whose work influenced generations of women. Her best-known poems feature animals and are written in precise, clear language.

Moore was born in Kirkwood, near St. Louis, but after her mentally ill father was institutionalized, her mother moved to Carlisle, Pennsylvania, where she supported the family by teaching. Moore was already writing poetry when she graduated from Bryn Mawr College at 22. For four years she taught typing and bookkeeping, and then, when she was 28, a journal in England accepted her poem on war called "To the Soul of Progress."

Moore then moved to New York City, where she lived with her mother in Greenwich Village and worked as a librarian. Her first poetry collection, *Poems*, was published in England when she was 34; *Observations* appeared in the U.S. three years later. At age 37 she became editor of *Dial* magazine, where she helped publish such writers as T.S. ELIOT and EZRA POUND. When *Dial* closed in 1929, Moore supported herself by writing. Her *Selected Poems* was highly praised by Eliot. In 1952 Moore received the **Pulitzer Prize** and the National Book Award for her *Collected Poems*. She dedicated the book to her mother, crediting her as an important influence.

A lifelong baseball fan, Moore was honored in 1968 with the role of throwing out the first ball to open the season at Yankee Stadium.

In addition to several volumes of poetry, Moore wrote essays on contemporary writers and artists and a translation of **fables** by JEAN DE LA FONTAINE.

WORKS INCLUDE

1921 *Poems*
1924 *Observations*
1935 *Selected Poems*
1941 *What Are Years*
1951 *Collected Poems*

1954 *The Fables of La Fontaine*
1955 *Predilections*
1961 *A Marianne Moore Reader*
1966 *Tell Me, Tell Me*
1969 *The Accented Syllable*

OTHER POETS 1900–40

AKHMATOVA, Anna
AUDEN, W.H.
DOOLITTLE, Hilda
ELIOT, T.S.
FROST, Robert
GRAVES, Robert
HUGHES, Langston
LOWELL, Amy

MASEFIELD, John
MILLAY, Edna St. Vincent
POUND, Ezra
SASSOON, Siegfried
TAGORE, Rabindranath
YEATS, W.B.

SEE INDEX FOR FULL LIST

WORLD EVENTS

Age	Contemporary Events
Born 1887 	**1895** Italian physicist Guglielmo Marconi invents radio **1903** American inventors Orville and Wilbur Wright make first airplane flight ❶
20 in 1907	**1908** Henry Ford introduces Model T car **1914–18** World War I ❷ **1917** Russian Revolution establishes Communist government **1926** British scientist John Logie Baird demonstrates television
40 in 1927	**1927** Joseph Stalin becomes dictator of Russia **1931** Empire State Building in New York City completed **1933** Nazi Party, led by Adolf Hitler, gains control in Germany **1939–45** World War II: allies, led by U.S. and Great Britain, fight axis powers, led by Germany and Japan **1945** U.S. drops first atomic bombs on Japan ❸
60 in 1947	**1950–53** Korean War: North Korea and China fight South Korea, the U.S., and United Nations troops **1960** John F. Kennedy elected president ❹ **1964–75** Vietnam War: war between communist North Vietnam and U.S. forces supporting South Vietnam
80 in 1967 **Dies 1972** ❺	**1967** Arabs and Israelis fight in Six Day War **1969** American astronaut walks on Moon ❺

© DIAGRAM

MORAVIA, Alberto

Italian novelist and short-story writer
Born Nov. 28, 1907
Died Sep. 26, 1990
Age at death 82

Book cover for Moravia's novel *The Empty Canvas*

Alberto Moravia was the pen name of Alberto Pincherle. Moravia is best known for his anti**fascist** novels and for his exploration of sexuality.

Moravia was born in Rome, Italy, into a middle-class family. As a boy he suffered from poor health and spent much of his enforced leisure reading. Later he became a journalist, traveled widely, and learned several languages.

Moravia's first novel, *Time of Indifference*, was published when he was 22. At that time the fascist dictator Benito Mussolini ruled Italy. Moravia's book caused a sensation for criticizing the ultraright-wing fascists, and it earned the disapproval of the authorities. This forced him to hide the true message of his stories by writing in an **allegorical** style. He was not quite successful in this, however, and his increasing involvement in politics led to his books being banned. Forced to disappear, he remained in hiding until Italy was liberated.

Several other popular novels followed toward the end of **World War II**, including his best-known, *The Woman of Rome*. Moravia was no brilliant stylist, but he could tell a good story and write excellent dialogue. His purpose was essentially serious. Some of his books, for example *The Woman of Rome*, include sympathetic portraits of prostitutes and other women, whom he generally regarded as being superior to men. Others attack right-wing politics, moralism, and corruption. Much of his work is concerned with the important question of the relationship of love to sex. In Moravia's view sex is the enemy of love.

WORKS INCLUDE

1929 *Time of Indifference*
1944 *Two Adolescents*
1947 *The Woman of Rome*
1949 *Conjugal Love*
1951 *The Conformist*

1954 *Roman Tales*
1957 *Two Women*
1960 *The Empty Canvas*
1978 *Time of Desecration*
1985 *The Voyeur*

OTHER ITALIAN WRITERS

ARIOSTO, Ludovico
CALVINO, Italo
CARDUCCI, Giosuè
D'ANNUNZIO, Gabriele
DANTE
ECO, Umberto
FO, Dario
LAMPEDUSA, Giuseppe di

LEVI, Primo
MANZONI, Alessandro
MONTALE, Eugenio
PIRANDELLO, Luigi
QUASIMODO, Salvatore
SVEVO, Italo

SEE INDEX FOR FULL LIST

WORLD EVENTS

Age	Contemporary Events
Born 1907 	**1908** Henry Ford introduces Model T car **1914–18** World War I ❶ **1917** Russian Revolution establishes Communist government **1926** British scientist John Logie Baird demonstrates television
20 in 1927 	**1927** Joseph Stalin becomes dictator of Russia **1933** Nazi Party, led by Adolf Hitler, gains control in Germany **1939–45** World War II: allies, led by U.S. and Great Britain, fight axis powers, led by Germany and Japan **1945** U.S. drops first atomic bombs on Japan ❷
40 in 1947 	**1950–53** Korean War: North Korea and China fight South Korea, the U.S., and United Nations troops **1957** Eisenhower sends troops to Little Rock, Arkansas, to ensure school desegregation **1960** John F. Kennedy elected president ❸ **1964–75** Vietnam War: war between communist North Vietnam and U.S. forces supporting South Vietnam
60 in 1967 	**1969** American astronaut walks on Moon ❹ **1979** Britain elects its first female prime minister, Margaret Thatcher **1981** U.S. launches first space shuttle ❺
80 in 1987 **Dies 1990**	**1989** Communist regimes fall throughout Eastern Europe

MORRIS, William

English poet and novelist
Born Mar. 24, 1834
Died Oct. 3, 1896
Age at death 62

Page from a beautiful book produced by Kelmscott Press

William Morris was one of the most popular poets of his time. Today he is remembered for founding the Arts and Crafts movement in England, which encouraged a return to handmade objects and away from industrialization. He is also known as a designer of furniture, fabrics, and wallpaper and as an artist.

Morris was born into a family with money. He originally planned to become a clergyman but turned to architecture instead. Friends persuaded him to switch to painting, and he became obsessed with **medieval** art. With his friends he started a company to design and make furniture, stained glass, and wallpaper. Later, he founded the Kelmscott Press, a publishing firm dedicated to producing beautiful books.

Morris's poems and other writings first appeared in a magazine. They were reprinted in *The Defence of Guenevere*, which he published when he was 24. Fame and success came with two long poems, *The Life and Death of Jason*, based on **ancient Greek** myths, and *The Earthly Paradise*, 24 tales from classical and medieval times. His greatest poetic book was *Sigurd the Volsung*, a retelling of ancient **sagas** from Iceland and Norway.

Most of Morris's later writings were in prose, and many were devoted to spreading his socialist views and ideas for a better future (for example, *News from Nowhere*). In 1887 he and GEORGE BERNARD SHAW led a political demonstration in London. He also wrote historical romances of times long past in northern Europe, including *The Roots of the Mountains* and *The Wood beyond the World*.

WORKS INCLUDE

1858 *The Defence of Guenevere*
1867 *The Life and Death of Jason*
1868–70 *The Earthly Paradise*
1876 *Sigurd the Volsung*
1882 *Hopes and Fears for Art*

1888 *A Dream of John Ball*
1890 *The Roots of the Mountains*
1891 *News from Nowhere*
1894 *The Wood beyond the World*

OTHER 19TH-CENTURY POETS

BROWNING, Elizabeth Barrett
BROWNING, Robert
BRYANT, William Cullen
BYRON, Lord
COLERIDGE, Samuel Taylor
DICKINSON, Emily
DUNBAR, Paul Laurence
HOUSMAN, A.E.

KEATS, John
LONGFELLOW, Henry Wadsworth
SHELLEY, Percy Bysshe
SWINBURNE, Algernon Charles
TENNYSON, Alfred
WHITMAN, Walt
WORDSWORTH, William

SEE INDEX FOR FULL LIST

WORLD EVENTS

Age	Contemporary Events
Born 1834 	**1834** American inventor Cyrus McCormick patents reaper, machine used to harvest grain ❶ **1837–1901** Queen Victoria reigns in Great Britain **1846** Mexican War: U.S. fights Mexico **1849** California gold rush draws thousands of people
20 in 1854	**1859** English naturalist Charles Darwin publishes his theories on evolution **1861–65** Civil War: North (Union) fights South (Confederacy) over issues of slavery and states' rights ❷ **1865** Pres. Abraham Lincoln assassinated ❸ **1869** U.S. transcontinental railroad completed
40 in 1874 	**1876** American scientist Alexander Graham Bell invents telephone **1876** Native American Sioux led by Crazy Horse kill Gen. George Armstrong Custer and his men at Battle of Little Bighorn ❹ **1877–79** American inventor Thomas Edison invents phonograph and electric lightbulb **1883** Brooklyn Bridge opens in New York
60 in 1894 **Dies 1896**	**1895** German physicist Wilhelm K. Roentgen discovers X-rays ❺ **1895** Italian physicist Guglielmo Marconi invents radio **1896** First modern Olympic Games held in Athens, Greece

© DIAGRAM

MORRISON, Toni

American novelist
Born Feb. 18, 1931

Toni Morrison is one of the world's most notable contemporary writers and only the second American woman to have won the **Nobel Prize** for literature.

Morrison was born Chloe Anthony Wofford in Lorain, Ohio. Her parents shared a love of African-American **folklore** and music with their children, and she was taught to read before she started school.

Morrison graduated from Howard University in 1953 (where she became known as "Toni") then received a master's degree from Cornell University in 1955. She married and had two sons, whom she raised on her own after her divorce in 1964. She became a book editor and eventually became responsible for the work of a number of leading black women writers, including TONI CADE BAMBARA and GAYL JONES. While working as an editor by day and caring for her children on her own, she wrote her first novel, *The Bluest Eye*, which was published when she was 39. It describes the experiences of young black girls struggling to define themselves. Part of their struggle is against "white" standards of beauty that are adopted even within the black community.

While compiling a book on "black life" in America from slavery to the 1940s called *The Black Book*, Morrison read documents that describe the lives of ordinary African Americans. Her novel *Beloved* is based on a story she discovered among these documents of a woman who tried to kill her children rather than allowing them to be sent back into slavery. The book earned her the **Pulitzer Prize** for fiction. She won the Nobel Prize for literature in 1993.

Book cover for Morrison's novel
Song of Solomon

WORKS INCLUDE

1970 *The Bluest Eye*
1973 *Sula*
1974 *The Black Book*
1977 *Song of Solomon*
1981 *Tar Baby*

1986 *Dreaming Emmett*
1987 *Beloved*
1992 *Jazz*
1998 *Paradise*

OTHER POST-1940 NOVELISTS

BALDWIN, James
BELLOW, Saul
CAMUS, Albert
GARCÍA MÁRQUEZ, Gabriel
GOLDING, William
HELLER, Joseph
IRVING, John
LESSING, Doris

SALINGER, J.D.
SINGER, Isaac Bashevis
SOLZHENITSYN, Aleksandr
UPDIKE, John
VIDAL, Gore
WALKER, Alice

SEE INDEX FOR FULL LIST

WORLD EVENTS

Age	Contemporary Events
Born 1931 	**1931** Empire State Building in New York City completed ❶ 
	1933 Nazi Party, led by Adolf Hitler, gains control in Germany ❷
	1939–45 World War II: allies, led by U.S. and Great Britain, fight axis powers, led by Germany and Japan
	1945 U.S. drops first atomic bombs on Japan
	1950–53 Korean War: North Korea and China fight South Korea, the U.S., and United Nations troops
20 in 1951 	**1957** Eisenhower sends troops to Little Rock, Arkansas, to ensure school desegregation
	1960 John F. Kennedy elected president ❸
	1964–75 Vietnam War: war between communist North Vietnam and U.S. forces supporting South Vietnam
	1969 American astronaut walks on Moon ❹
40 in 1971	**1980** Ronald Reagan elected president ❺
	1989 Communist regimes fall throughout Eastern Europe
60 in 1991	**1991** Gulf War: UN forces, led by U.S., defeat Iraq and free Kuwait
	1992 Bill Clinton elected president
	1994 First multiracial elections in South Africa end years of white minority rule. They are won by Nelson Mandela, African National Congress leader

© DIAGRAM

MOSLEY, Walter

American crime writer
Born 1952

Walter Mosley is the most well-known African-American crime writer in the U.S. today. President Clinton has called him his favorite crime novelist.

The son of a black father and a white Jewish mother, Mosley grew up in the tough Watts area of Los Angeles. His father was a school janitor. Mosley later moved to New York, where he worked as a painter, a caterer, and a computer programmer before becoming a full-time writer. Today Mosley still lives in New York, but his novels are set in Los Angeles.

Mosley's first work of fiction, *Gone Fishin'*, was not a crime novel. It failed to find a publisher, and Mosley turned to the more commercial thriller **genre** instead. He wrote his first crime novel, *Devil in a Blue Dress*, when he was 38. It was an immediate success and was made into a film starring Denzel Washington.

In the series of novels that follow, Mosley offers a history of black Los Angeles, starting in the 1940s just after **World War II**, when African Americans migrated from the Southern states to work in California. He then moves on to the 1950s, a period when American society was obsessed with the fear of **communism**. His later books are set in the 1960s against a background of social rebellion during the **civil rights movement**.

The main character in Mosley's novels is Easy Rawlins, a school janitor (like Mosley's father) and a reluctant private detective. His friend Mouse is loyal but extremely violent. Like the **hard-boiled** detectives before him – such as RAYMOND CHANDLER's Philip Marlowe – Easy struggles to build a decent life for himself but becomes increasingly cynical about human nature.

Novel featuring Mosley's detective hero Easy Rawlins

WORKS INCLUDE

1990 *Devil in a Blue Dress*
1991 *A Red Death*
1992 *White Butterfly*
1994 *Black Betty*
1996 *A Little Yellow Dog*

1997 *Always Outnumbered, Always Outgunned*

CHANDLER, Raymond
CHRISTIE, Agatha
DOYLE, Arthur Conan
GARDNER, Erle Stanley
GRAFTON, Sue
GRISHAM, John
HAMMETT, Dashiell
HIGHSMITH, Patricia

JAMES, P.D.
Le CARRÉ, John
LEONARD, Elmore
McBAIN, Ed
PARETSKY, Sara
RENDELL, Ruth
THOMPSON, Jim

SEE INDEX FOR FULL LIST

WORLD EVENTS

Age	Contemporary Events
Born 1952 ❶	**1957** Eisenhower sends troops to Little Rock, Arkansas, to ensure school desegregation **1960** John F. Kennedy elected president ❶
10 in 1962 ❷ ❸	**1963** Led by Rev. Martin Luther King, Jr., thousands march on Washington DC to press for civil rights for African Americans **1964–75** Vietnam War: war between communist North Vietnam and U.S. forces supporting South Vietnam ❷ **1967** Arabs and Israelis fight in Six Day War **1969** American astronaut walks on Moon ❸
20 in 1972 ❹	**1975–79** Communist forces murder hundreds of thousands in Cambodia **1980** Ronald Reagan elected president ❹ **1981** U.S. launches first space shuttle ❺
30 in 1982 ❺	**1987** Gorbachev begins reforms in USSR: perestroika (restructuring) and glasnost (openness) ❻ **1989** Communist regimes fall throughout Eastern Europe **1991** Gulf War: UN forces, led by U.S., defeat Iraq and free Kuwait
40 in 1992 ❻	**1992** Bill Clinton elected president **1994** First multiracial elections in South Africa end years of white minority rule. They are won by Nelson Mandela, African National Congress leader

© DIAGRAM

MPHAHLELE, Es'kia

South African novelist, short-story writer, and poet
Born Dec. 17, 1919

Book cover for a collection of Mphahlele's stories

Es'kia (formerly Ezekiel) Mphahlele, one of Africa's leading writers in English, wrote the classic novel *Down Second Avenue.*

Mphahlele was born in the slums of Pretoria, one of South Africa's major cities. From the age of 12 he lived with his grandmother and aunt, who made sure that Mphahlele could finally start school at the age of 13. He went on to be a teacher but was banned from teaching in 1952 after criticizing the government's planned Bantu Education Act. At that time the white South Africans controlled the government and all the major industries. Racist laws restricted where black people could live and what work they could do. While continuing his studies, Mphahlele took a variety of jobs instead of teaching.

Mphahlele began writing short stories, but his work was banned by the white government, so he left South Africa. For 20 years he lived abroad in Nigeria, France, Kenya, the U.S., and Zambia. He worked as a college teacher while writing novels, poems, and essays. Based on his years growing up in Pretoria, the novel *Down Second Avenue* came out when Mphahlele was 40. It describes the harm caused by racist **apartheid** policies. *Chirundu* is based on his time in Zambia, telling of the ups and downs of life in a newly independent country. His prizewinning *The Wanderers* is based on his years of exile. Mphahlele returned to South Africa in 1977. Back home, he continued the story of his life in *Africa My Music* and became head of African literature at the University of Witwatersrand in Johannesburg.

WORKS INCLUDE

1947 *Man Must Live*
1959 *Down Second Avenue*
1961 *The Living and Dead*
1967 *In Corner B*
1971 *The Wanderers*

1972 *Voices in the Whirlwind*
1980 *Chirundu*
1984 *Africa My Music*
1984 *Father Come Home*
1985 *Let's Talk Writing*

OTHER AFRICAN WRITERS

ACHEBE, Chinua
CLARK-BEKEDEREMO, John Pepper
COETZEE, J.M.
FUGARD, Athol
GORDIMER, Nadine
HEAD, Bessie
MAHFOUZ, Naguib
NETO, Agostinho

NGUGI wa Thiong'o
NWAPA, Flora
OKRI, Ben
PATON, Alan
ROBERT, Shaaban
SENGHOR, Léopold Sédar
SOYINKA, Wole

SEE INDEX FOR FULL LIST

WORLD EVENTS

Age	Contemporary Events
Born 1919 	**1927** Joseph Stalin becomes dictator of Russia **1931** Empire State Building in New York City completed **1933** Nazi Party, led by Adolf Hitler, gains control in Germany ❶
20 in 1939 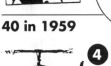 	**1939–45** World War II: allies, led by U.S. and Great Britain, fight axis powers, led by Germany and Japan **1945** U.S. drops first atomic bombs on Japan **1950–53** Korean War: North Korea and China fight South Korea, the U.S., and United Nations troops **1957** Eisenhower sends troops to Little Rock, Arkansas, to ensure school desegregation ❷
40 in 1959 	**1960** John F. Kennedy elected president ❸ **1964–75** Vietnam War: war between communist North Vietnam and U.S. forces supporting South Vietnam ❹ **1967** Arabs and Israelis fight in Six Day War **1969** American astronaut walks on Moon ❺
60 in 1979 	**1980** Ronald Reagan elected president ❻ **1981** U.S. launches first space shuttle ❼ **1991** Gulf War: UN forces, led by U.S., defeat Iraq and free Kuwait **1992** Bill Clinton elected president **1994** First multiracial elections in South Africa end years of white minority rule. They are won by Nelson Mandela, African National Congress leader

© DIAGRAM

MQHAYI, Samuel

South African novelist, short-story writer, and poet
Born Dec. 1, 1875
Died Jul. 29, 1945
Age at death 69

U-DON JADU

" *UkuHamba yimFundo.* "

Imbali yokukhuthaza uManyano nenKqubela-
Phambili.

IBALWE NGU-
S. E. KTUNE MQHAYI.

THE LOVEDALE PRESS

Mqhayi's book *U-Don Jadu*,
written in the Xhosa language

Samuel Mqhayi is the most famous South African writer in the Xhosa language.

Mqhayi was born in the British Cape Colony, South Africa. Descended from a chief and the son of a teacher, he belonged to a high-ranking Xhosa family. The Xhosa are one of South Africa's main ethnic groups. When he was nine, the Cape was hit by famine, so his family moved northeast to Transkei. They settled near one of Mqhayi's uncles, a Xhosa chief. Listening to the tales of Xhosa warriors and attending meetings at the local court made a great impression on the young Mqhayi. He later used these memories in his classic novel *The Case of the Twins*.

When he was 22, Mqhayi's poems appeared in the newspaper *The Voice of the People*. Like most of his poetry, they were based on Xhosa praise-poems sung in honor of others. Mqhayi continued to work on this newspaper in between teaching jobs. Then, when he was 39, *The Case of the Twins* was published and made him famous. About the conflict between twin sons to decide who was born first and could, therefore, claim their father's estate, this novel shows how well African justice systems worked before the introduction of European laws. During Mqhayi's lifetime he had seen white South Africans become increasingly powerful at the expense of the rights of black Africans. His novel *U-Don Jadu* looks toward a future without racism.

Mqhayi would recite poems at important events and came to be known as the praise-poet of the entire Xhosa nation. He also translated many books into Xhosa, recorded Xhosa praise-poems, and standardized Xhosa spelling and grammar.

WORKS INCLUDE

1914 *The Case of the Twins*
c. 1920 *The Heroes of the Mendi*
1923 *The Church of the People*
1927 *Songs of Exaltation*
1929 *U-Don Jadu*

1937 *Hintza the Great*
1939 *Mqhayi from the Mountain of Glory*
1942 *Reward*

OTHER AFRICAN WRITERS

ACHEBE, Chinua
CLARK-BEKEDEREMO, John Pepper
COETZEE, J.M.
FUGARD, Athol
GORDIMER, Nadine
HEAD, Bessie
MAHFOUZ, Naguib
NETO, Agostinho

NGUGI wa Thiong'o
NWAPA, Flora
OKRI, Ben
PATON, Alan
ROBERT, Shaaban
SENGHOR, Léopold Sédar
SOYINKA, Wole

SEE INDEX FOR FULL LIST

WORLD EVENTS

Age	Contemporary Events
Born 1875	**1876** American scientist Alexander Graham Bell invents telephone
	1876 Native American Sioux led by Crazy Horse kill Gen. George Armstrong Custer and his men at Battle of Little Bighorn ❶
	1877–79 American inventor Thomas Edison invents phonograph and electric lightbulb
	1883 Brooklyn Bridge opens in New York
20 in 1895	**1895** Italian physicist Guglielmo Marconi invents radio ❷
	1903 American inventors Orville and Wilbur Wright make first airplane flight
	1908 Henry Ford introduces Model T car
	1914–18 World War I
40 in 1915	**1917** Russian Revolution establishes Communist government
	1919 Prohibition introduced in U.S. ❸
	1926 British scientist John Logie Baird demonstrates television
	1927 Joseph Stalin becomes dictator of Russia
	1931 Empire State Building in New York City completed ❹
	1933 Nazi Party, led by Adolf Hitler, gains control in Germany
60 in 1935	**1935** Italy invades Abyssinia (Ethiopia)
	1939–45 World War II: allies, led by U.S. and Great Britain, fight axis powers, led by Germany and Japan
Dies 1945	**1945** U.S. drops first atomic bombs on Japan

© DIAGRAM

MUNRO, Alice

**Canadian
short-story writer
Born** Jul. 10, 1931

ALICE
MUNRO

Lives OF
Girls AND
Women

Munro's second collection of
short stories

Alice Munro is known for the way she captures the details of ordinary rural lives in her short stories.

Munro was born in the small town of Wingham in rural Ontario. She grew up on a farm with her sister and brother. Her mother had been a teacher, and her father raised foxes, then worked as a watchman, then farmed. Munro also was expected to farm when she grew up, but she had other plans; by age 12 she had decided to become a writer.

Munro attended the University of Western Ontario on a scholarship. In 1951 she married a fellow student and moved with him to Vancouver, where she found herself trying to combine writing with being a suburban wife and mother. She published a few stories in literary magazines, and in the 1960s she and her husband started a bookstore.

It was not until she was 37 that Munro published a book – a collection of 15 stories called *Dance of the Happy Shades*. It was highly praised and won her Canada's prestigious Governor General's Award. But it was *Lives of Girls and Women*, Munro's second collection, that earned her international attention. The linked stories describe the childhood of a young woman in rural Canada who wants to become a writer. The book was made into a TV movie starring Munro's daughter Jenny.

Influenced by writers such as EUDORA WELTY and FLANNERY O'CONNOR, Munro writes about the peculiarities and customs of small-town life. However, the issues she addresses are broad and relevant to all of humanity.

WORKS INCLUDE

1968 *Dance of the Happy Shades*
1971 *Lives of Girls and Women*
1974 *Something I've Been Meaning to Tell You*
1978 *The Beggar Maid*

1982 *The Moons of Jupiter*
1986 *The Progress of Love*
1990 *Friend of My Youth*
1994 *Open Secrets*

OTHER POST-1940 WRITERS

BALDWIN, James
BELLOW, Saul
CAMUS, Albert
GARCÍA MÁRQUEZ, Gabriel
GOLDING, William
HELLER, Joseph
IRVING, John
LESSING, Doris

MORRISON, Toni
SALINGER, J.D.
SINGER, Isaac Bashevis
SOLZHENITSYN, Aleksandr
UPDIKE, John
VIDAL, Gore
WALKER, Alice

SEE INDEX FOR FULL LIST

WORLD EVENTS

Age	Contemporary Events
Born 1931  	**1931** Empire State Building in New York City completed
	1933 Nazi Party, led by Adolf Hitler, gains control in Germany
	1939–45 World War II: allies, led by U.S. and Great Britain, fight axis powers, led by Germany and Japan
	1945 U.S. drops first atomic bombs on Japan
	1950–53 Korean War: North Korea and China fight South Korea, the U.S., and United Nations troops ❶
20 in 1951	**1957** Eisenhower sends troops to Little Rock, Arkansas, to ensure school desegregation ❷
	1960 John F. Kennedy elected president ❸
	1964–75 Vietnam War: war between communist North Vietnam and U.S. forces supporting South Vietnam
	1967 Arabs and Israelis fight in Six Day War
	1969 American astronaut walks on Moon ❹
40 in 1971 	**1981** U.S. launches first space shuttle
	1989 Communist regimes fall throughout Eastern Europe
60 in 1991 	**1991** Gulf War: UN forces, led by U.S., defeat Iraq and free Kuwait ❺
	1992 Bill Clinton elected president
	1994 First multiracial elections in South Africa end years of white minority rule. They are won by Nelson Mandela, African National Congress leader

© DIAGRAM

MURASAKI Shikibu

**Japanese poet
and novelist**
Born c. 978
Died c. 1026
Age at death c. 48

Japanese classic written by
Murasaki Shikibu

Murasaki Shikibu is the pen name of the author of *The Tale of Genji*, which has been described as the greatest work in the history of Japanese literature.

Little is known about Murasaki's life, not even her real name. She was born into a powerful aristocratic family and was educated along with her brothers in the arts of poetry. It was not uncommon for aristocratic women to be educated in literature at this time in Japan.

In 999 Murasaki was married to a man so much older than herself that he already had a son who was older than she was. Around this time she began to keep a diary detailing life at the court of a Japanese empress. Murasaki's husband died within two years. The empress came to hear of her talents as a poet and appointed her to the imperial court.

The Tale of Genji was based on Murasaki's experiences of court life. It is about the romances of Prince Genji and the lives of his descendants. Set in a world of complex social ritual, elegance, and beauty, it is a very long and complicated tale that follows the intricate social lives and love affairs of its characters. Although there is no real central story, the skill with which the author describes the emotions and thoughts of the many characters, especially the women, was far ahead of any other writer of the period. For this reason many scholars describe *The Tale of Genji* as the first true novel.

The Tale of Genji became known in the West more than 900 years after it was written when an English poet published a translation in the 1920s.

WORKS INCLUDE

c. 1010 *The Tale of Genji*

OTHER ASIAN AND MIDDLE EASTERN WRITERS

BASHO, Matsuo
DESAI, Anita
DING LING
DU FU
HAYASHI Fumiko
KALIDASA
KAWABATA Yasunari
MISHIMA Yukio

NARAYAN, R.K.
OZ, Amos
SHIMAZAKI Toson
TAGORE, Rabindranath
TANIZAKI Junichiro
WU CHENGEN

SEE INDEX FOR FULL LIST

WORLD EVENTS

Age	Contemporary Events
Before her birth	**874–986** Vikings settle Iceland and Greenland ❶
	882 Kiev becomes capital of Russia
	900 Anasazi people begin building pueblos in southwestern North America
	c. 900 Castles become headquarters of European nobility
	c. 900 Chinese begin using paper money
	900–1100 Toltecs flourish in Central America ❷
	942 Arabs introduce trumpets in Europe
	969 Fatimids, Syrian Arabs, conquer Egypt
Born **c. 978** ❷ **Dies c. 1026**	**c. 1000** Chinese invent gunpowder
	1001 Stephen I crowned king of Hungary
	1002 Viking leader Leif Ericson explores Newfoundland
After her death	**c. 1050** Chinese and Arabs use compass
	1050–1105 Almoravids, Berbers from the western Sahara, conquer Spain
	1052 Building begins on Westminster Abbey in London, England
	1054 Christian Church divided into Roman Catholic and Orthodox
	1063 St. Mark's Basilica completed in Venice, Italy
	1066 French Normans, under William the Conqueror, defeat English Saxons at Battle of Hastings in England ❸
	1071 Muslim Turks stop Christian pilgrimages to Jerusalem
	1086 William the Conqueror conducts survey of England recorded in *Domesday Book*

MURDOCH, Iris

Anglo-Irish novelist, philosopher, and playwright
Born Jul. 15, 1919

Book cover for one of Murdoch's popular novels

Iris Murdoch is one of the most important writers of her generation. She has written many books on **philosophy**, and even her fiction has been described as "novels of ideas." In recognition of her work she was made a dame in 1987 (a title equivalent to knighthood).

Murdoch was born in Dublin, Ireland, but was brought up in England. Her mother was Irish and her father English. After graduating from Oxford University, she worked for the United Nations as an administrative officer. From 1948 to 1963 she taught philosophy at Oxford.

Murdoch's first book was about philosophy. She began writing stories as a hobby, and her first novel, *Under the Net*, came out when she was 35. It was an instant success, and she has since followed it by over 20 others as well as more philosophical works.

The Bell, whose subject is an unofficial religious community, is regarded as one of her best novels. *A Severed Head*, first published as a novel, was turned into a play with the help of J.B. PRIESTLEY. She later wrote several more plays.

Murdoch's novels combine realistic characters with extraordinary situations, often bordering on the fantastic. Many of them have a religious or philosophical theme. For example, *The Time of the Angels* features a priest in an inner-city parish who goes in for devil worship. Some critics describe her novels as "psychological detective stories" because of the way in which they investigate in great detail the motives and consequences of the characters' behavior.

WORKS INCLUDE

1954 *Under the Net*
1958 *The Bell*
1961 *A Severed Head*
1966 *The Time of the Angels*
1972 *The Two Arrows*

1974 *The Sacred and Profane Love Machine*
1978 *The Sea, the Sea*
1983 *The Philosopher's Pupil*
1995 *Jackson's Dilemma*

OTHER POST-1940 NOVELISTS

BALDWIN, James
BELLOW, Saul
CAMUS, Albert
GARCÍA MÁRQUEZ, Gabriel
GOLDING, William
HELLER, Joseph
IRVING, John
LESSING, Doris

MORRISON, Toni
SALINGER, J.D.
SINGER, Isaac Bashevis
SOLZHENITSYN, Aleksandr
UPDIKE, John
VIDAL, Gore
WALKER, Alice

SEE INDEX FOR FULL LIST

WORLD EVENTS

Age	Contemporary Events
Born 1919 	**1927** Joseph Stalin becomes dictator of Russia **1931** Empire State Building in New York City completed **1933** Nazi Party, led by Adolf Hitler, gains control in Germany ❶
20 in 1939 	**1939–45** World War II: allies, led by U.S. and Great Britain, fight axis powers, led by Germany and Japan **1945** U.S. drops first atomic bombs on Japan **1950–53** Korean War: North Korea and China fight South Korea, the U.S., and United Nations troops **1957** Eisenhower sends troops to Little Rock, Arkansas, to ensure school desegregation ❷
40 in 1959 	**1960** John F. Kennedy elected president ❸ **1964–75** Vietnam War: war between communist North Vietnam and U.S. forces supporting South Vietnam ❹ **1967** Arabs and Israelis fight in Six Day War **1969** American astronaut walks on Moon ❺
60 in 1979 	**1980** Ronald Reagan elected president ❻ **1981** U.S. launches first space shuttle ❼ **1991** Gulf War: UN forces, led by U.S., defeat Iraq and free Kuwait **1992** Bill Clinton elected president **1994** First multiracial elections in South Africa end years of white minority rule. They are won by Nelson Mandela, African National Congress leader

NABOKOV, Vladimir

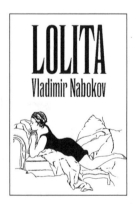

**Russian-born
American novelist
Born** Apr. 23, 1899
Died Jul. 2, 1977
Age at death 78

Book cover for Nabokov's
controversial novel *Lolita*

Vladimir Nabokov was an outstanding 20th-century writer. He is best known for his novel *Lolita*.

Nabokov was born in St. Petersburg, Russia, into an aristocratic family. An intelligent child, he learned to speak English and French as well as his native Russian. His first poems were published before he was 20.

Nabokov's family lost its wealth during the **Russian Revolution** and in 1919 moved abroad. Nabokov studied at Cambridge University, England, and from 1922 until 1940 lived first in Germany and then Paris, France, where he met the great novelist JAMES JOYCE and mixed with Russian refugees. During these years he published nine novels, writing in Russian under the pen name Vladimir Serin. His reputation as an inventive novelist grew, but he earned little money and survived by teaching.

In 1940 Nabokov, his wife, and son moved to America, where he took citizenship in 1945. His first novel in English was *The Real Life of Sebastian Knight*, published when he was 42; from then on he wrote all his books in English. From 1948 to 1959 he taught at Cornell University, using this experience for his novel *Pnin*, a comic account of a Russian professor at an American college.

When he was in his mid-50s, Nabokov's masterpiece, *Lolita*, was published. It tells the story of a middle-aged man and his passion for his 12-year-old stepdaughter. The novel's subject matter shocked many people, but its humor and literary style were praised by critics. *Lolita* was an instant success; it shot Nabokov to fame and enabled him to devote himself to writing.

WORKS INCLUDE

1926 *Mary*
1928 *King, Queen, Knave*
1932 *Laughter in the Dark*
1936 *Despair*
1937–38 *The Gift*

1938 *Invitation to a Beheading*
1941 *The Real Life of Sebastian Knight*
1947 *Bend Sinister*
1955 *Lolita*
1957 *Pnin*

OTHER POST-1940 NOVELISTS

BALDWIN, James
BELLOW, Saul
CAMUS, Albert
GARCÍA MÁRQUEZ, Gabriel
GOLDING, William
HELLER, Joseph
IRVING, John
LESSING, Doris

MORRISON, Toni
SALINGER, J.D.
SINGER, Isaac Bashevis
SOLZHENITSYN, Aleksandr
UPDIKE, John
VIDAL, Gore
WALKER, Alice

SEE INDEX FOR FULL LIST

WORLD EVENTS

Age	Contemporary Events
Born 1899	**1903** American inventors Orville and Wilbur Wright make first airplane flight **1908** Henry Ford introduces Model T car **1914–18** World War I **1917** Russian Revolution establishes Communist government **1917** U.S. enters World War I ❶
20 in 1919 	**1926** British scientist John Logie Baird demonstrates television **1927** Joseph Stalin becomes dictator of Russia ❷ **1931** Empire State Building in New York City completed ❸ **1933** Nazi Party, led by Adolf Hitler, gains control in Germany
40 in 1939 	**1939–45** World War II: allies, led by U.S. and Great Britain, fight axis powers, led by Germany and Japan **1945** U.S. drops first atomic bombs on Japan **1950–53** Korean War: North Korea and China fight South Korea, the U.S., and United Nations troops ❹ **1957** Eisenhower sends troops to Little Rock, Arkansas, to ensure school desegregation
60 in 1959 **Dies 1977**	**1960** John F. Kennedy elected president **1964–75** Vietnam War: war between communist North Vietnam and U.S. forces supporting South Vietnam ❺ **1967** Arabs and Israelis fight in Six Day War **1969** American astronaut walks on Moon

© DIAGRAM

NAIPAUL, V.S.

Many consider V.S. Naipaul to be one of the world's most gifted novelists. He has written about many different cultures and problems faced by ordinary people all over the world.

Vidiadhar Surajprasad Naipaul was born in Trinidad to Indian parents. He went to England to study at Oxford University and settled in that country.

Naipaul's first three books are lighthearted novels about Trinidadian life, starting with *The Mystic Masseur*, which came out when Naipaul was 25. He came to fame at the age of 29 with his fourth novel, *A House for Mr. Biswas*, also set in Trinidad. Its central character was based on his father, a mild-mannered journalist.

From then on Naipaul moved the setting of his novels to other places. *Mr. Stone and the Knights Companion* is set in London. He returned to the Caribbean in *The Mimic Men*, in which the action takes place on a fictitious island, and in *Guerrillas*, which describes a violent uprising on yet another island.

Naipaul has become increasingly absorbed with the problems of less-developed countries. In *A Bend in the River* he traces, with the expectance of a bad outcome, the development of a West African state whose dictator-president tries to control events through periods of revolution and counterrevolution.

Besides his novels, Naipaul has written several books about travel and politics. Among them are three studies of India since independence, including *India: A Wounded Civilization* (1977) and *Among the Believers: An Islamic Journey* (1981).

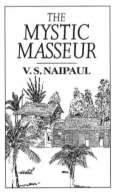

Trinidadian-born British novelist Born Aug. 17, 1932

Book cover for one of Naipaul's early novels

WORKS INCLUDE

1957 The Mystic Masseur
1958 The Suffrage of Elvira
1961 A House for Mr. Biswas
1963 Mr. Stone and the Knights
Companion

1967 The Mimic Men
1971 In a Free State
1975 Guerrillas
1979 A Bend in the River
1994 A Way in the World

OTHER POST-1940 NOVELISTS

BALDWIN, James
BELLOW, Saul
CAMUS, Albert
GARCÍA MÁRQUEZ, Gabriel
GOLDING, William
HELLER, Joseph
IRVING, John
LESSING, Doris

MORRISON, Toni
SALINGER, J.D.
SINGER, Isaac Bashevis
SOLZHENITSYN, Aleksandr
UPDIKE, John
VIDAL, Gore
WALKER, Alice

SEE INDEX FOR FULL LIST

WORLD EVENTS

Age	Contemporary Events
Born 1932 	**1933** Nazi Party, led by Adolf Hitler, gains control in Germany **1939–45** World War II: allies, led by U.S. and Great Britain, fight axis powers, led by Germany and Japan **1945** U.S. drops first atomic bombs on Japan ❶ **1945** Cold War begins between USSR and U.S. **1950–53** Korean War: North Korea and China fight South Korea, the U.S., and United Nations troops
20 in 1952 	**1957** Eisenhower sends troops to Little Rock, Arkansas, to ensure school desegregation ❷ **1960** John F. Kennedy elected president **1964–75** Vietnam War: war between communist North Vietnam and U.S. forces supporting South Vietnam **1967** Arabs and Israelis fight in Six Day War **1969** American astronaut walks on Moon
40 in 1972  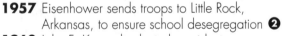	**1980** Ronald Reagan elected president ❸ **1981** U.S. launches first space shuttle ❹ **1989** Communist regimes fall throughout Eastern Europe **1991** Gulf War: UN forces, led by U.S., defeat Iraq and free Kuwait ❺
60 in 1992 ❺	**1992** Bill Clinton elected president **1994** First multiracial elections in South Africa end years of white minority rule. They are won by Nelson Mandela, African National Congress leader

NARAYAN, R.K.

**Indian novelist,
short-story writer,
and essayist
Born** Oct. 10, 1906

R.K. Narayan is an outstanding Indian novelist recognized as a writer of international importance.

Narayan was born Rasipuram Krishnaswami Narayanswami in Madras in the south of India and was raised by his grandmother. He was educated in Madras and at the Maharaja's College in Mysore. He worked as a teacher before becoming a full-time writer, choosing to write in English, the language of educated Indians.

Narayan's 11 novels are set in the imaginary town of Malgudi. The last seven of the series are works of the first rank, revealing his wisdom, sophistication, and power. His style is simple, elegant, and has a delicate humor. As the greatest Hindu novelist who has written in English, he provides an insight into the values and traditions of Hinduism. His books deal with the realities of life, with moral questions, human relationships, and the conflict between traditional and modern urban life.

Narayan believes in the Hindu doctrine of reincarnation (being reborn after death), and this is an important theme in his later fiction. He is concerned with the process of human improvement – the characters that interest him most are those people who are "insane" because of their lack of knowledge about themselves.

Many critics regard *The Guide* as his best work. It is a part-comedy, part-**tragedy** about the conversion to holiness of a con man. Narayan has also written short stories, travel and children's books, essays, and his memoirs.

Book cover for one of Narayan's popular novels set in India

WORKS INCLUDE

1935 *Swami and Friends*
1937 *The Bachelor of Arts*
1938 *The Dark Room*
1945 *Grateful to Love and Death*
1949 *The Printer of Malgudi*

1958 *The Guide*
1961 *The Man-Eater of Malgudi*
1967 *The Vendor of Sweets*
1977 *The Painter of Signs*
1990 *The World of Nagaraj*

OTHER ASIAN AND MIDDLE EASTERN WRITERS

BASHO, Matsuo
DESAI, Anita
DING LING
DU FU
HAYASHI Fumiko
KALIDASA
KAWABATA Yasunari
MISHIMA Yukio

MURASAKI Shikibu
NARAYAN, R.K.
OZ, Amos
SHIMAZAKI Toson
TAGORE, Rabindranath
TANIZAKI Junichiro
WU CHENGEN

SEE INDEX FOR FULL LIST

WORLD EVENTS

Age	Contemporary Events
Born **1906**	**1914–18** World War I **1917** Russian Revolution establishes Communist government
20 in **1926**	**1927** Joseph Stalin becomes dictator of Russia ❶ **1933** Nazi Party, led by Adolf Hitler, gains control in Germany ❷ **1939–45** World War II: allies, led by U.S. and Great Britain, fight axis powers, led by Germany and Japan **1945** U.S. drops first atomic bombs on Japan
40 in 1946 	**1950–53** Korean War: North Korea and China fight South Korea, the U.S., and United Nations troops **1960** John F. Kennedy elected president ❸ **1964–75** Vietnam War: war between communist North Vietnam and U.S. forces supporting South Vietnam ❹
60 in 1966 	**1969** American astronaut walks on Moon ❺ **1981** U.S. launches first space shuttle
80 in 1986	**1989** Communist regimes fall throughout Eastern Europe **1991** Gulf War: UN forces, led by U.S., defeat Iraq and free Kuwait ❻ **1992** Bill Clinton elected president **1994** First multiracial elections in South Africa end years of white minority rule. They are won by Nelson Mandela, African National Congress leader

© DIAGRAM

105

NASH, Ogden

Ogden Nash was an original and funny poet whose work has often been imitated, but few other poets of light verse have been as popular. He used simple, oddly spelled, unusually rhymed verse to mock, surprise, or just raise a laugh. Some of his lines, such as "Candy is dandy, but liquor is quicker," have become established parts of American culture.

Nash was born in Rye, New York, to parents of Southern stock. He was raised in Savannah, Georgia, and several other cities because the family moved around with his father's business. Between 1917 and 1920 he attended St. George's School in Newport, Rhode Island, then Harvard College from 1920 to 1921, when he left to earn a living. He went back to St. George's to teach, then to Wall Street to work as a bond salesman. He admits he sold only one bond, to his godmother, and wisely moved into advertising. Nash did well in advertising, having an original and clever sense of humor.

In his spare time he tried his hand at serious poetry. He wanted to write about beauty, truth, eternity, and pain, like the poets he admired, such as JOHN KEATS and LORD BYRON. He decided later that he was better at humorous verse. His first published work, *The Cricket of Carador*, was a children's book. After a few years of scribbling down verses on office paper, Nash published his first book of humorous verse, *Hard Lines*, when he was 29. It was so successful that Nash soon quit his job in advertising and within four years was able to concentrate on his writing alone. Other well-known works include *Happy Days* and *The Bad Parents' Garden of Verse*.

American poet
Born Aug. 19, 1902
Died May 19, 1971
Age at death 68

The *Cricket* *of Carador*

BY JOSEPH ALGER
& OGDEN NASH

ILLUSTRATIONS BY
CHRISTOPHER RULE

Published by DOUBLEDAY, PAGE & CO., Garden City, New York
1925

Book cover for Nash's first published work

WORKS INCLUDE

1925 *The Cricket of Carador*
1931 *Hard Lines*
1931 *Free Wheeling*
1936 *The Bad Parents' Garden of Verse*
1938 *I'm a Stranger Here Myself*
1953 *The Private Dining Room, and Other New Verses*
1959 *Verse from 1929 On*
1959 *Custard the Dragon*

OTHER POETS 1900–40

AKHMATOVA, Anna
AUDEN, W.H.
DOOLITTLE, Hilda
ELIOT, T.S.
FROST, Robert
GRAVES, Robert
HUGHES, Langston
LOWELL, Amy

MASEFIELD, John
MILLAY, Edna St. Vincent
MOORE, Marianne
POUND, Ezra
SASSOON, Siegfried
TAGORE, Rabindranath
YEATS, W.B.

SEE INDEX FOR FULL LIST

WORLD EVENTS

Age	Contemporary Events
Born 1902 	**1903** American inventors Orville and Wilbur Wright make first airplane flight
	1908 Henry Ford introduces Model T car
	1912 Luxury liner *Titanic* sinks
	1914–18 World War I ❶
	1917 Russian Revolution establishes Communist government
20 in 1922 	**1926** British scientist John Logie Baird demonstrates television
	1927 Joseph Stalin becomes dictator of Russia ❷
	1931 Empire State Building in New York City completed
	1933 Nazi Party, led by Adolf Hitler, gains control in Germany ❸
	1939–45 World War II: allies, led by U.S. and Great Britain, fight axis powers, led by Germany and Japan ❹
40 in 1942 	**1945** U.S. drops first atomic bombs on Japan ❺
	1950–53 Korean War: North Korea and China fight South Korea, the U.S., and United Nations troops
	1957 Eisenhower sends troops to Little Rock, Arkansas, to ensure school desegregation
	1960 John F. Kennedy elected president
60 in 1962 	**1964–75** Vietnam War: war between communist North Vietnam and U.S. forces supporting South Vietnam ❻
Dies 1971	**1967** Arabs and Israelis fight in Six Day War
	1969 American astronaut walks on Moon

NAYLOR, Gloria

American novelist
Born Jan. 25, 1950

Book cover for Naylor's
fourth novel

The strength of women working together to fight racism is one of the themes of Gloria Naylor's novels, which convey both the sufferings and the triumphs of African-American women. When she was 38, Naylor became one of the few African-American women writers to win a prestigious Guggenheim fellowship.

Although she was born in New York, the South had a big influence on Naylor. Her parents – a telephone operator and a transit worker – had worked as sharecroppers in Mississippi until just before she was born, and she grew up with stories of life there.

After high school Naylor worked as a Jehovah's Witness missionary for seven years then enrolled in Brooklyn College. While there she read TONI MORRISON's *The Bluest Eye*, which made a huge impression on her; it was the first time she saw her own experience as a black woman reflected in literature, and it made her want to write.

While in college Naylor supported herself as a telephone operator in New York hotels. After graduating in 1981, she went to Yale, where she received her master's degree in 1983. She had also been working on her first novel, which she published when she was 32. In seven separate but interlocking stories *The Women of Brewster Place* tells of a community of women who live on a run-down street in a black ghetto. They struggle together to break down the walls of racism that keep them poor and oppressed. It won the National Book Award for best first novel and was made into a television movie starring Oprah Winfrey.

WORKS INCLUDE

1982 *The Women of Brewster Place*
1985 *Linden Hills*
1988 *Mama Day*
1992 *Bailey's Café*

OTHER POST-1940 NOVELISTS

BALDWIN, James
BELLOW, Saul
CAMUS, Albert
GARCÍA MÁRQUEZ, Gabriel
GOLDING, William
HELLER, Joseph
IRVING, John
LESSING, Doris

MORRISON, Toni
SALINGER, J.D.
SINGER, Isaac Bashevis
SOLZHENITSYN, Aleksandr
UPDIKE, John
VIDAL, Gore
WALKER, Alice

SEE INDEX FOR FULL LIST

WORLD EVENTS

Age	Contemporary Events
Born 1950 	**1950–53** Korean War: North Korea and China fight South Korea, the U.S., and United Nations troops ❶ **1957** Eisenhower sends troops to Little Rock, Arkansas, to ensure school desegregation
10 in 1960  	**1960** John F. Kennedy elected president **1963** Led by Rev. Martin Luther King, Jr., thousands march on Washington DC to press for civil rights for African Americans ❷ **1964–75** Vietnam War: war between communist North Vietnam and U.S. forces supporting South Vietnam ❸ **1967** Arabs and Israelis fight in Six Day War **1969** American astronaut walks on Moon
20 in 1970 	**1974** Pres. Richard M. Nixon resigns presidency **1975–79** Communist forces murder hundreds of thousands in Cambodia ❹
30 in 1980 	**1980** Ronald Reagan elected president **1981** U.S. launches first space shuttle **1989** Communist regimes fall throughout Eastern Europe ❺
40 in 1990 ❻	**1991** Gulf War: UN forces, led by U.S., defeat Iraq and free Kuwait ❻ **1992** Bill Clinton elected president **1994** First multiracial elections in South Africa end years of white minority rule. They are won by Nelson Mandela, African National Congress leader

© DIAGRAM

NELLIGAN, Emile

Canadian poet
Born Dec. 24, 1879
Died Nov. 18, 1941
Age at death 61

EMILE
NELLIGAN

Complete
Works

Book cover for an English
translation of Nelligan's poetry

Emile Nelligan wrote all his poems in a period of three years between the ages of 17 and 20. He is famous not only for the brilliance of these poems but also for bringing French-Canadian poetry into the modern age.

Nelligan was born in Montreal, Quebec, where he and his two sisters attended school. Doted on by his French-Canadian mother, he enjoyed a blissfully happy childhood. At age 17 he quit school and joined the now famous L'École Littéraire de Montréal, a circle of young writers who met weekly to discuss the arts and to try to revive the French cultural life of Quebec. At the circle's meetings he read his poems to great acclaim. In 1899, however, a minor French critic spoke harshly of his work. Nelligan was so devastated that he withdrew into his own private world and threatened to commit suicide. A year later he was diagnosed as suffering from mental illness and at age 20 was admitted to a hospital, where he remained until his death 40 years later.

Nelligan's poems were considered modern because, unlike other French-Canadian poets of the time, he did not write about overused, impersonal subjects such as patriotism and the glories of old France. Instead, he explored the dark corners of his own tortured soul and turned to his dreams and his childhood memories for inspiration and escape from the difficulties of the world. His poems were first published four years after he was hospitalized. He made such an impact in his short creative life that more than 600 critical writings on his work have appeared in print.

WORKS INCLUDE

1903 Emile Nelligan and His Work
Published after he died
1952 Complete Poems: 1896–99
1960 Selected Poems
1983 The Complete Poems of Emile Nelligan

OTHER POETS 1900–40

AKHMATOVA, Anna
AUDEN, W.H.
DOOLITTLE, Hilda
ELIOT, T.S.
FROST, Robert
GRAVES, Robert
HUGHES, Langston
LOWELL, Amy

MASEFIELD, John
MILLAY, Edna St. Vincent
MOORE, Marianne
POUND, Ezra
SASSOON, Siegfried
TAGORE, Rabindranath
YEATS, W.B.

SEE INDEX FOR FULL LIST

WORLD EVENTS

Age	Contemporary Events
Born 1879 	**1883** Brooklyn Bridge opens in New York **1895** Italian physicist Guglielmo Marconi invents radio
20 in 1899	**1903** American inventors Orville and Wilbur Wright make first airplane flight **1908** Henry Ford introduces Model T car **1914–18** World War I **1917** Russian Revolution establishes Communist government **1917** U.S. enters World War I
40 in 1919  Berlin 1936	**1919** Prohibition introduced in U.S. ❶ **1926** British scientist John Logie Baird demonstrates television **1927** American aviator Charles A. Lindbergh makes first solo flight across Atlantic ❷ **1927** Joseph Stalin becomes dictator of Russia ❸ **1931** Empire State Building in New York City completed ❹ **1933** Nazi Party, led by Adolf Hitler, gains control in Germany **1936** African-American track star Jesse Owens wins four gold medals at Olympics in Hitler's Germany ❺ **1936–39** Spanish Civil War: conservative forces overthrow government
60 in 1939 **Dies 1941**	**1939–45** World War II: allies, led by U.S. and Great Britain, fight axis powers, led by Germany and Japan **1941** Germany invades USSR

© DIAGRAM

NEMEROV, Howard

**American poet,
short-story writer,
and novelist**
Born Mar. 1, 1920
Died Jul. 5, 1991
Age at death 71

Inside the Onion

Howard Nemerov

A collection of Nemerov's
award-winning poetry

Howard Nemerov is highly respected for his witty
and often **ironic** poetry. He was also a successful
novelist and short-story writer. His achievements
both as a poet and an educator earned him many
awards, including the post of **Poet Laureate** of
America from 1988 to 1990.

Nemerov was born in New York City and educated at
the Fieldston School. He graduated from Harvard in
1941 and during **World War II** served in both the
Royal Canadian and U.S. air forces. After the war he
taught at various colleges and for two years was poetry
consultant at the Library of Congress. He taught at
Washington University, St. Louis, from 1969, and for
the last 14 years of his life he was titled Distinguished
Professor of English there.

Nemerov's first volume of poetry, *The Image and the
Law*, was published when he was 27. His early poetry
was influenced by the great Irish poet W.B. YEATS and
by WALLACE STEVENS. Like them, Nemerov saw poetry
as a shield from the chaos that is the natural world.
The poems of Nemerov's collections *The Next Room of
the Dream* and *The Blue Swallows* show a new clarity and
directness and reflect the mood of rapid change in
1960s America. Nemerov himself identified influences
of more radical poets, such as T.S. ELIOT.

The Collected Poems, published when Nemerov was
57, contained verse from all his previous books and
caused a reevaluation of Nemerov's status. He was
awarded the **Pulitzer Prize** the following year. *Trying
Conclusions* was published in the year of his death and
contained many new poems. It is the companion
volume to *The Collected Poems*.

WORKS INCLUDE

1947 *The Image and the Law*
1950 *Guide to the Ruins*
1957 *The Homecoming Game*
1960 *New and Selected Poems*
1962 *The Next Room of the Dream*

1967 *The Blue Swallows*
1973 *Gnomes and Occasions*
1977 *The Collected Poems*
1984 *Inside the Onion*
1991 *Trying Conclusions*

ANGELOU, Maya
BISHOP, Elizabeth
BRODSKY, Joseph
DUNCAN, Robert
GINSBERG, Allen
HAYDEN, Robert
HEANEY, Seamus
HUGHES, Ted

LOWELL, Robert
PAZ, Octavio
PLATH, Sylvia
SEXTON, Anne
THOMAS, Dylan
WALCOTT, Derek
YEVTUSHENKO, Yevgeny

SEE INDEX FOR FULL LIST

WORLD EVENTS

Age	Contemporary Events
Born 1920 	**1926** British scientist John Logie Baird demonstrates television **1927** Joseph Stalin becomes dictator of Russia ❶ **1933** Nazi Party, led by Adolf Hitler, gains control in Germany ❷ **1939–45** World War II: allies, led by U.S. and Great Britain, fight axis powers, led by Germany and Japan
20 in 1940 	**1941** Germany invades USSR ❸ **1945** U.S. drops first atomic bombs on Japan **1950–53** Korean War: North Korea and China fight South Korea, the U.S., and United Nations troops **1957** Eisenhower sends troops to Little Rock, Arkansas, to ensure school desegregation
40 in 1960 	**1960** John F. Kennedy elected president **1961** East Germans build Berlin Wall **1962** Cuban Missile Crisis erupts after the U.S. discovers Soviet missiles on island ❹ **1964–75** Vietnam War: war between communist North Vietnam and U.S. forces supporting South Vietnam **1967** Arabs and Israelis fight in Six Day War **1969** American astronaut walks on Moon
60 in 1980  **Dies 1991**	**1981** U.S. launches first space shuttle ❺ **1989** Communist regimes fall throughout Eastern Europe **1991** Gulf War: UN forces, led by U.S., defeat Iraq and free Kuwait

© DIAGRAM

113

NERUDA, Pablo

Chilean poet
Born Jul. 12, 1904
Died Sep. 23, 1973
Age at death 69

ELEMENTARY ODES

Pablo Neruda

Book cover for a collection of Neruda's poetry

Pablo Neruda was one of the greatest South American poets and is certainly the best known. His poems have been translated into many languages, and he was awarded the **Nobel Prize** for literature in 1971.

Neruda was born in Chile, the son of a poor railroad worker. He was named Naftalí Reyes, and he began writing poetry when he was ten years old. He did not use the name by which he is now known until he published his first poems in student magazines as a teenager.

In 1921 Neruda went to study at teachers' college in Santiago, the capital city. Almost immediately he established himself as a powerful new voice in Chilean poetry. When he was 20, he published *Twenty Love Poems and a Song of Despair*, the collection that first brought him international fame.

At the age of only 23 Neruda was appointed by the Chilean government as a consul in Burma (now Myanmar). This was the start of a diplomatic career that took him all over Asia and South America and to Spain, where he became close friends with the poet FEDERICO GARCÍA LORCA. When García Lorca was executed soon after the outbreak of the **Spanish Civil War**, Neruda's poetry grew increasingly political, and he became a committed **communist**.

Soon after **World War II** Neruda's politics almost cost him his life when the Chilean government was taken over by right-wing extremists. He escaped by crossing the Andes Mountains on horseback. Neruda returned to Chile in 1952 and lived there for the rest of his life, writing and campaigning.

WORKS INCLUDE

1924 *Twenty Love Poems and a Song of Despair*
1933 *Residence on Earth*
1945 *The Heights of Macchu Picchu*
1950 *Canto General*

1954 *Elementary Odes*
1967 *Twenty Poems*
1972 *Captain's Verses*
1977 *Memoirs* (published after he died)

OTHER LATIN AMERICAN WRITERS

ALEGRÍA, Claribel
ALLENDE, Isabel
ASTURIAS, Miguel Angel
BENEDETTI, Mario
BORGES, Jorge Luis
CABRERA INFANTE, Guillermo
FUENTES, Carlos
GARCÍA MÁRQUEZ, Gabriel

MACHADO de ASSIS, Joaquim Maria
ONETTI, Juan Carlos
PAZ, Octavio
ROA BASTOS, Augusto
RULFO, Juan
VARGAS LLOSA, Mario

SEE INDEX FOR FULL LIST

WORLD EVENTS

Age	Contemporary Events
Born 1904	**1908** Henry Ford introduces Model T car **1914–18** World War I **1917** Russian Revolution establishes Communist government
20 in 1924  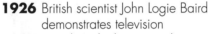	**1926** British scientist John Logie Baird demonstrates television **1927** Joseph Stalin becomes dictator of Russia **1931** Empire State Building in New York City completed ❶ **1933** Nazi Party, led by Adolf Hitler, gains control in Germany ❷ **1939–45** World War II: allies, led by U.S. and Great Britain, fight axis powers, led by Germany and Japan
40 in 1944	**1945** U.S. drops first atomic bombs on Japan **1950–53** Korean War: North Korea and China fight South Korea, the U.S., and United Nations troops **1957** Eisenhower sends troops to Little Rock, Arkansas, to ensure school desegregation **1960** John F. Kennedy elected president **1961** East Germans build Berlin Wall **1962** Cuban Missile Crisis erupts after the U.S. discovers Soviet missiles on island ❸
60 in 1964  **Dies 1973**	**1964–75** Vietnam War: war between communist North Vietnam and U.S. forces supporting South Vietnam ❹ **1967** Arabs and Israelis fight in Six Day War **1969** American astronaut walks on Moon

© DIAGRAM

115

NESBIT, E.

E. Nesbit was an English writer who is remembered for her stories for children. Her most famous book is *The Railway Children.*

Edith Nesbit was born in London, England, the last of six children. Her father, a scientist, died when she was young, and she was sent to a boarding school for her education, which she hated. Memories of her early life as part of a large family later inspired Nesbit's writings for children.

When she was 22 and living back in London, Nesbit married. Soon after the wedding her husband was cheated in a business deal, and the couple found themselves with little money and a young son to support. Nesbit had already had a few poems published, and she turned to writing articles and stories to earn money for the family.

Nesbit had always wanted to be a poet, and her first collection of poems, *Lays and Legends*, was published when she was 28. Her poetry was never successful, and she did not become known until she began to write children's stories in her mid-30s.

Nesbit started writing a series of books about the adventures of six brothers and sisters called the Bastables. The first of these, *The Story of the Treasure Seekers*, was published when she was 41. The Bastable family was very like Nesbit's own, and their adventures were set in the real world. *The Railway Children* was another realistic adventure, based on Nesbit's memories of a childhood home that had a railroad nearby. She also wrote fantasy stories, such as *Five Children and It* and *The Phoenix and the Carpet*, which are full of magic and mystery.

English children's writer
Born Aug. 15, 1858
Died May 4, 1924
Age at death 65

Illustration of a scene from *The Railway Children*

WORKS INCLUDE

1886 *Lays and Legends*
1899 *The Story of the Treasure Seekers*
1901 *Nine Unlikely Tales for Children*
1901 *The Wouldbegoods*
1902 *Five Children and It*

1904 *The Phoenix and the Carpet*
1904 *The New Treasure Seekers*
1906 *The Railway Children*
1928 *The Bastable Children* (published after she died)

OTHER CHILDREN'S WRITERS

ADAMS, Harriet Stratemeyer
ALCOTT, Louisa May
ANDERSEN, Hans Christian
BARRIE, J.M.
BLYTON, Enid
CARLE, Eric
CARROLL, Lewis
DAHL, Roald

KIPLING, Rudyard
LEAR, Edward
MILNE, A.A.
POTTER, Beatrix
REID BANKS, Lynne
SENDAK, Maurice
TWAIN, Mark

SEE INDEX FOR FULL LIST

WORLD EVENTS

Age	Contemporary Events
Born 1858   	**1859** English naturalist Charles Darwin publishes his theories on evolution **1861–65** Civil War: North (Union) fights South (Confederacy) over issues of slavery and states' rights ❶ **1865** Pres. Abraham Lincoln assassinated ❷ **1869** U.S. transcontinental railroad completed **1876** American scientist Alexander Graham Bell invents telephone **1876** Native American Sioux led by Crazy Horse kill Gen. George Armstrong Custer and his men at Battle of Little Bighorn ❸ **1877–79** American inventor Thomas Edison invents phonograph and electric lightbulb
20 in 1878 	**1883** Brooklyn Bridge opens in New York **1888** George Eastman perfects "Kodak" box camera **1895** Italian physicist Guglielmo Marconi invents radio ❹
40 in 1898 	**1903** American inventors Orville and Wilbur Wright make first airplane flight ❺ **1908** Henry Ford introduces Model T car ❻ **1914–18** World War I **1917** Russian Revolution establishes Communist government
60 in 1918 **Dies 1924**	**1919** English physicist Ernest Rutherford splits atom **1924** George Gershwin composes *Rhapsody in Blue*

© DIAGRAM

NETO, Agostinho

Agostinho Neto was Angola's leading poet as well as that country's first president.

Neto was born in a village near Luanda, the capital of Angola, which was then a Portuguese colony. He studied at local schools before becoming a nurse at the age of 22. For three years he saved money to study medicine, and during that time he helped set up a cultural association which became increasingly anticolonial. With his savings and extra help from his village and friends, he traveled to Portugal to study medicine in 1947.

Neto's studies in Portugal were interrupted three times by arrest and imprisonment. He became involved in various anticolonial political movements and began writing poetry that reflected his political views. His poems, some of which were published when he was 26, deal with freedom, and many were smuggled out of jail. His writings brought him much attention, and after being arrested for the third time, international outcry forced the Portuguese to release him. Neto finally returned to Angola as a doctor in 1958.

In 1959 Neto was made leader of the MPLA (Popular Movement for the Liberation of Angola). A year later he was arrested and held in prisons and under house arrest. He managed to escape in 1962 and lead the MPLA in the armed struggle against Portuguese rule. Angola finally became independent in 1975 with Neto as its first president. By that time, however, the struggle had turned into a civil war, and Neto was never to rule over a unified Angola; he died of cancer four years later.

Angolan poet
Born Sep. 17, 1922
Died Sep. 10, 1979
Age at death 56

Book cover for a collection of Neto's poetry

WORKS INCLUDE

1961 Collected Poems
1963 With Dry Eyes
1974 Sacred Hope
1979 Poems from Angola

OTHER AFRICAN WRITERS

ACHEBE, Chinua
CLARK-BEKEDEREMO, John Pepper
COETZEE, J.M.
FUGARD, Athol
GORDIMER, Nadine
HEAD, Bessie
MAHFOUZ, Naguib
NGUGI wa Thiong'o

NWAPA, Flora
OKRI, Ben
PATON, Alan
ROBERT, Shaaban
SENGHOR, Léopold Sédar
SOYINKA, Wole

SEE INDEX FOR FULL LIST

WORLD EVENTS

Age	Contemporary Events
Born 1922 	**1926** British scientist John Logie Baird demonstrates television **1927** Joseph Stalin becomes dictator of Russia ❶ **1931** Empire State Building in New York City completed **1933** Nazi Party, led by Adolf Hitler, gains control in Germany **1939–45** World War II: allies, led by U.S. and Great Britain, fight axis powers, led by Germany and Japan ❷
20 in 1942 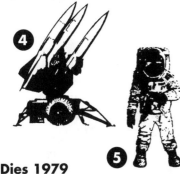	**1945** U.S. drops first atomic bombs on Japan ❸ **1950–53** Korean War: North Korea and China fight South Korea, the U.S., and United Nations troops **1957** Eisenhower sends troops to Little Rock, Arkansas, to ensure school desegregation **1960** John F. Kennedy elected president **1961** East Germans build Berlin Wall
40 in 1962   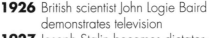 **Dies 1979**	**1962** Cuban Missile Crisis erupts after the U.S. discovers Soviet missiles on island ❹ **1964–75** Vietnam War: war between communist North Vietnam and U.S. forces supporting South Vietnam **1966** Mao Zedong launches Cultural Revolution, using millions of young Chinese to secure his power **1967** Arabs and Israelis fight in Six Day War **1969** American astronaut walks on Moon ❺ **1975–79** Communist forces murder hundreds of thousands in Cambodia

© DIAGRAM

NGUGI wa Thiong'o

**Kenyan novelist,
short-story writer,
and playwright**
Born Jan. 5, 1938

Book cover for one of Ngugi's
famous novels

Ngugi wa Thiong'o (formerly known as James Ngugi) is East Africa's most important writer. He wrote the first major English language novel, *Weep Not, Child*, to be published by an East African author.

Ngugi was born near Nairobi, the capital of Kenya, which was then a British colony. His family was poor and belonged to Kenya's largest ethnic group, the Kikuyu. His mother managed to send him to school, and he attended college in Kampala, now the capital of neighboring Uganda. After graduating in 1964, Ngugi worked as a reporter before traveling to England to study at the University of Leeds.

Together, his three famous novels of the 1960s chart the history of Kenya from before British rule to independence. *The River Between* tells of a time when European missionaries, but not European rule, had come to East Africa. *Weep Not, Child* tells of the impact the anti-British Mau Mau rebellion during the mid-1950s had on a poor boy's family. *A Grain of Wheat* deals with the social, moral, and racial issues in the struggle for independence and in the early days of independence.

Ngugi returned to Kenya at age 29 and became the head of the literature department at the University of Nairobi five years later. In 1977 he published *Petals of Blood* and cowrote the play *I Will Marry When I Want*, both of which criticized the leaders of Kenya. For this he was imprisoned for nearly a year without trial and lost his job. He now writes full time but deplores the fact that most of the Kenyans about whom he writes cannot read his books. He has since tried to overcome this by writing only in Kikuyu.

WORKS INCLUDE

1964 *Weep Not, Child*	**1977** *Petals of Blood*
1965 *The River Between*	**1977** *I Will Marry When I Want*
1967 *A Grain of Wheat*	**1980** *Devil on the Cross*
1974 *Secret Lives*	**1981** *Detained: A Writer's Prison Diary*
1977 *Trial of Dedan Kimathi*	**1986** *Matigari*

OTHER AFRICAN WRITERS

ACHEBE, Chinua
CLARK-BEKEDEREMO, John Pepper
COETZEE, J.M.
FUGARD, Athol
GORDIMER, Nadine
HEAD, Bessie
MAHFOUZ, Naguib
NETO, Agostinho

NWAPA, Flora
OKRI, Ben
PATON, Alan
ROBERT, Shaaban
SENGHOR, Léopold Sédar
SOYINKA, Wole

SEE INDEX FOR FULL LIST

WORLD EVENTS

Age	Contemporary Events
Born 1938	**1939–45** World War II: allies, led by U.S. and Great Britain, fight axis powers, led by Germany and Japan
	1945 U.S. drops first atomic bombs on Japan ❶
	1945 Cold War begins between USSR and U.S.
	1950–53 Korean War: North Korea and China fight South Korea, the U.S., and United Nations troops
	1957 Eisenhower sends troops to Little Rock, Arkansas, to ensure school desegregation ❷
20 in 1958	**1960** John F. Kennedy elected president
	1963 Led by Rev. Martin Luther King, Jr., thousands march on Washington DC to press for civil rights for African Americans ❸
	1964–75 Vietnam War: war between communist North Vietnam and U.S. forces supporting South Vietnam
	1967 Arabs and Israelis fight in Six Day War
	1969 American astronaut walks on Moon ❹
40 in 1978	**1980** Ronald Reagan elected president
	1981 U.S. launches first space shuttle
	1989 Communist regimes fall throughout Eastern Europe
	1991 Gulf War: UN forces, led by U.S., defeat Iraq and free Kuwait
	1992 Bill Clinton elected president
	1994 First multiracial elections in South Africa end years of white minority rule. They are won by Nelson Mandela, African National Congress leader ❺

© DIAGRAM

NICHOLS, Grace

Guyanese-British poet and children's writer
Born Jan. 18, 1950

Grace Nichols is one of Britain's most respected and popular contemporary poets. She often uses the landscapes and language of her native Guyana in her work.

Nichols was born in Georgetown, the capital of Guyana in South America, where she attended the University of Guyana. At 17 she began working as a teacher, then as a journalist for several years. At age 27 she moved to Britain, where she became known initially for her writing for children. Her first book, the children's story collection *Trust You, Wriggly*, was published when she was 30, and four years later she published a children's novel, *Leslyn in London*.

It was when she was 33 that Nichols first came to the attention of adult readers with her poetry collection, *i Is a Long Memoried Woman*. The book won an important literary prize and launched Nichols's career as a "serious" writer. Since then she has written for both children and adults.

In much of her work Nichols explores Guyanese life and issues of race and gender. In *The Fat Black Woman's Poems* she argues against the "jovial Jemima" image often used to **stereotype** black women, and her character celebrates her large body: "my thighs are twin seals / fat slick pups." At age 36 she wrote her first novel for adults, *Whole of a Morning Sky*, based on her childhood in Guyana.

Nichols uses humor in her work and language that reflects the way people speak rather than read. She is married to John Agard, another poet from Guyana, and they have one daughter. In 1994 she and Agard edited the poetry collection *A Black Dozen*.

Book cover for Nichols's first collection of poetry

WORKS INCLUDE

1980 *Trust You, Wriggly*
1983 *i Is a Long Memoried Woman*
1984 *Leslyn in London*
1984 *The Fat Black Woman's Poems*
1986 *Whole of a Morning Sky*

1988 *Come On into My Tropical Garden*
1989 *Lazy Thoughts of a Lazy Woman*
1994 *Give Yourself a Hug*

OTHER POST-1940 POETS

ANGELOU, Maya
BISHOP, Elizabeth
BRODSKY, Joseph
DUNCAN, Robert
GINSBERG, Allen
HAYDEN, Robert
HEANEY, Seamus
HUGHES, Ted

LOWELL, Robert
PAZ, Octavio
PLATH, Sylvia
SEXTON, Anne
THOMAS, Dylan
WALCOTT, Derek
YEVTUSHENKO, Yevgeny

SEE INDEX FOR FULL LIST

WORLD EVENTS

Age		Contemporary Events
Born 1950		**1950–53** Korean War: North Korea and China fight South Korea, the U.S., and United Nations troops **1957** Eisenhower sends troops to Little Rock, Arkansas, to ensure school desegregation ❶
10 in 1960		**1960** John F. Kennedy elected president **1964–75** Vietnam War: war between communist North Vietnam and U.S. forces supporting South Vietnam **1967** Arabs and Israelis fight in Six Day War **1969** American astronaut walks on Moon
20 in 1970		**1974** Pres. Richard M. Nixon resigns presidency **1975–79** Communist forces murder hundreds of thousands in Cambodia ❷
30 in 1980	 	**1980** Ronald Reagan elected president **1981** U.S. launches first space shuttle ❸ **1987** Gorbachev begins reforms in USSR: perestroika (restructuring) and glasnost (openness) ❹ **1989** Communist regimes fall throughout Eastern Europe
40 in 1990		**1991** Gulf War: UN forces, led by U.S., defeat Iraq and free Kuwait ❺ **1992** Bill Clinton elected president **1994** First multiracial elections in South Africa end years of white minority rule. They are won by Nelson Mandela, African National Congress leader

© DIAGRAM

NIETZSCHE, Friedrich

Friedrich Nietzsche was an important German **philosopher** whose work had a strong influence on politics and literature.

Nietzsche was born in a small German village. His father died when he was five, and he and his younger sister were brought up by their mother. At college in the German city of Bonn he studied theology at first but soon switched to philosophy.

Nietzsche was a brilliant student, and at the age of just 24 became a professor at the University of Basel in Switzerland. At Basel he became a close friend of the great German composer Richard Wagner, who shared his views about politics and society – views Nietzsche made clear in his *Untimely Meditations*, which contains strong criticisms of German culture and institutions.

In famous books such as *Thus Spoke Zarathustra* and *Beyond Good and Evil* Nietzsche set out his radical ideas. He believed that Christianity no longer had a place in society, and individuals must create their own ideas about what is right and wrong, a view he summed up in his famous phrase "God is dead." Many writers have been both fascinated and horrified by Nietzsche's ideas. The ideal human being described by Nietzsche – a passionate person who controls his passion and puts it to creative use – became the hero of many late 19th-century novels and plays.

Nietzsche acquired a bad reputation when his ideas were taken up by German **Nazis** in the 1930s to justify their anti-Jewish policies, although this was never part of his philosophy.

German philosopher and writer
Born Oct. 15, 1844
Died Aug. 25, 1900
Age at death 55

Title page for *Thus Spoke Zarathustra*

WORKS INCLUDE

1872 *The Birth of Tragedy*
1873–76 *Untimely Meditations*
1878–90 *Human, All-Too-Human*
1883–85 *Thus Spoke Zarathustra*
1886 *Beyond Good and Evil*

1887 *On the Genealogy of Morals*
1889 *Twilight of the Idols*
Published after he died
1901 *The Will to Power*
1908 *Ecce Homo*

OTHER GERMAN-SPEAKING WRITERS

BÖLL, Heinrich
BRECHT, Bertolt
GOETHE, Johann Wolfgang von
GRASS, Günter
HAUPTMANN, Gerhart
HEINE, Heinrich
HESSE, Hermann
HOFFMANN, E.T.A.

JÜNGER, Ernst
MANN, Thomas
NIETZSCHE, Friedrich
REMARQUE, Erich Maria
RILKE, Rainer Maria
SCHILLER, Friedrich von
WOLF, Christa

SEE INDEX FOR FULL LIST

WORLD EVENTS

Age	Contemporary Events
Born 1844 	**1846** Mexican War: U.S. fights Mexico **1848** Revolutions throughout Europe **1849** California gold rush draws thousands of people ❶ **1859** English naturalist Charles Darwin publishes his theories on evolution **1861** Italy unified **1861–65** Civil War: North (Union) fights South (Confederacy) over issues of slavery and states' rights
20 in 1864 	**1865** Pres. Abraham Lincoln assassinated ❷ **1869** U.S. transcontinental railroad completed **1876** American scientist Alexander Graham Bell invents telephone **1876** Native American Sioux led by Crazy Horse kill Gen. George Armstrong Custer and his men at Battle of Little Bighorn **1877–79** American inventor Thomas Edison invents phonograph and electric lightbulb ❸ **1883** Brooklyn Bridge opens in New York
40 in 1884  **Dies 1900**	**1886** Statue of Liberty erected in New York harbor **1888** George Eastman perfects "Kodak" box camera **1895** German physicist Wilhelm K. Roentgen discovers X-rays ❹ **1895** Italian physicist Guglielmo Marconi invents radio ❺ **1896** First modern Olympic Games held in Athens, Greece

NIN, Anaïs

**French-born
American writer
Born** Feb. 21, 1903
Died Jan. 14, 1977
Age at death 73

Part of the *Diary of Anaïs Nin* covering the 1920s

Anaïs Nin is most famous for her eight-volume *Diary of Anaïs Nin.* Combining truth and fiction, the diaries relate her inner journey of self-discovery and also give a fascinating account of the era from 1914 to the 1970s. The diaries also made Nin a major figure in the 1970s **women's movement**.

Nin was born to artistic parents near Paris, France. After her father deserted the family when Nin was 11, they moved to New York City. She left school when she was 15 and taught herself in public libraries. Nin moved back to Paris in the 1920s and studied the workings of the mind with the famous doctor Otto Rank. In the 1930s Nin, already a published author, became friends with a group of well-known writers and artists, including HENRY MILLER. Lifelong friends, Nin and Miller both influenced each other in their work. When **World War II** broke out, she returned to New York and set up the Gemor Press to print her own books. Nin had been writing **lyrical** books about women for over 30 years before becoming famous with the publication of the first volume of her diary when she was 63. She died 11 years later, at the height of her fame.

The *House of Incest* has been called Nin's best fiction. It combines prose and poetry to retell a woman's nightmare. One of her largest projects was the five-volume *Cities of the Interior,* which follows the lives of three women. After trying to find happiness through lovers, art, and analysis, only one manages to reach acceptance of herself. The bestselling *Delta of Venus* collects sexually explicit stories that Nin wrote for a dollar a page while poor in the 1940s.

WORKS INCLUDE

1936 *House of Incest*
1939 *Winter of Artifice*
1944 *Under a Glass Bell*
1946–61 *Cities of the Interior* (5 vols.)
1964 *Collages*

1966–80 *Diary of Anaïs Nin* (8 vols, some after she died)
1977 *Delta of Venus* (published after she died)

OTHER POST-1940 WRITERS

BALDWIN, James
BELLOW, Saul
CAMUS, Albert
GARCÍA MÁRQUEZ, Gabriel
GOLDING, William
HELLER, Joseph
IRVING, John
LESSING, Doris

MORRISON, Toni
SALINGER, J.D.
SINGER, Isaac Bashevis
SOLZHENITSYN, Aleksandr
UPDIKE, John
VIDAL, Gore
WALKER, Alice

SEE INDEX FOR FULL LIST

WORLD EVENTS

Age	Contemporary Events
Born 1903 	**1903** American inventors Orville and Wilbur Wright make first airplane flight **1908** Henry Ford introduces Model T car ❶ **1909 1914–18** World War I **1917** Russian Revolution establishes Communist government
20 in 1923  	**1926** British scientist John Logie Baird demonstrates television **1927** Joseph Stalin becomes dictator of Russia **1931** Empire State Building in New York City completed ❷ **1933** Nazi Party, led by Adolf Hitler, gains control in Germany ❸ **1939–45** World War II: allies, led by U.S. and Great Britain, fight axis powers, led by Germany and Japan
40 in 1943 	**1945** U.S. drops first atomic bombs on Japan ❹ **1950–53** Korean War: North Korea and China fight South Korea, the U.S., and United Nations troops **1957** Eisenhower sends troops to Little Rock, Arkansas, to ensure school desegregation **1960** John F. Kennedy elected president
60 in 1963 **Dies 1977**	**1964–75** Vietnam War: war between communist North Vietnam and U.S. forces supporting South Vietnam ❺ **1967** Arabs and Israelis fight in Six Day War **1969** American astronaut walks on Moon **1974** Pres. Richard M. Nixon resigns presidency

© DIAGRAM

NIXON, Joan Lowery

American young-adults' writer
Born Feb. 3, 1927

Joan Lowery Nixon has been called the "grande dame" of young-adult mystery writers. She is the first author to have won the EDGAR ALLAN POE Award for the best mystery book of the year four times.

Nixon was born Joan Lowery in Los Angeles. She had a happy and creative childhood and published her first poem in the magazine *Children's Playmate* when she was just ten. She grew up in Hollywood and attended local public schools before studying journalism at the University of Southern California. After graduating in 1947, she found it difficult to find work as a journalist since she was a woman competing against men returning from **World War II**. She took a job teaching elementary school and liked it so much that she trained to be teacher. In 1949 she married, becoming Joan Lowery Nixon, qualified as a teacher, and began teaching third grade. Over much of the next two decades Nixon was busy raising her four children and teaching.

The family often moved due to her husband's work. While they were living in Texas, Nixon went to a writers' conference, which inspired her to try writing fiction for children. Her daughters insisted that she include them in her book, which should be a mystery. Nixon had always enjoyed mystery books even as a child, and her first book, *The Mystery of Hurricane Castle*, came out when she was 37. She gave up teaching soon afterward and focused on writing. Nixon has since written over 100 books for children and young adults, mostly mysteries and historical fiction. She is known for well-written characters, fast-paced plots, and for mixing suspense with humor.

Book cover for one of Nixon's thrillers for young adults

WORKS INCLUDE

1964 The Mystery of Hurricane Castle
1979 The Kidnapping of Christina Lattimore
1980 The Seance
1986 The Other Side of Dark

1988 A Family Apart
1989 In the Face of Danger
1992 Land of Hope
1993 The Name of the Game Was Murder

OTHER CHILDREN'S WRITERS

ADAMS, Harriet Stratemeyer
ALCOTT, Louisa May
ANDERSEN, Hans Christian
BARRIE, J.M.
BLYTON, Enid
CARLE, Eric
CARROLL, Lewis
DAHL, Roald

KIPLING, Rudyard
LEAR, Edward
MILNE, A.A.
POTTER, Beatrix
REID BANKS, Lynne
SENDAK, Maurice
TWAIN, Mark

SEE INDEX FOR FULL LIST

WORLD EVENTS

Age	Contemporary Events
Born 1927 	**1927** Joseph Stalin becomes dictator of Russia **1933** Nazi Party, led by Adolf Hitler, gains control in Germany **1939–45** World War II: allies, led by U.S. and Great Britain, fight axis powers, led by Germany and Japan **1945** U.S. drops first atomic bombs on Japan ❶
20 in 1947  	**1950–53** Korean War: North Korea and China fight South Korea, the U.S., and United Nations troops ❷ **1957** Eisenhower sends troops to Little Rock, Arkansas, to ensure school desegregation **1960** John F. Kennedy elected president **1964–75** Vietnam War: war between communist North Vietnam and U.S. forces supporting South Vietnam
40 in 1967 	**1967** Arabs and Israelis fight in Six Day War **1969** American astronaut walks on Moon ❸ **1980** Ronald Reagan elected president **1981** U.S. launches first space shuttle ❹
60 in 1987	**1989** Communist regimes fall throughout Eastern Europe **1991** Gulf War: UN forces, led by U.S., defeat Iraq and free Kuwait **1992** Bill Clinton elected president **1994** First multiracial elections in South Africa end years of white minority rule. They are won by Nelson Mandela, African National Congress leader ❺

© DIAGRAM

129

NORMAN, Marsha

American playwright
Born Sep. 21, 1947

Marsha Norman won the 1983 **Pulitzer Prize** for her play *'Night Mother* and has been described as one of America's most promising new playwrights. Most of her plays focus on women and their search for identity. Several explore the relationship between mother and daughter.

Before becoming a playwright, Norman held a variety of jobs. After graduating from the University of Louisville, Kentucky, she taught emotionally disturbed children and worked as a writer for television and as a journalist.

Although from the South (she was born in Louisville, Kentucky), Norman insists that she is not a "Southern woman." She writes from a universally American point of view and makes sure that her plays are not obviously set in a particular region. *Getting Out*, first staged when Norman was 30, is now one of her most popular plays and has won several awards. It attacks the failure both of a daughter's relationship with her mother and of the prison system. Arlene, the main character, is released from prison supposedly reformed, yet it becomes clear that she has left one prison for another.

Among Norman's many plays, her most famous is *'Night Mother*. This powerful play has only two characters, a mother and her daughter. The daughter, Jessie, commits suicide, but this action is portrayed as an act of triumph. There was great controversy over this treatment of suicide when the play first appeared.

Norman has also written a musical, *The Secret Garden*, based on FRANCES HODGSON BURNETT's famous children's book, and a novel, *The Fortune Teller*.

IIIIIII

GETTING OUT

A play by
Marsha Norman

Poster for Norman's early play

WORKS INCLUDE

1977 *Getting Out*	**1984** *Traveler in the Dark*
1978 *Third and Oak: The Laundromat*	**1987** *The Fortune Teller*
1979 *Circus Valentine*	**1988** *Sarah and Abraham*
1980–83 *The Holdup*	**1991** *The Secret Garden*
1983 *'Night Mother*	**1992** *D. Boone*

OTHER POST-1940 PLAYWRIGHTS

ALBEE, Edward
BECKETT, Samuel
BRECHT, Bertolt
FUGARD, Athol
GENET, Jean
KUSHNER, Tony
MAMET, David
MILLER, Arthur

OSBORNE, John
PINTER, Harold
SHEPARD, Sam
SIMON, Neil
SOYINKA, Wole
WILLIAMS, Tennessee

SEE INDEX FOR FULL LIST

WORLD EVENTS

Age	Contemporary Events
Born 1947 	**1950–53** Korean War: North Korea and China fight South Korea, the U.S., and United Nations troops ❶
	1957 Eisenhower sends troops to Little Rock, Arkansas, to ensure school desegregation
	1960 John F. Kennedy elected president ❷
	1962 Cuban Missile Crisis erupts after the U.S. discovers Soviet missiles on island
	1964–75 Vietnam War: war between communist North Vietnam and U.S. forces supporting South Vietnam ❸
20 in 1967 	**1967** Arabs and Israelis fight in Six Day War
	1969 American astronaut walks on Moon
	1975–79 Communist forces murder hundreds of thousands in Cambodia
	**1979** Britain elects its first female prime minister, Margaret Thatcher
	1981 U.S. launches first space shuttle
40 in 1987	**1987** Gorbachev begins reforms in USSR: perestroika (restructuring) and glasnost (openness)
	1989 Communist regimes fall throughout Eastern Europe ❹
	1991 Gulf War: UN forces, led by U.S., defeat Iraq and free Kuwait
	1992 Bill Clinton elected president
	**1994** First multiracial elections in South Africa end years of white minority rule. They are won by Nelson Mandela, African National Congress leader ❺

© DIAGRAM

NORRIS, Frank

American novelist
Born Mar. 5, 1870
Died Oct. 25, 1902
Age at death 32

Book cover for Norris's realistic novel about a murder

Frank Norris has been called the first important naturalistic American novelist. He pioneered the literary style of **realism** in his books about social injustice.

Shortly after his birth in Chicago, Norris and his family moved to San Francisco, where he spent his early years. From 1887 to 1889 Norris studied art in Paris, France. Once back in the United States, he attended the University of California, where he was greatly influenced by the writings of French novelist EMILE ZOLA. He also studied at Harvard, where his professors encouraged him to write.

From 1895 to 1896 Norris covered the **Boer War** in South Africa for the *San Francisco Chronicle* and *Collier's* magazine. When he was 28, he moved to New York City to write for *McClure's Magazine* and was sent to Cuba to report on the **Spanish-American War**.

These experiences inspired Norris to develop a realistic literary style to portray the effects of modern technology on society. His first major novel was *McTeague*, which was published when he was 29. It is about a drunken dentist who murders his wife.

Toward the end of his life Norris began to write a **trilogy** called *Epic of the Wheat*. The first volume, *The Octopus*, highlights the struggle between railroad interests and wheat farmers in California. The second volume, *The Pit*, describes wheat speculation on the Chicago Board of Trade. Norris died of complications following an operation for appendicitis before he was able to begin the third volume, *The Wolf*, which was to be about wheat and food distribution.

WORKS INCLUDE

1898 *Moran of the Lady Letty*	**Published after he died**
1899 *McTeague*	**1903** *The Pit*
1899 *Blix*	**1903** *A Deal in Wheat*
1900 *A Man's Woman*	**1909** *The Third Circle*
1901 *The Octopus*	**1914** *Vandover and the Brute*

OTHER 19TH-CENTURY NOVELISTS

AUSTEN, Jane
BRONTË, Charlotte, Emily, and Anne
COOPER, James Fenimore
DICKENS, Charles
ELIOT, George
HARDY, Thomas
HAWTHORNE, Nathaniel
HUGO, Victor

JAMES, Henry
MELVILLE, Herman
SCOTT, Sir Walter
STEVENSON, Robert Louis
STOWE, Harriet Beecher
TOLSTOY, Leo
ZOLA, Émile

SEE INDEX FOR FULL LIST

WORLD EVENTS

Age	Contemporary Events
Born 1870	**1876** American scientist Alexander Graham Bell invents telephone **1876** Native American Sioux led by Crazy Horse kill Gen. George Armstrong Custer and his men at Battle of Little Bighorn ❶ **1877–79** American inventor Thomas Edison invents phonograph and electric lightbulb
10 in 1880	**1883** Brooklyn Bridge opens in New York **1886** Statue of Liberty erected in New York harbor **1888** George Eastman perfects "Kodak" box camera ❷
20 in 1890	**1890** Last major battle of the Indian Wars is fought at Wounded Knee, South Dakota **1894–95** Following war with China, Japan occupies Korea **1895** German physicist Wilhelm K. Roentgen discovers X-rays ❸ **1895** Italian physicist Guglielmo Marconi invents radio ❹ **1896** First modern Olympic Games held in Athens, Greece **1898** French physicists Marie and Pierre Curie discover radioactive element, radium **1898** Spanish-American War: U.S. fights Spain
30 in 1900 **Dies 1902**	**1901** Theodore Roosevelt becomes president following assassination of William McKinley **1901** Edward VII crowned king of England

© DIAGRAM

133

NWAPA, Flora

**Nigerian novelist
and short-story
writer**
Born Jan. 18, 1931

Nwapa's powerful stories about women's lives

Flora Nwapa has been called the mother of modern African literature. Her novel *Efuru*, the first published by a woman in Nigeria (West Africa), was one of the first works of African literature to concentrate on the experiences of women.

Nwapa was born in Oguta, eastern Nigeria, which was then a British colony. She was educated at various Nigerian schools before training to be a teacher at the University of Edinburgh in Britain. On her return to Nigeria she worked as an education officer for women and as a teacher and was assistant registrar at the University of Lagos. After the **Biafran War**, a civil war in Nigeria in the late 1960s, Nwapa was employed by the Ministry of Health and Welfare in the war-torn eastern part of the country. Her tasks included finding homes for 2,000 war orphans. *Never Again*, her novel written in remembrance of the war, tells of the vital role that women played.

After five years Nwapa retired from her work for the state government. Soon after this, however, she founded her own printing press and a publishing company. Her aims are to publish African-language books, to guide African children, and to educate non-Africans about Africa.

Many of Nwapa's books focus on the lives and roles of women. *Efuru*, *Idu*, and *One Is Enough* are stories of women searching for fulfillment. Efuru and Idu want more than just to have children. Efuru loses two husbands and a child but eventually finds happiness as an independent, single woman and follower of the goddess Uhamiri, who gives her worshipers wealth and beauty but few children.

WORKS INCLUDE

1966 *Efuru*
1970 *Idu*
1971 *This Is Lagos and Other Stories*
1975 *Never Again*
1979 *Mammywater*

1980 *Wives at War and Other Stories*
1981 *One Is Enough*
1986 *Women Are Different*

OTHER AFRICAN WRITERS

ACHEBE, Chinua
CLARK-BEKEDEREMO, John Pepper
COETZEE, J.M.
FUGARD, Athol
GORDIMER, Nadine
HEAD, Bessie
MAHFOUZ, Naguib
NETO, Agostinho

NGUGI wa Thiong'o
OKRI, Ben
PATON, Alan
ROBERT, Shaaban
SENGHOR, Léopold Sédar
SOYINKA, Wole

SEE INDEX FOR FULL LIST

WORLD EVENTS

Age	Contemporary Events
Born 1931 	**1931** Empire State Building in New York City completed
	1933 Nazi Party, led by Adolf Hitler, gains control in Germany
	1939–45 World War II: allies, led by U.S. and Great Britain, fight axis powers, led by Germany and Japan
	1945 U.S. drops first atomic bombs on Japan
	1950–53 Korean War: North Korea and China fight South Korea, the U.S., and United Nations troops ❶
20 in 1951  	**1957** Eisenhower sends troops to Little Rock, Arkansas, to ensure school desegregation ❷
	1960 John F. Kennedy elected president ❸
	1964–75 Vietnam War: war between communist North Vietnam and U.S. forces supporting South Vietnam
	1967 Arabs and Israelis fight in Six Day War
	1969 American astronaut walks on Moon ❹
40 in 1971 	**1981** U.S. launches first space shuttle
	1989 Communist regimes fall throughout Eastern Europe
60 in 1991 	**1991** Gulf War: UN forces, led by U.S., defeat Iraq and free Kuwait ❺
	1992 Bill Clinton elected president
	1994 First multiracial elections in South Africa end years of white minority rule. They are won by Nelson Mandela, African National Congress leader

OATES, Joyce Carol

**American novelist
and short-story
writer
Born** Jun. 16, 1938

Book cover for one of Oates's
novels about women's lives

Joyce Carol Oates is one of America's most respected and prolific contemporary writers, having published more than 55 books since 1963.

Oates was born in Lockport, New York, and was raised a Catholic in an Irish-American, working-class family. Her elementary school was a one-room schoolhouse. She began writing at age 14, after being given a typewriter. Oates received a scholarship to Syracuse University, and while there she wrote a novel each semester. She earned a master's degree in 1961, and that year she married. She and her husband settled in Detroit. The city's social turmoil at that time had an enormous influence on her early career.

Oates published her first book, the short-story collection *By the North Gate*, at age 25. For the next few years, in addition to teaching full time at a nearby university, she wrote two or three books a year, including the National Book Award-winning *Them*. Like much of her work it features violence, in particular men's violence against women.

In 1978 Oates and her husband moved to Princeton, New Jersey, where they founded a literary magazine, *The Ontario Review*. She teaches creative writing at Princeton University and continues to write. In addition to novels she writes short stories; one of her stories that often appears in short-story collections is "Where Are You Going, Where Have You Been." Her novels cover a range of literary **genres**, including gloomy **gothic** stories, romances, and thrillers (the latter published under the pen name Rosamond Smith). She is also a boxing fan, an interest reflected in her collection of essays entitled *On Boxing* (1987).

WORKS INCLUDE

1967 *A Garden of Earthly Delights*
1968 *Expensive People*
1969 *Them*
1973 *Do With Me What You Will*
1980 *Bellefleur*

1986 *Marya: A Life*
1992 *Black Water*
1993 *Foxfire: Confessions of a Girl Gang*
1997 *Man Crazy*

OTHER POST-1940 NOVELISTS

BALDWIN, James	**MORRISON**, Toni
BELLOW, Saul	**SALINGER**, J.D.
CAMUS, Albert	**SINGER**, Isaac Bashevis
GARCÍA MÁRQUEZ, Gabriel	**SOLZHENITSYN**, Aleksandr
GOLDING, William	**UPDIKE**, John
HELLER, Joseph	**VIDAL**, Gore
IRVING, John	**WALKER**, Alice
LESSING, Doris	

SEE INDEX FOR FULL LIST

WORLD EVENTS

Age	Contemporary Events
Born 1938 	**1939–45** World War II: allies, led by U.S. and Great Britain, fight axis powers, led by Germany and Japan **1945** U.S. drops first atomic bombs on Japan ❶ **1950–53** Korean War: North Korea and China fight South Korea, the U.S., and United Nations troops ❷ **1957** Eisenhower sends troops to Little Rock, Arkansas, to ensure school desegregation
20 in 1958 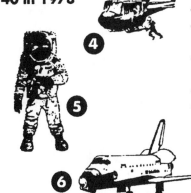	**1960** John F. Kennedy elected president ❸ **1964–75** Vietnam War: war between communist North Vietnam and U.S. forces supporting South Vietnam ❹ **1967** Arabs and Israelis fight in Six Day War **1969** American astronaut walks on Moon ❺ **1975–79** Communist forces murder hundreds of thousands in Cambodia
40 in 1978	**1980** Ronald Reagan elected president **1981** U.S. launches first space shuttle ❻ **1989** Communist regimes fall throughout Eastern Europe **1991** Gulf War: UN forces, led by U.S., defeat Iraq and free Kuwait **1992** Bill Clinton elected president **1994** First multiracial elections in South Africa end years of white minority rule. They are won by Nelson Mandela, African National Congress leader

© DIAGRAM

O'BRIAN, Patrick

**Irish novelist
and biographer
Born** 1914

Patrick O'Brian is celebrated for his exciting sea stories set during the **Napoleonic Wars**.

O'Brian was born in Ireland to Anglo-Irish parents. As a child he suffered ill-health. He also moved about a good deal and was partly self-taught. O'Brian learned French, Catalan, and Spanish, and this knowledge helped his secret intelligence-gathering work during **World War II**. After the war he lived in Wales with his wife Mary, and later they moved to a French village on the Mediterranean Sea, close to Spain.

From his home in France O'Brian wrote short stories and reviews and translated some of the works of SIMONE DE BEAUVOIR. His first novel, *Testimonies*, appeared when he was 38, but he earned little from writing until the first of his series of historical naval novels was published 18 years later. *Master and Commander* introduced readers to the adventures of Captain "Lucky" Jack Aubrey of the Royal Navy and his oddball friend Stephen Maturin, an Irish-Catalan doctor, naturalist, and British government spy.

O'Brian's own background helped him invent believable sea stories set in the past. They are filled with unexpected incidents and lively details that show how sailors talked, thought, ate, slept, worked, and fought two centuries ago.

By the age of 83 O'Brian had produced 18 Aubrey-Maturin stories set in various parts of the world. Some critics consider them among the finest of all historical novels. O'Brian's other works include his **biography** of the artist Pablo Picasso, who was a friend and neighbor in France.

Illustration for O'Brian's novel
The Thirteen-Gun Salute

WORKS INCLUDE

1952 *Testimonies*	**1981** *The Ionian Mission*
1970 *Master and Commander*	**1984** *The Far Side of the World*
1972 *Post Captain*	**1989** *The Thirteen-Gun Salute*
1973 *HMS Surprise*	**1990** *The Letter of Marque*
1977 *The Mauritius Command*	**1997** *The Yellow Admiral*

OTHER POST-1940 NOVELISTS

BALDWIN, James
BELLOW, Saul
CAMUS, Albert
GARCÍA MÁRQUEZ, Gabriel
GOLDING, William
HELLER, Joseph
IRVING, John
LESSING, Doris

MORRISON, Toni
SALINGER, J.D.
SINGER, Isaac Bashevis
SOLZHENITSYN, Aleksandr
UPDIKE, John
VIDAL, Gore
WALKER, Alice

SEE INDEX FOR FULL LIST

WORLD EVENTS

Age	Contemporary Events
Born 1914 	**1914–18** World War I **1917** Russian Revolution establishes Communist government **1927** Joseph Stalin becomes dictator of Russia ❶ **1933** Nazi Party, led by Adolf Hitler, gains control in Germany
20 in 1934	**1939–45** World War II: allies, led by U.S. and Great Britain, fight axis powers, led by Germany and Japan **1945** U.S. drops first atomic bombs on Japan ❷ **1950–53** Korean War: North Korea and China fight South Korea, the U.S., and United Nations troops
40 in 1954 	**1960** John F. Kennedy elected president ❸ **1964–75** Vietnam War: war between communist North Vietnam and U.S. forces supporting South Vietnam ❹ **1969** American astronaut walks on Moon
60 in 1974 	**1981** U.S. launches first space shuttle ❺ **1989** Communist regimes fall throughout Eastern Europe **1991** Gulf War: UN forces, led by U.S., defeat Iraq and free Kuwait **1992** Bill Clinton elected president
80 in 1994 	**1994** First multiracial elections in South Africa end years of white minority rule. They are won by Nelson Mandela, African National Congress leader

© DIAGRAM

O'BRIEN, Edna

Irish novelist, short-story writer, and playwright
Born Dec. 15, 1932

Book cover for one of O'Brien's novels about Ireland

Edna O'Brien is best known for her stories of girls and women living in Ireland.

O'Brien was born a farmer's daughter, in Tuamgraney, a Catholic village in the west of Ireland. She received a strict Catholic education at a convent school in the town of Loughrea. At 16 she left to work in a Dublin pharmacy, studying at the Pharmaceutical College in her spare time. At 20 she married the novelist Ernest Gebler. The couple moved to London when O'Brien was 25, but divorced when she was in her early 30s. By then she had two sons.

O'Brien had written tales while a child but was 28 when she published her first novel. *The Country Girls* tells of two Irish girls: soft-hearted and trusting Caithleen and bolder and spiteful Baba. Like O'Brien herself, both are strictly brought up in a small, narrow-minded village community and excited when they become old enough to find work and romance in the city of Dublin. O'Brien's next books, *The Lonely Girl* and *Girls in Their Married Bliss*, take both grown-up girls to London, where they live after making unhappy marriages – as O'Brien herself did.

Many of O'Brien's stories attack the harsh way girls like her were brought up in Ireland or tell of a heroine's loneliness and sad love affairs. Her musical language conveys a strong feeling of what Ireland and the Irish are like.

A Fanatic Heart and other collections of short stories by O'Brien also deal with feelings of love, loss, and guilt. She has written several plays and a book of fairy stories for children based on Irish **folklore**.

WORKS INCLUDE

1960 *The Country Girls*	**1972** *Night*
1962 *The Lonely Girl*	**1982** *Returning*
1964 *Girls in Their Married Bliss*	**1984** *A Fanatic Heart*
1968 *The Love Object*	**1986** *Tales for the Telling*
1970 *A Pagan Place*	**1994** *The House of Splendid Isolation*

OTHER POST-1940 NOVELISTS

BALDWIN, James
BELLOW, Saul
CAMUS, Albert
GARCÍA MÁRQUEZ, Gabriel
GOLDING, William
HELLER, Joseph
IRVING, John
LESSING, Doris

MORRISON, Toni
SALINGER, J.D.
SINGER, Isaac Bashevis
SOLZHENITSYN, Aleksandr
UPDIKE, John
VIDAL, Gore
WALKER, Alice

SEE INDEX FOR FULL LIST

WORLD EVENTS

Age	Contemporary Events
Born 1932 	**1933** Nazi Party, led by Adolf Hitler, gains control in Germany **1939–45** World War II: allies, led by U.S. and Great Britain, fight axis powers, led by Germany and Japan ❶ **1945** U.S. drops first atomic bombs on Japan **1950–53** Korean War: North Korea and China fight South Korea, the U.S., and United Nations troops
20 in 1952 	**1957** Eisenhower sends troops to Little Rock, Arkansas, to ensure school desegregation ❷ **1960** John F. Kennedy elected president **1961** East Germans build Berlin Wall ❸ **1964–75** Vietnam War: war between communist North Vietnam and U.S. forces supporting South Vietnam **1967** Arabs and Israelis fight in Six Day War **1969** American astronaut walks on Moon ❹
40 in 1972 	**1981** U.S. launches first space shuttle **1988** George Bush elected president **1989** Communist regimes fall throughout Eastern Europe **1991** Gulf War: UN forces, led by U.S., defeat Iraq and free Kuwait
60 in 1992 	**1992** Bill Clinton elected president **1994** First multiracial elections in South Africa end years of white minority rule. They are won by Nelson Mandela, African National Congress leader ❺

© DIAGRAM

O'BRIEN, Flann

**Irish novelist
and journalist
Born** Oct. 5, 1911
Died Apr. 1, 1966
Age at death 54

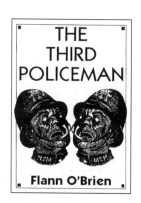

O'Brien's second
experimental novel

Flann O'Brien was the pen name of Brian Ó Nualláin, who was best known for his remarkable **experimental** comic novel *At Swim-Two-Birds.*

O'Brien was born in Strabane, now in Northern Ireland, one of 12 children of a customs and excise officer. Although the family moved frequently, O'Brien spent most of his childhood in or near Dublin. He was educated by priests there and went to University College, Dublin, at the age of 18. He remained a student for six years, and during this time he also spent a year in Germany.

At age 24 O'Brien got a job as a civil servant. His first novel, which was influenced by the experimental novels of the great Irish author JAMES JOYCE, is a clever mix of fantasy, farce, legend, **folklore**, **satire**, and poetry; it is about a man who is writing a novel about a man who is writing a novel. *At Swim-Two-Birds* (the title is a translation of an Irish place name) was published when O'Brien was 28, but was ignored until it was republished to great praise 21 years later.

O'Brien's next novel, *The Third Policeman*, was rejected by his publisher as too unusual but was published after he died. It is both serious and funny: one of the characters is concerned that the water he drinks is too strong and asks if it can be diluted!

For over 20 years from 1940 O'Brien wrote a successful column of comic and serious pieces in the *Irish Times* under the name Myles na Gopaleen. A selection was later published as *The Best of Myles.* One of O'Brien's other novels, *The Dalkey Archive*, was made into a successful play, *When the Saints Go Cycling In.*

WORKS INCLUDE

1939 *At Swim-Two-Birds*
1941 *The Poor Mouth*
1943 *Faustus Kelly*
1961 *The Hard Life*
1964 *The Dalkey Archive*

Published after he died
1967 *The Third Policeman*
1968 *The Best of Myles*
1976 *The Hair of the Dogma*

OTHER POST-1940 NOVELISTS

BALDWIN, James
BELLOW, Saul
CAMUS, Albert
GARCÍA MÁRQUEZ, Gabriel
GOLDING, William
HELLER, Joseph
IRVING, John
LESSING, Doris

MORRISON, Toni
SALINGER, J.D.
SINGER, Isaac Bashevis
SOLZHENITSYN, Aleksandr
UPDIKE, John
VIDAL, Gore
WALKER, Alice

SEE INDEX FOR FULL LIST

WORLD EVENTS

Age	Contemporary Events
Born 1911 	**1914–18** World War I ❶ **1917** Russian Revolution establishes Communist government **1926** British scientist John Logie Baird demonstrates television **1927** Joseph Stalin becomes dictator of Russia
20 in 1931 	**1931** Empire State Building in New York City completed **1933** Nazi Party, led by Adolf Hitler, gains control in Germany **1939–45** World War II: allies, led by U.S. and Great Britain, fight axis powers, led by Germany and Japan **1941** Germany invades USSR ❷ **1945** U.S. drops first atomic bombs on Japan **1950–53** Korean War: North Korea and China fight South Korea, the U.S., and United Nations troops
40 in 1951   **Dies 1966**	**1957** Eisenhower sends troops to Little Rock, Arkansas, to ensure school desegregation **1960** John F. Kennedy elected president **1961** East Germans build Berlin Wall **1962** Cuban Missile Crisis erupts after the U.S. discovers Soviet missiles on island ❸ **1964–75** Vietnam War: war between communist North Vietnam and U.S. forces supporting South Vietnam **1966** Mao Zedong launches Cultural Revolution, using millions of young Chinese to secure his power ❹

O'CASEY, Sean

Irish playwright
Born Mar. 30, 1880
Died Sep. 18, 1964
Age at death 84

Sean O'Casey was an important Irish playwright. He is best known for his dramas about the political unrest in Ireland during the early years of the 20th century.

O'Casey was born in Dublin, the youngest of 13 children in a poor, working-class family. He received almost no education and taught himself to read and write. He also developed a love of the theater through attending amateur productions.

The early death of O'Casey's father left the family in poverty, and O'Casey had to work as a laborer from the age of 14. In 1913 he helped found the Irish Citizen Army, a radical organization dedicated to improving conditions for the poor and achieving independence from the British, who ruled all of Ireland at the time. He left the following year when it became clear that the other leaders were interested more in war than in social reform.

Between 1916 and 1921 Irish nationalists fought the British in a bitter war. O'Casey sympathized with the aims of the nationalists but was horrified by the effects of the fighting. Although Ireland achieved independence, a civil war followed that brought more bloodshed and sadness. His first successful play, *The Shadow of a Gunman*, produced when he was 43, shows the tragic consequences for poor families.

Because O'Casey's plays showed the negative side of the struggle for independence, he was very controversial. His play *The Plough and the Stars* caused several days of rioting. He left the country soon after to live in England, where he continued writing about Irish themes and the futility of war.

Scene from a production of *Juno and the Paycock*

WORKS INCLUDE

1923 *The Shadow of a Gunman*	**1940** *The Star Turns Red*
1924 *Juno and the Paycock*	**1940** *Purple Dust*
1926 *The Plough and the Stars*	**1955** *The Bishop's Bonfire*
1928 *The Silver Tassie*	**1956** *Mirror in My House*
1933 *Within the Gates*	**1958** *The Drums of Father Ned*

OTHER PLAYWRIGHTS 1900–40

AKINS, Zoë
COWARD, Noël
GARCÍA LORCA, Federico
GREEN, Paul
GREGORY, Lady
KAUFMAN, George. S
ODETS, Clifford
O'NEILL, Eugene

PIRANDELLO, Luigi
PRIESTLEY, J.B.
SHAW, George Bernard
SHERWOOD, Robert E.
SYNGE, John Millington
WILDER, Thornton

SEE INDEX FOR FULL LIST

WORLD EVENTS

Age	Contemporary Events
Born 1880	**1895** Italian physicist Guglielmo Marconi invents radio
20 in 1900	**1903** American inventors Orville and Wilbur Wright make first airplane flight **1908** Henry Ford introduces Model T car ❶ **1914–18** World War I **1917** Russian Revolution establishes Communist government
40 in 1920	**1926** British scientist John Logie Baird demonstrates television **1927** Joseph Stalin becomes dictator of Russia **1931** Empire State Building in New York City completed **1933** Nazi Party, led by Adolf Hitler, gains control in Germany ❷ **1939–45** World War II: allies, led by U.S. and Great Britain, fight axis powers, led by Germany and Japan
60 in 1940	**1945** U.S. drops first atomic bombs on Japan ❸ **1950–53** Korean War: North Korea and China fight South Korea, the U.S., and United Nations troops ❹ **1957** Eisenhower sends troops to Little Rock, Arkansas, to ensure school desegregation
80 in 1960 **Dies 1964**	**1960** John F. Kennedy elected president **1964–75** Vietnam War: war between communist North Vietnam and U.S. forces supporting South Vietnam ❺

© DIAGRAM

145

O'CONNOR, Flannery

Flannery O'Connor is best known for part tragic, part comic stories that combine a cartoonlike quality with serious criticisms of Southern society. She once wrote that "all comic novels that are any good must be about matters of life and death."

O'Connor was born in Savannah, Georgia, the only child of Southern Catholic parents. When her father was diagnosed with lupus, a rare disease, the family moved to a town called Milledgeville.

O'Connor began writing at a young age, and she had her first story published when she was 21, a year after graduating from Georgia State College for Women. In 1947 she attended the Writers' Workshop at the University of Iowa, where she earned a master's degree. Her first novel, *Wise Blood*, arose from her work while at Iowa.

At age 25 O'Connor was also diagnosed with lupus, and she became an invalid in her 30s. She returned to Milledgeville, where she lived with her mother and raised peacocks. She continued to write until her early death at age 39.

O'Connor's Southern background and her Catholicism both influenced her writing. Themes in her stories include religion in general and the piety of religious individuals. Her characters are exaggerated in their awfulness, demonstrating the dangers of pride. She uses the same characters to expose prejudice in society, as in her two novels *Wise Blood* and *The Violent Bear It Away*. In 1959 O'Connor received a Ford Foundation grant to help her to continue writing. Her *Complete Stories* received the National Book Award in 1972.

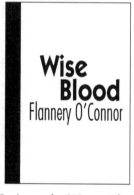

American novelist and short-story writer
Born Mar. 25, 1925
Died Aug. 3, 1964
Age at death 39

Wise Blood
Flannery O'Connor

Book cover for O'Connor's first novel, *Wise Blood*

WORKS INCLUDE

1952 *Wise Blood*
1955 *A Good Man Is Hard to Find*
1960 *The Violent Bear It Away*

Published after she died
1965 *Everything That Rises Must Converge*
1969 *Mystery and Manners*
1971 *Complete Stories*
1979 *The Habit of Being*

OTHER POST-1940 NOVELISTS

BALDWIN, James
BELLOW, Saul
CAMUS, Albert
GARCÍA MÁRQUEZ, Gabriel
GOLDING, William
HELLER, Joseph
IRVING, John
LESSING, Doris

MORRISON, Toni
SALINGER, J.D.
SINGER, Isaac Bashevis
SOLZHENITSYN, Aleksandr
UPDIKE, John
VIDAL, Gore
WALKER, Alice

SEE INDEX FOR FULL LIST

WORLD EVENTS

Age	Contemporary Events
Born 1925 	**1926** British scientist John Logie Baird demonstrates television **1927** Joseph Stalin becomes dictator of Russia **1929** Stock Market crash ushers in Great Depression **1931** Empire State Building in New York City completed **1933** Nazi Party, led by Adolf Hitler, gains control in Germany ❶
10 in 1935 	**1936–39** Spanish Civil War: conservative forces overthrow government ❷ **1939–45** World War II: allies, led by U.S. and Great Britain, fight axis powers, led by Germany and Japan ❸
20 in 1945 	**1945** U.S. drops first atomic bombs on Japan ❹ **1950–53** Korean War: North Korea and China fight South Korea, the U.S., and United Nations troops **1953** New Zealand explorer Edmund Hillary climbs Mount Everest
30 in 1955   **Dies 1964**	**1957** Eisenhower sends troops to Little Rock, Arkansas, to ensure school desegregation **1960** John F. Kennedy elected president ❺ **1963** Led by Rev. Martin Luther King, Jr., thousands march on Washington DC to press for civil rights for African Americans **1964–75** Vietnam War: war between communist North Vietnam and U.S. forces supporting South Vietnam ❻

© DIAGRAM

O'DELL, Scott

American young-adults' writer
Born May 23, 1898
Died Oct. 15, 1989
Age at death 91

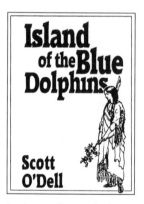

Book cover for O'Dell's first historical children's novel

Scott O'Dell is one of America's best-known writers of historical fiction for young adults. He won every major award in children's literature and sold millions of copies of books. The yearly Scott O'Dell Award for historical fiction is his legacy to children's literature.

O'Dell was born near Los Angeles. His father's job with the railroad meant that the family often had to move, and he grew up all over southern California. Between 1919 and 1921 he studied at various colleges so that he could see the country but never completed a degree. He then moved to Hollywood, where he worked as a cameraman. O'Dell traveled to Italy to help film the 1925 silent classic *Ben Hur* and decided to study at the University of Rome. He then returned to California and worked as a book reviewer and book editor.

O'Dell had planned to become a writer while still a college student. He wrote his first book when he was in Italy, but it was never published. His first published work, *Woman of Spain*, a novel for adults, came out when he was 36. His first historical novel for young adults was not published until 26 years later, when he was 62. *Island of the Blue Dolphins* was a great success and is still one of his most popular books. It is based on the true story of a Native-American woman who survives for 18 years alone on an island. It is written in simple sentences as if told by the woman herself – a style that became O'Dell's trademark. He followed this success with many other stories based on actual events, most often from American history, and some with more modern settings. He was still writing at the age of 91.

WORKS INCLUDE

1934 *Woman of Spain*	**1969** *Journey to Jericho*
1960 *Island of the Blue Dolphins*	**1970** *Sing Down the Moon*
1966 *The King's Fifth*	**1974** *Child of Fire*
1967 *The Black Pearl*	**1980** *Sarah Bishop*
1968 *The Dark Canoe*	**1983** *The Amethyst Ring*

OTHER CHILDREN'S WRITERS

ADAMS, Harriet Stratemeyer
ALCOTT, Louisa May
ANDERSEN, Hans Christian
BARRIE, J.M.
BLYTON, Enid
CARLE, Eric
CARROLL, Lewis
DAHL, Roald

KIPLING, Rudyard
LEAR, Edward
MILNE, A.A.
POTTER, Beatrix
REID BANKS, Lynne
SENDAK, Maurice
TWAIN, Mark

SEE INDEX FOR FULL LIST

WORLD EVENTS

Age	Contemporary Events
Born 1898 	**1903** American inventors Orville and Wilbur Wright make first airplane flight **1908** Henry Ford introduces Model T car **1914–18** World War I ❶ **1917** Russian Revolution establishes Communist government
20 in 1918 	**1927** Joseph Stalin becomes dictator of Russia ❷ **1933** Nazi Party, led by Adolf Hitler, gains control in Germany
40 in 1938	**1939–45** World War II: allies, led by U.S. and Great Britain, fight axis powers, led by Germany and Japan **1945** U.S. drops first atomic bombs on Japan ❸ **1950–53** Korean War: North Korea and China fight South Korea, the U.S., and United Nations troops **1957** Eisenhower sends troops to Little Rock, Arkansas, to ensure school desegregation
60 in 1958 	**1960** John F. Kennedy elected president **1961** East Germans build Berlin Wall **1964–75** Vietnam War: war between communist North Vietnam and U.S. forces supporting South Vietnam ❹ **1967** Arabs and Israelis fight in Six Day War **1969** American astronaut walks on Moon ❺
80 in 1978 **Dies 1989**	**1981** U.S. launches first space shuttle **1989** Communist regimes fall throughout Eastern Europe

© DIAGRAM

ODETS, Clifford

American playwright and screenwriter
Born Jul. 18, 1906
Died Aug. 14, 1963
Age at death 57

Scene from a production of Odets's play *Waiting for Lefty*

Clifford Odets's best-known plays, *Waiting for Lefty* and *Awake and Sing!*, are about the suffering of those who have to fight to make a living.

Raised in a middle-class family in New York City, Odets left school when he was 15 to become an actor. At age 24 he joined the Group Theater, which later put on many of his plays.

Waiting for Lefty, produced when Odets was 29, won him national fame. About a cab drivers' strike, it focuses on the struggles of the working class. His next play, *Awake and Sing!*, is the story of a poor Jewish family. These and others of Odets's early plays were written during the **Great Depression**. They are about people who try to keep their sense of identity in an often hostile world. Their social concerns reflect Odets's belief in the family and in the dignity of human beings.

Odets moved to Hollywood in 1935 to write screenplays. Rejecting the love for money and corruption he found there, he returned to New York City and continued to write plays on social themes. *Golden Boy* and *Clash by Night* concern the frustration felt by those who have no financial security. *Golden Boy*, his greatest commercial success, is about a man who gives up a career as a violinist to become a boxer and realizes too late how much he has sacrificed for success. Odets's later plays were less well received, except for *The Country Girl*, which tells the story of a wife's support of her alcoholic husband.

During the 1940s and '50s Odets returned to Hollywood and wrote screenplays for such movies as *The Sweet Smell of Success*.

WORKS INCLUDE

1935 *Waiting for Lefty*
1935 *Awake and Sing!*
1935 *Till the Day I Die*
1935 *Paradise Lost*
1937 *Golden Boy*

1941 *Clash by Night*
1949 *The Big Knife*
1950 *The Country Girl*
1954 *The Flowering Peach*
1957 *The Sweet Smell of Success*

OTHER PLAYWRIGHTS 1900–40

AKINS, Zoë
COWARD, Noël
GARCÍA LORCA, Federico
GREEN, Paul
GREGORY, Lady
KAUFMAN, George. S
O'CASEY, Sean
O'NEILL, Eugene

PIRANDELLO, Luigi
PRIESTLEY, J.B.
SHAW, George Bernard
SHERWOOD, Robert E.
SYNGE, John Millington
WILDER, Thornton

SEE INDEX FOR FULL LIST

WORLD EVENTS

Age	Contemporary Events
Born 1906 	**1908** Henry Ford introduces Model T car ❶ **1914–18** World War I **1917** Russian Revolution establishes Communist government
20 in 1926  	**1926** British scientist John Logie Baird demonstrates television **1927** Joseph Stalin becomes dictator of Russia ❷ **1931** Empire State Building in New York City completed **1933** Nazi Party, led by Adolf Hitler, gains control in Germany ❸ **1939–45** World War II: allies, led by U.S. and Great Britain, fight axis powers, led by Germany and Japan **1941** Germany invades USSR **1945** U.S. drops first atomic bombs on Japan **1945** United Nations (UN), organization working for betterment of humanity, founded
40 in 1946 **Dies 1963**	**1950–53** Korean War: North Korea and China fight South Korea, the U.S., and United Nations troops ❹ **1957** Eisenhower sends troops to Little Rock, Arkansas, to ensure school desegregation **1960** John F. Kennedy elected president **1961** East Germans build Berlin Wall **1962** Cuban Missile Crisis erupts after the U.S. discovers Soviet missiles on island ❺ **1963** Led by Rev. Martin Luther King, Jr., thousands march on Washington DC to press for civil rights for African Americans ❻

© DIAGRAM

151

OE Kenzaburo

Japanese novelist and short-story writer
Born Jan. 31, 1935

Book cover for Oe's novel about Japan *The Silent Cry*

Oe Kenzaburo writes novels about the conflict between Japanese traditions and modern Western culture and ideas. He was awarded the **Nobel Prize** for literature in 1994.

Oe was born in a mountain village on Shikoku, smallest of the four main Japanese islands. He graduated from the University of Tokyo in 1959, having published a number of award-winning short stories. His senior thesis was on the French writer JEAN-PAUL SARTRE, and he has been deeply influenced by Western literature, especially the work of ALBERT CAMUS and NORMAN MAILER.

In his early writings Oe focused on young people who use sex and violence to numb feelings of rootlessness and despair in the insecure world of post-**World War II** Japan. By the 1960s his stories were challenging the policies of the Japanese government. He still campaigns against nuclear weapons and the censorship of writers.

In 1963 Oe's first son, Hikari, was born severely brain damaged. Doctors advised Oe and his wife to let Hikari die, but after speaking with someone who had treated the victims of the atomic bombing of Hiroshima, Oe rejected their advice. His seventh novel (the first to be published in English), *A Personal Matter*, is a fictional account of his life with Hikari; much of his later writing centers around the relationships between disabled and nondisabled people. After receiving the Nobel Prize, Oe announced that his novel *A Flaming Tree* would be his last.

WORKS INCLUDE

1958 "Prize Stock"
1958 *Nip the Buds, Shoot the Kids*
1964 *A Personal Matter*
1967 *The Silent Cry*
1973 *The Deluge Flooded into My Soul*

1977 *Teach Us to Outgrow Our Madness*
1984 *The Crazy Iris and Other Stories of the Atomic Aftermath*
1994 *A Flaming Tree*

OTHER ASIAN AND MIDDLE EASTERN WRITERS

BASHO, Matsuo
DESAI, Anita
DING LING
DU FU
HAYASHI Fumiko
KALIDASA
KAWABATA Yasunari
MISHIMA Yukio

MURASAKI Shikibu
NARAYAN, R.K.
OZ, Amos
SHIMAZAKI Toson
TAGORE, Rabindranath
TANIZAKI Junichiro
WU CHENGEN

SEE INDEX FOR FULL LIST

WORLD EVENTS

Age	Contemporary Events
Born 1935 	**1939–45** World War II: allies, led by U.S. and Great Britain, fight axis powers, led by Germany and Japan ❶ **1941** Germany invades USSR **1945** U.S. drops first atomic bombs on Japan **1950–53** Korean War: North Korea and China fight South Korea, the U.S., and United Nations troops ❷
20 in 1955	**1957** Eisenhower sends troops to Little Rock, Arkansas, to ensure school desegregation **1960** John F. Kennedy elected president **1964–75** Vietnam War: war between communist North Vietnam and U.S. forces supporting South Vietnam ❸ **1967** Arabs and Israelis fight in Six Day War **1969** American astronaut walks on Moon ❹
40 in 1975	**1980** Ronald Reagan elected president ❺ **1981** U.S. launches first space shuttle ❻ **1989** Communist regimes fall throughout Eastern Europe **1991** Gulf War: UN forces, led by U.S., defeat Iraq and free Kuwait **1992** Bill Clinton elected president **1994** First multiracial elections in South Africa end years of white minority rule. They are won by Nelson Mandela, African National Congress leader
60 in 1995	**1996** Jumbo jet TWA 800 explodes off Long Island in New York

© DIAGRAM

O'FAOLAIN, Sean

**Irish short-story
writer and novelist
Born** Feb. 22, 1900
Died Apr. 20, 1991
Age at death 91

THE
B E L L
Edited by Peadar O'Donnell
Contributors to this issue include
SEAN O'FAOLAIN
BRYAN McMAHON
JOHN HEWITT
JOHN O'CONNOR
R. WYSE JACKSON
LIAM O'LAOGHAIRE
One Shilling and Sixpence

Cover for an edition of
O'Faolain's literary magazine

Sean O'Faolain is one of Ireland's most celebrated
writers. He is known particularly for his short stories,
which realistically portray the lives and struggles of
ordinary Irish people.

O'Faolain was born in Cork, southern Ireland,
which was then under British rule. His name at birth
was John Whelan, but he later changed this to its Irish
equivalent. O'Faolain was educated at University
College, Cork, where he joined the Irish nationalist
movement that later became the Irish Republican
Army (IRA). When British rule ended, Ireland was
divided into Northern Ireland and the Irish Free State
and civil war broke out. O'Faolain served with the
IRA, but the republicans were defeated.

Disillusioned, O'Faolain studied English literature
at Harvard (1926–29). While there he married a
former IRA comrade, Eileen Gould. He then taught
literature in the U.S. and England for a few years,
planning to earn enough to return home.

O'Faolain's first published book, *Midsummer Night
Madness and Other Stories*, came out when he was 32.
Its success allowed him to write full time and return
to Ireland. His work reflects his political concerns,
drawing initially on his youthful revolutionary
activities and, later, on his views about the new Irish
state. As well as fiction, he wrote an analysis of the
Irish national character and **biographies** of important
Irish figures. He founded a literary magazine, *The Bell*,
and used it to encourage young writers to comment
on social conditions and to campaign against
Ireland's strict censorship laws.

WORKS INCLUDE

1932 *Midsummer Night Madness and
Other Stories*
1933 *A Nest of Simple Folk*
1936 *Bird Alone*
1940 *Come Back to Erin*

1947 *The Irish*
1964 *Vive Moi!*
1976 *Foreign Affairs and Other Stories*
1980 *Collected Stories*

WORLD EVENTS

Age	Contemporary Events
Born 1900 	**1908** Henry Ford introduces Model T car **1914–18** World War I ❶ **1917** Russian Revolution establishes Communist government
20 in 1920 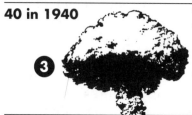	**1927** Joseph Stalin becomes dictator of Russia **1933** Nazi Party, led by Adolf Hitler, gains control in Germany **1939–45** World War II: allies, led by U.S. and Great Britain, fight axis powers, led by Germany and Japan ❷
40 in 1940 	**1945** U.S. drops first atomic bombs on Japan ❸ **1950–53** Korean War: North Korea and China fight South Korea, the U.S., and United Nations troops **1957** Eisenhower sends troops to Little Rock, Arkansas, to ensure school desegregation
60 in 1960 	**1960** John F. Kennedy elected president **1964–75** Vietnam War: war between communist North Vietnam and U.S. forces supporting South Vietnam ❹ **1969** American astronaut walks on Moon **1974** Pres. Richard M. Nixon resigns presidency ❺
80 in 1980  **Dies 1991**	**1980** Ronald Reagan elected president **1981** U.S. launches first space shuttle ❻ **1989** Communist regimes fall throughout Eastern Europe **1991** Gulf War: UN forces, led by U.S., defeat Iraq and free Kuwait

© DIAGRAM

OGOT, Grace

Kenyan novelist and short-story writer
Born May 15, 1930

THE OTHER WOMAN
Grace Ogot

Book cover for a collection of Ogot's short stories

Grace Ogot is Kenya's most famous female writer. With the publication of her first novel, *The Promised Land*, she became one of the founders of modern African women's literature.

Ogot was born in Kenya's central Nyana region at a time when the country was a British colony. She went to local schools before studying to be a nurse in neighboring Uganda and then England in the late 1950s. While studying in London, she began writing short stories after a friend commented on her well-written letters. She was also inspired by the lack of East African work at the 1962 African Writers' conference in Uganda.

Ogot's work often explores the conflicts brought about by British rule in Kenya. She has written several books in Luo – her mother tongue – to preserve the language and make her work readable to her own people. *The Promised Land*, published when Ogot was 36, is set in the colonial period and centers on the experience of a new bride, her feelings of isolation in her husband's village, and the couple's migration to a new region.

In 1975 the Kenyan president appointed Ogot to Kenya's seat at the United Nations. She was made a member of the Kenyan parliament in 1983 but resigned two years later to fight for her seat in elections. She won and later became assistant minister of culture. Similar to Ogot's experiences, her novel *The Graduate* tells of a female politician's fight to be judged on her ability, not on her sex. In the 1992 elections Ogot lost her seat, and she now owns two clothing stores in Nairobi, the Kenyan capital.

WORKS INCLUDE

1966 *The Promised Land*
1968 *Land without Thunder*
1976 *The Other Woman*
1980 *The Graduate*
1980 *The Island of Tears*

1983 *Miaha*
1989 *The Strange Bride*

OTHER AFRICAN WRITERS

ACHEBE, Chinua
CLARK-BEKEDEREMO, John Pepper
COETZEE, J.M.
FUGARD, Athol
GORDIMER, Nadine
HEAD, Bessie
MAHFOUZ, Naguib
NETO, Agostinho

NGUGI wa Thiong'o
NWAPA, Flora
OKRI, Ben
PATON, Alan
ROBERT, Shaaban
SENGHOR, Léopold Sédar
SOYINKA, Wole

SEE INDEX FOR FULL LIST

WORLD EVENTS

Age	Contemporary Events
Born 1930 	**1931** Empire State Building in New York City completed **1933** Nazi Party, led by Adolph Hitler, gains control in Germany **1939–45** World War II: allies, led by U.S. and Great Britain, fight axis powers, led by Germany and Japan **1945** U.S. drops first atomic bombs on Japan ❶
20 in 1950 	**1950–53** Korean War: North Korea and China fight South Korea, the U.S., and United Nations troops ❷ **1960** John F. Kennedy elected president **1964–75** Vietnam War: war between communist North Vietnam and U.S. forces supporting South Vietnam **1967** Arabs and Israelis fight in Six Day War **1969** American astronaut walks on Moon
40 in 1970 	**1979** Britain elects its first female prime minister, Margaret Thatcher **1981** U.S. launches first space shuttle **1989** Communist regimes fall throughout Eastern Europe ❸
60 in 1990 	**1991** Gulf War: UN forces, led by U.S., defeat Iraq and free Kuwait **1992** Bill Clinton elected president **1994** First multiracial elections in South Africa end years of white minority rule. They are won by Nelson Mandela, African National Congress leader ❹

© DIAGRAM

157

O'HARA, John

American novelist and short-story writer
Born Jan. 31, 1905
Died Apr. 11, 1970
Age at death 65

One of O'Hara's bestselling novels about American life

John O'Hara was a popular author best known for writing about the morals, prejudices, and anxieties of upper-middle-class Americans. By his death 20 million copies of his books had been sold.

O'Hara was born in Pottsville, Pennsylvania. His school career was a disaster: he was "honorably dismissed" from Fordham Preparatory School in New York and expelled from the Keystone State Normal School near Pottsville. When his father, a physician, died suddenly, leaving the family poor, O'Hara worked for several newspapers and magazines; because he drank too much, the jobs did not last long. His unstable behavior was also responsible for the breakup of his first marriage. Finally, he isolated himself in a Manhattan hotel, determined to write and make something of his life.

O'Hara's first novel, *Appointment in Samarra*, was published when he was 29 and was an instant success. It covers the last three days in the life of the main character. The themes of this novel became familiar in all O'Hara's later work: the power of certain social classes to exclude people they consider "outsiders"; the power of lust over love in human relationships; and the failures of parents.

Although O'Hara's fiction was hugely popular, critics never rated him highly. He claimed to be the hardest working author in the U.S., turning out some 37 books, most of them after he gave up drinking in 1949; he even conquered Broadway when he helped produce the musical adaptation of his *Pal Joey* stories. In 1956 he won the National Book Award for *Ten North Frederick*.

WORKS INCLUDE

1934 *Appointment in Samarra*
1935 *Butterfield 8*
1938 *Hope of Heaven*
1940 *Pal Joey*
1949 *A Rage to Live*

1955 *Ten North Frederick*
1958 *From the Terrace*
1960 *Sermons and Soda Water*
1963 *The Hat on the Bed*
1967 *Waiting for Winter*

OTHER POST-1940 NOVELISTS

BALDWIN, James
BELLOW, Saul
CAMUS, Albert
GARCÍA MÁRQUEZ, Gabriel
GOLDING, William
HELLER, Joseph
IRVING, John
LESSING, Doris

MORRISON, Toni
SALINGER, J.D.
SINGER, Isaac Bashevis
SOLZHENITSYN, Aleksandr
UPDIKE, John
VIDAL, Gore
WALKER, Alice

SEE INDEX FOR FULL LIST

WORLD EVENTS

Age	Contemporary Events
Born 1905	**1908** Henry Ford introduces Model T car
	1914–18 World War I
	1917 Russian Revolution establishes Communist government
20 in 1925	**1926** British scientist John Logie Baird demonstrates television
	1927 Joseph Stalin becomes dictator of Russia
	1931 Empire State Building in New York City completed ❶
	1933 Nazi Party, led by Adolf Hitler, gains control in Germany ❷
	1939–45 World War II: allies, led by U.S. and Great Britain, fight axis powers, led by Germany and Japan
40 in 1945	**1945** U.S. drops first atomic bombs on Japan
	1950–53 Korean War: North Korea and China fight South Korea, the U.S., and United Nations troops
	1957 Eisenhower sends troops to Little Rock, Arkansas, to ensure school desegregation ❸
	1960 John F. Kennedy elected president
	1961 East Germans build Berlin Wall
	1962 Cuban Missile Crisis erupts after the U.S. discovers Soviet missiles on island ❹
	1964–75 Vietnam War: war between communist North Vietnam and U.S. forces supporting South Vietnam
60 in 1965 **Dies 1970**	**1967** Arabs and Israelis fight in Six Day War
	1969 American astronaut walks on Moon ❺

© DIAGRAM

159

OKIGBO, Christopher

Nigerian poet
Born Aug. 16, 1932
Died Aug. 1967
Age at death c. 35

CHRISTOPHER
OKIGBO

**COLLECTED
POEMS**

Book cover for a collection of
Okigbo's poetry

Christopher Okigbo was one of Nigeria's best poets. Written in English, his work can be difficult but has inspired many African writers.

Okigbo was born near Onitsha in eastern Nigeria (West Africa), which at the time was a British colony. His family was Christian but still followed the Igbo religion. Okigbo's grandfather had been a priest of the river god Idoto, and Okigbo, who was believed to be his grandfather reborn, took over this role at the same time he decided to become a poet. Okigbo studied Greek and Latin at the University of Ibadan, Nigeria, and then took a variety of jobs, including civil servant, Latin teacher, and librarian. Soon, however, he decided that he could not be anything but a poet. Any job Okigbo held he saw just as a way to earn money to support his family.

Okigbo's first volume of poetry, *Heavensgate*, was published when he was 30. He was influenced by both European literature and his African upbringing. Having been educated when Nigeria was a colony, he felt he belonged to both the European and African worlds and tried to unite the two in his work.

In 1966 Okigbo won the poetry prize at the Festival of Negro Arts in Dakar, Senegal (West Africa). He refused the prize because he felt that his work and not his race should be judged. Okigbo's work slowly became more political. *Silences* mourns the troubles of newly independent Nigeria, and *Path of Thunder* predicted the **Biafran War** that split Nigeria. In July 1967 Okigbo joined the forces fighting for the independence of Biafra – the Igbo region of eastern Nigeria. He was killed in action one month later.

WORKS INCLUDE

1962 *Heavensgate*	Published after he died
1964 *Limits*	**1968** *Path of Thunder*
1964 *Distances*	**1971** *Labyrinths*
1965 *Silences*	**1986** *Collected Poems*

OTHER AFRICAN WRITERS

ACHEBE, Chinua
CLARK-BEKEDEREMO, John Pepper
COETZEE, J.M.
FUGARD, Athol
GORDIMER, Nadine
HEAD, Bessie
MAHFOUZ, Naguib
NETO, Agostinho

NGUGI wa Thiong'o
NWAPA, Flora
OKRI, Ben
PATON, Alan
ROBERT, Shaaban
SENGHOR, Léopold Sédar
SOYINKA, Wole

SEE INDEX FOR FULL LIST

WORLD EVENTS

Age	Contemporary Events
Born 1932  	**1933** Nazi Party, led by Adolf Hitler, gains control in Germany ❶
	1934 Mao Zedong becomes head of Chinese Communist Party and leads Long March of Communists to northern China
	1935 Italy invades Abyssinia (Ethiopia)
	1936 African-American track star Jesse Owens wins four gold medals at Olympics in Hitler's Germany ❷
	1936–39 Spanish Civil War: conservative forces overthrow government
	1939–45 World War II: allies, led by U.S. and Great Britain, fight axis powers, led by Germany and Japan ❸
	1941 Germany invades USSR
10 in 1942 	**1945** U.S. drops first atomic bombs on Japan
	1945 United Nations (UN), organization working for betterment of humanity, founded ❹
	1950–53 Korean War: North Korea and China fight South Korea, the U.S., and United Nations troops
20 in 1952 	**1957** Eisenhower sends troops to Little Rock, Arkansas, to ensure school desegregation
	1960 John F. Kennedy elected president
	1961 East Germans build Berlin Wall ❺
30 in 1962 **Dies 1967**	**1964–75** Vietnam War: war between communist North Vietnam and U.S. forces supporting South Vietnam ❻
	1967 Arabs and Israelis fight in Six Day War

OKRI, Ben

**Nigerian novelist,
poet, and short-
story writer
Born** Mar. 15, 1959

Book cover for Okri's
prizewinning novel

Ben Okri is one of Nigeria's most famous younger writers. In 1991 his novel *The Famished Road* won the **Booker Prize**, which is given each year to the best book published in Britain.

Okri was born in Nigeria (West Africa) just before the country became independent from British rule. As a child he read widely, anything from English literature to African myths and **folklore**. His father brought many books back from his time in England, where he had studied law, and his mother told him many African stories.

As early as the age of 17 Okri knew that he wanted to be a writer. At first he wrote articles on social and political issues, most of which he could not get published. When he wrote short stories based on these articles, however, he found that they were well received. These first short stories appeared in Nigerian journals and newspapers. Okri's first novel, *Flowers and Shadows*, published when he was only 21, grew out of one of these short stories. It is about a successful businessman whose jealous relatives try to destroy him. Okri moved to southern England when he was 19 to study at the University of Essex. He has since settled in London.

Okri's most famous book, *The Famished Road*, is set in Nigeria. It is the story of Azaro, a spirit child, who is supposed to die soon after being born. On this occasion, however, Azaro decides to remain in the real world, while keeping one foot in the spirit world. Like much of Okri's work it combines magic, fantasy, and reality. The story continues in the sequel *Songs of Enchantment*.

WORKS INCLUDE

1980 *Flowers and Shadows*
1981 *The Landscapes Within*
1986 *Incidents at the Shrine*
1988 *Stars of the New Curfew*
1991 *The Famished Road*

1992 *An African Elegy*
1993 *Songs of Enchantment*
1995 *Astonishing the Gods*
1996 *Dangerous Love*

OTHER AFRICAN WRITERS

ACHEBE, Chinua
CLARK-BEKEDEREMO, John Pepper
COETZEE, J.M.
FUGARD, Athol
GORDIMER, Nadine
HEAD, Bessie
MAHFOUZ, Naguib
NETO, Agostinho

NGUGI wa Thiong'o
NWAPA, Flora
PATON, Alan
ROBERT, Shaaban
SENGHOR, Léopold Sédar
SOYINKA, Wole

SEE INDEX FOR FULL LIST

WORLD EVENTS

Age	Contemporary Events
Born 1959	**1960** John F. Kennedy elected president
	1962 Cuban Missile Crisis erupts after the U.S. discovers Soviet missiles on island ❶
	1963 Led by Rev. Martin Luther King, Jr., thousands march on Washington DC to press for civil rights for African Americans
	1964–75 Vietnam War: war between communist North Vietnam and U.S. forces supporting South Vietnam
	1967 Arabs and Israelis fight in Six Day War
10 in 1969	**1969** American astronaut walks on Moon
	1974 Pres. Richard M. Nixon resigns presidency
	1975–79 Communist forces murder hundreds of thousands in Cambodia ❷
20 in 1979	**1980** Ronald Reagan elected president
	1981 U.S. launches first space shuttle
	1987 Gorbachev begins reforms in USSR: perestroika (restructuring) and glasnost (openness) ❸
30 in 1989	**1989** Communist regimes fall throughout Eastern Europe ❹
	1990 Cold War between USSR and U.S. ends
	1991 Gulf War: UN forces, led by U.S., defeat Iraq and free Kuwait ❺
	1992 Bill Clinton elected president
	1994 First multiracial elections in South Africa end years of white minority rule. They are won by Nelson Mandela, African National Congress leader

© DIAGRAM

163

OLIVER, Mary

American poet
Born Sep. 10, 1935

Book cover for Oliver's award-winning poetry collection

Mary Oliver is famous for her powerful poetry that often describes natural forces and wildlife but also deals with important human concerns that affect everyone. In 1984 she won the **Pulitzer Prize** for her collection of poetry called *American Primitive*.

The daughter of a teacher, Oliver was born in Cleveland, Ohio, and raised in the countryside. She studied at Ohio State University for one year and for a further year at Vassar College, New York. Her first collection of poetry, *No Voyage*, came out when she was 28. It was first published in England and was highly praised by critics. Despite the title, the poems are set in various parts of the world, including Ohio, New England, England, and Scotland. The title poem won an award from the Poetry Society of America in 1963, and since then Oliver has regularly won prizes for her work. These prizes, awards, and fellowships have allowed her to support herself by writing.

In 1980 Oliver took her first college teaching job – as visiting professor at the Case Western Reserve University in Cleveland. Since 1991 she has been writer-in-residence at Sweet Briar College, Virginia.

Oliver's early poems focus on nature. She is passionate about the natural world and uses images drawn from it to explore human experience. She often compares humans to animals in a way that makes her poetry more than simply descriptive. Her work has gradually come to include more references to herself, her relatives, and her life. This has added to the depth and power of her verse.

WORKS INCLUDE

1963 No Voyage
1972 The River Styx, Ohio, and Other Poems
1978 The Night Traveler
1978 Twelve Moons
1979 Sleeping in the Forest
1983 American Primitive
1986 Dream Work
1990 Provincetown
1992 New and Selected Poems

OTHER POST-1940 POETS

ANGELOU, Maya
BISHOP, Elizabeth
BRODSKY, Joseph
DUNCAN, Robert
GINSBERG, Allen
HAYDEN, Robert
HEANEY, Seamus
HUGHES, Ted

LOWELL, Robert
PAZ, Octavio
PLATH, Sylvia
SEXTON, Anne
THOMAS, Dylan
WALCOTT, Derek
YEVTUSHENKO, Yevgeny

SEE INDEX FOR FULL LIST

WORLD EVENTS

Age	Contemporary Events
Born 1935	**1939–45** World War II: allies, led by U.S. and Great Britain, fight axis powers, led by Germany and Japan
	1941 Germany invades USSR ❶
	1945 U.S. drops first atomic bombs on Japan
	1950–53 Korean War: North Korea and China fight South Korea, the U.S., and United Nations troops ❷
20 in 1955	**1957** Eisenhower sends troops to Little Rock, Arkansas, to ensure school desegregation
	1960 John F. Kennedy elected president
	1964–75 Vietnam War: war between communist North Vietnam and U.S. forces supporting South Vietnam ❸
	1967 Arabs and Israelis fight in Six Day War
	1969 American astronaut walks on Moon ❹
40 in 1975	**1980** Ronald Reagan elected president ❺
	1981 U.S. launches first space shuttle ❻
	1989 Communist regimes fall throughout Eastern Europe
	1991 Gulf War: UN forces, led by U.S., defeat Iraq and free Kuwait
	1992 Bill Clinton elected president
	1994 First multiracial elections in South Africa end years of white minority rule. They are won by Nelson Mandela, African National Congress leader
60 in 1995	**1996** Jumbo jet TWA 800 explodes off Long Island in New York

OLSEN, Tillie

American novelist, essayist, and short-story writer
Born Jan. 14, 1913

Book cover for Olsen's first novel about women's lives

Although she has published relatively little, Tillie Olsen has had a huge impact on women's writing in America through her fiction, essays, and teaching. Her first novel, *Yonnondio*, has been described as one of the best novels to come out of the 1930s.

The second of seven children, Olsen was born Tillie Lerner in Wahoo, Nebraska. Her parents were poor Russian-Jewish immigrants. Olsen inherited her father's socialist beliefs and from a young age was politically active. After being forced to leave school early, she held a variety of low-paid jobs. This did not stop her from fighting to improve workers' lives, and she twice spent time in jail for her union activities.

While Olsen was still in her 20s, she managed to publish two poems and several political essays and begin writing *Yonnondio*. In 1936 she married and started a family, which prevented her from writing for the next two decades. She began writing again in her late 40s after winning a grant for a creative-writing course. In this time she wrote the short stories that later appeared in *Tell Me a Riddle* but had to return to work in 1957 when the money ran out. After this book was published a few years later, Olsen won various grants and teaching jobs.

Yonnondio was finally published when she was 61. About the fortunes of a working-class family during the **Great Depression**, it shows how women suffered even more than their unemployed husbands. Olsen has since worked to rediscover the voices of writers silenced by their race, class, or gender, as hers was for so many years.

WORKS INCLUDE

1934 *There Is a Reason*
1934 *I Want You Women up North to Know*
1961 *Tell Me a Riddle*
1974 *Yonnondio*

1978 *Silences*
1981 *I Stand Here Ironing*

OTHER POST-1940 NOVELISTS

BALDWIN, James
BELLOW, Saul
CAMUS, Albert
GARCÍA MÁRQUEZ, Gabriel
GOLDING, William
HELLER, Joseph
IRVING, John
LESSING, Doris

MORRISON, Toni
SALINGER, J.D.
SINGER, Isaac Bashevis
SOLZHENITSYN, Aleksandr
UPDIKE, John
VIDAL, Gore
WALKER, Alice

SEE INDEX FOR FULL LIST

WORLD EVENTS

Age	Contemporary Events
Born 1913	**1914–18** World War I ❶ **1917** Russian Revolution establishes Communist government ❷ **1927** Joseph Stalin becomes dictator of Russia
20 in 1933 	**1933** Nazi Party, led by Adolf Hitler, gains control in Germany ❸ **1939–45** World War II: allies, led by U.S. and Great Britain, fight axis powers, led by Germany and Japan **1945** U.S. drops first atomic bombs on Japan **1950–53** Korean War: North Korea and China fight South Korea, the U.S., and United Nations troops
40 in 1953	**1960** John F. Kennedy elected president **1964–75** Vietnam War: war between communist North Vietnam and U.S. forces supporting South Vietnam ❹ **1967** Arabs and Israelis fight in Six Day War **1969** American astronaut walks on Moon
60 in 1973	**1981** U.S. launches first space shuttle ❺ **1989** Communist regimes fall throughout Eastern Europe **1991** Gulf War: UN forces, led by U.S., defeat Iraq and free Kuwait
80 in 1993	**1994** First multiracial elections in South Africa end years of white minority rule. They are won by Nelson Mandela, African National Congress leader ❻

We Demand... DEMOCRACY

© DIAGRAM

167

OMAR KHAYYAM

Persian poet
Born May 18, 1048
Died Dec. 4, 1131
Age at death 83

THE
RUBAIYAT
OF
OMAR
KHAYYAM

Book cover for Khayyam's world famous poem

The Rubaiyat of Omar Khayyam is one of the world's most famous poetic works. Its author, Omar Khayyam, was a great scholar in the ancient Muslim kingdom of Persia almost a thousand years ago.

Omar Khayyam was born in Nishapur, Persia (now Iran). At that time Persian civilization was far more advanced than that of Europe, and as a young man Omar Khayyam learned about astronomy, mathematics, **philosophy**, and medicine.

When one of Omar Khayyam's student friends became an important official at the court of a powerful ruler, Omar Khayyam traveled there and was allowed to live and study at the court. Between the years 1074 and 1079 he worked on a project to reform the Islamic calendar according to highly accurate astronomical observations. He also wrote an important book on the branch of math known as algebra.

It is not known when Omar Khayyam wrote the 200 or so four-line verses for which he has become famous. They were probably composed at different stages of his life. His work became known outside the Muslim world when the English poet Edward Fitzgerald published a translation of his collected poems as *The Rubaiyat of Omar Khayyam* more than 700 years after his death. The book became extremely popular – readers loved its descriptions of luxury and pleasure and its sense of ancient wisdom. The images it conjured up of beautiful gardens and mysterious veiled women became the **stereotyped** Western idea of Muslim culture. *The Rubaiyat* has since been translated into most of the world's languages.

WORKS INCLUDE

1859 *The Rubaiyat of Omar Khayyam*
(published after he died)

OTHER ASIAN AND MIDDLE EASTERN WRITERS

BASHO, Matsuo
DESAI, Anita
DING LING
DU FU
HAYASHI Fumiko
KALIDASA
KAWABATA Yasunari
MISHIMA Yukio

MURASAKI Shikibu
NARAYAN, R.K.
OZ, Amos
SHIMAZAKI Toson
TAGORE, Rabindranath
TANIZAKI Junichiro
WU CHENGEN

SEE INDEX FOR FULL LIST

WORLD EVENTS

Age	Contemporary Events
Before his birth	**1001** Stephen I crowned king of Hungary
	1002 Viking leader Leif Ericson explores Newfoundland
Born 1048	**c. 1050** Chinese and Arabs use compass
	1050–1105 Almoravids, Berbers from the western Sahara, conquer Spain
PLGNIS	**1052** Building begins on Westminster Abbey in London, England
	1054 Christian Church divided into Roman Catholic and Orthodox
	1063 St. Mark's Basilica completed in Venice, Italy
	1066 French Normans, under William the Conqueror, defeat English Saxons at Battle of Hastings in England ❶
	1071 Muslim Turks stop Christian pilgrimages to Jerusalem
	1078 Building begins on Tower of London, England
	1086 William the Conqueror conducts survey of England recorded in *Domesday Book*
	1096 Christian rulers from Europe go on First Crusade to recapture Holy Land (Palestine) from Muslims
	1099 Crusaders capture Jerusalem ❷
Dies 1131	**c. 1100** Viking raids end
After his death	**1147–49** Turks defeat Christian soldiers of Second Crusade
	1154 Henry II becomes king of England and controls land in England and France

ONDAATJE, Michael

Michael Ondaatje is a Canadian writer who uses poetic, sensual language in **experimental** ways; the results are well received by both literary critics and readers.

Born in Sri Lanka, where his grandfather owned a tea plantation, Ondaatje's parents divorced, and he went to England with his mother when he was nine. Unhappy with the British higher education system, he emigrated to Canada in 1962, where he studied at Bishop's, Toronto, and Queen's universities before gaining a teaching position at York University, Toronto in 1971.

Ondaatje married in 1964, and his family inspired many poems for his first volume, *The Dainty Monsters*, which came out when he was 24. It depicts domestic life peppered with bizarre occurrences – cars chewing up bushes and dragons in the backyard. He also wrote a study of LEONARD COHEN, who has been a major influence on his writing.

He won two major Canadian awards for subsequent volumes, one of which was based on the life of Billy the Kid. Poems, prose, and illustrations combine Billy's experiences with Ondaatje's to produce a work of art. He repeats this process in *Coming Through Slaughter*, drawn from the life of a New Orleans jazz musician who went mad. *Running in the Family*, written after a return to Sri Lanka, explores the links between the island's past under British rule and his own family history. The novel *The English Patient* depicts four characters in an abandoned **World War II** Italian hospital surrounded by unexploded mines. It was made into an Academy Award-winning film.

Sri Lankan-born Canadian novelist and poet
Born Sep. 12, 1943

Book cover for one of Ondaatje's novels

WORKS INCLUDE

1967 *The Dainty Monsters*
1970 *The Collected Works of Billy the Kid: Left-Handed Poems*
1970 *Leonard Cohen*
1973 *Rat Jelly*

1976 *Coming Through Slaughter*
1982 *Running in the Family*
1987 *In the Skin of a Lion*
1991 *The Cinnamon Peeler*
1992 *The English Patient*

OTHER POST-1940 NOVELISTS

BALDWIN, James
BELLOW, Saul
CAMUS, Albert
GARCÍA MÁRQUEZ, Gabriel
GOLDING, William
HELLER, Joseph
IRVING, John
LESSING, Doris

MORRISON, Toni
SALINGER, J.D.
SINGER, Isaac Bashevis
SOLZHENITSYN, Aleksandr
UPDIKE, John
VIDAL, Gore
WALKER, Alice

SEE INDEX FOR FULL LIST

WORLD EVENTS

Age	Contemporary Events
Born 1943 	**1945** U.S. drops first atomic bombs on Japan **1950–53** Korean War: North Korea and China fight South Korea, the U.S., and United Nations troops **1957** Eisenhower sends troops to Little Rock, Arkansas, to ensure school desegregation **1960** John F. Kennedy elected president ❶ **1961** East Germans build Berlin Wall
20 in 1963 	**1963** Led by Rev. Martin Luther King, Jr., thousands march on Washington DC to press for civil rights for African Americans ❷ **1964–75** Vietnam War: war between communist North Vietnam and U.S. forces supporting South Vietnam **1967** Arabs and Israelis fight in Six Day War **1969** American astronaut walks on Moon **1974** Pres. Richard M. Nixon resigns presidency **1975–79** Communist forces murder hundreds of thousands in Cambodia ❸ **1980** Ronald Reagan elected president **1981** U.S. launches first space shuttle
40 in 1983 	**1989** Communist regimes fall throughout Eastern Europe ❹ **1991** Gulf War: UN forces, led by U.S., defeat Iraq and free Kuwait **1992** Bill Clinton elected president **1994** First multiracial elections in South Africa end years of white minority rule. They are won by Nelson Mandela, African National Congress leader ❺

© DIAGRAM

171

O'NEILL, Eugene

American playwright and poet
Born Oct. 16, 1888
Died Nov. 27, 1953
Age at death 65

Scene from O'Neill's play
The Iceman Cometh

Eugene O'Neill was a leading American playwright. His drama is famous for its **realism** and for its depressing stories of people who have no hope of controlling their destinies. He was awarded the **Nobel Prize** for literature in 1936.

O'Neill was born in New York City, the son of an actor, and his early childhood was spent touring with his father. He was educated at a Catholic boarding school in Connecticut and spent a year at Princeton University before leaving to begin traveling.

O'Neill was a passionate man prone to depression, and he spent much of his youth drifting from job to job and living in poverty. His experiences during this period, particularly his time spent at sea, form the basis for much of his later work. Returning to America in 1912, he was admitted to a hospital, suffering from tuberculosis. During this period of enforced rest he started writing. The following year, when he was 25, he wrote his first play, *The Web.* By 1920 O'Neill was already becoming recognized as a serious playwright, winning his first **Pulitzer Prize** for *Beyond the Horizon.* He went on to win three more Pulitzers: one in 1922 for *Anna Christie*; another in 1928 for *Strange Interlude*; and the last was awarded in 1957, after he had died, for *Long Day's Journey into Night.*

O'Neill's plays often deal with characters looking for a meaning to life. His most famous work, *The Iceman Cometh,* performed when he was 58, is set in a dockside bar where characters discuss their hopeless lives. Altogether he wrote 45 plays, which range in style from **satire** to **tragedy.**

WORKS INCLUDE

1920 *Beyond the Horizon*
1920 *The Emperor Jones*
1921 *Anna Christie*
1922 *The Hairy Ape*
1924 *Desire under the Elms*

1928 *Strange Interlude*
1931 *Mourning Becomes Electra*
1946 *The Iceman Cometh*
1956 *Long Day's Journey into Night*
(published after he died)

OTHER PLAYWRIGHTS 1900–40

AKINS, Zoë
COWARD, Noël
GARCÍA LORCA, Federico
GREEN, Paul
GREGORY, Lady
KAUFMAN, George. S
O'CASEY, Sean
ODETS, Clifford

PIRANDELLO, Luigi
PRIESTLEY, J.B.
SHAW, George Bernard
SHERWOOD, Robert E.
SYNGE, John Millington
WILDER, Thornton

SEE INDEX FOR FULL LIST

WORLD EVENTS

Age	Contemporary Events
Born 1888	**1888** George Eastman perfects "Kodak" box camera ❶ **1895** Italian physicist Guglielmo Marconi invents radio **1903** American inventors Orville and Wilbur Wright make first airplane flight
20 in 1908  	**1908** Henry Ford introduces Model T car **1912** Luxury liner *Titanic* sinks **1914–18** World War I **1917** Russian Revolution establishes Communist government ❷ **1917** U.S. enters World War I ❸ **1926** British scientist John Logie Baird demonstrates television **1927** Joseph Stalin becomes dictator of Russia
40 in 1928 	**1931** Empire State Building in New York City completed **1933** Nazi Party, led by Adolf Hitler, gains control in Germany **1939–45** World War II: allies, led by U.S. and Great Britain, fight axis powers, led by Germany and Japan **1945** U.S. drops first atomic bombs on Japan ❹ **1945** United Nations (UN), organization working for betterment of humanity, founded ❺ **1945** Cold War begins between USSR and U.S.
60 in 1948 **Dies 1953**	**1950–53** Korean War: North Korea and China fight South Korea, the U.S., and United Nations troops

© DIAGRAM

ONETTI, Juan Carlos

**Uruguayan novelist
and short-story
writer**
Born Jul. 1, 1909
Died May 30, 1994
Age at death 84

One of Onetti's novels about
modern urban life

Juan Carlos Onetti, one of Latin America's finest writers, is notable for a series of brilliant novels that describe the breakdown of modern town life. Although often pessimistic and complex, his stories are rich in creativity and imagination.

Onetti was born in Montevideo, Uruguay, where his schooling was brief, and he then survived on various low-paid jobs. Later, he studied at the university in Buenos Aires, Argentina.

In Montevideo, at the age of 30, Onetti got a job on the important weekly journal *Marcha*. He then moved to Buenos Aires, where he worked as a journalist for 12 years. Returning to Montevideo in 1957, he was appointed director of the city's municipal libraries.

Onetti's first novel, *The Pit*, was published when he was 30. It is a study of aimlessness, isolation, and the failure of human communication. A succession of remarkable novels followed, including *The Shipyard*, about a worker who attempts to improve his social position by courting the shipyard owner's daughter but doesn't realize that the society he aspires to has disintegrated. Onetti's best-known novel, *A Brief Life*, was published when he was 41 and describes a man who copes with a series of tragedies by disappearing into a fantasy world.

In 1974 Onetti left Uruguay for Spain after being imprisoned for publishing a young writer's story that had upset the military government. He died in Madrid.

WORKS INCLUDE

1939 *The Pit*
1941 *No Man's Land*
1950 *A Brief Life*
1951 *A Dream Fulfilled*
1961 *The Shipyard*

1964 *Body Snatcher*
1974 *Complete Stories 1933–50*
1990 *Goodbye and Stories*
1996 *Let the Wind Speak* (published after he died)

OTHER LATIN AMERICAN WRITERS

ALEGRÍA, Claribel
ALLENDE, Isabel
ASTURIAS, Miguel Angel
BENEDETTI, Mario
BORGES, Jorge Luis
CABRERA INFANTE, Guillermo
FUENTES, Carlos
GARCÍA MÁRQUEZ, Gabriel

MACHADO de ASSIS, Joaquim Maria
NERUDA, Pablo
PAZ, Octavio
ROA BASTOS, Augusto
RULFO, Juan
VARGAS LLOSA, Mario

SEE INDEX FOR FULL LIST

WORLD EVENTS

Age	Contemporary Events
Born 1909 	**1914–18** World War I
	1917 Russian Revolution establishes Communist government
	1927 Joseph Stalin becomes dictator of Russia ❶
20 in 1929	**1933** Nazi Party, led by Adolf Hitler, gains control in Germany
	1939–45 World War II: allies, led by U.S. and Great Britain, fight axis powers, led by Germany and Japan ❷
	1945 U.S. drops first atomic bombs on Japan
40 in 1949	**1950–53** Korean War: North Korea and China fight South Korea, the U.S., and United Nations troops
	1957 Eisenhower sends troops to Little Rock, Arkansas, to ensure school desegregation
	1960 John F. Kennedy elected president ❸
	1964–75 Vietnam War: war between communist North Vietnam and U.S. forces supporting South Vietnam
	1967 Arabs and Israelis fight in Six Day War
60 in 1969 	**1969** American astronaut walks on Moon
	1981 U.S. launches first space shuttle ❹
80 in 1989 	**1991** Gulf War: UN forces, led by U.S., defeat Iraq and free Kuwait ❺
Dies 1994	**1994** First multiracial elections in South Africa end years of white minority rule. They are won by Nelson Mandela, African National Congress leader

© DIAGRAM

175

OPPEN, George

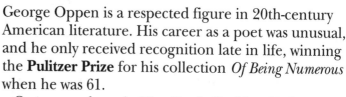

American poet
Born Apr. 24, 1908
Died Jul. 7, 1984
Age at death 76

George Oppen is a respected figure in 20th-century American literature. His career as a poet was unusual, and he only received recognition late in life, winning the **Pulitzer Prize** for his collection *Of Being Numerous* when he was 61.

Oppen was born in New Rochelle, New York, and grew up in San Francisco, California. He briefly attended Oregon State University, where he met his wife. In 1929, two years after their marriage, they moved to France, where many young American artists and writers lived at that time. In France they started their own publishing company and published other American poets such as EZRA POUND and WILLIAM CARLOS WILLIAMS.

When they returned to New York in 1933, Oppen, then 25, published his first book, *Discrete Series*. The poems in this collection have been described as "objectivist" because they are strictly concerned with real objects and make no mention of emotion or human involvement. He then decided to put his own writing aside and work with the **Communist** Party. During **World War II** Oppen served in the army and was badly wounded, and after the war, like many other artists in the **McCarthy Era**, he was forced to flee to Mexico because of FBI harassment over his political activities. He only began to write again when he returned to the United States eight years later.

Oppen's second collection of poems, *The Materials*, came out when he was 54, almost 30 years after his first book. These poems are more connected to his own life and emotions.

Book cover for a collection of Oppen's award-winning poems

WORKS INCLUDE

1934 *Discrete Series*
1962 *The Materials*
1965 *This in Which*
1968 *Of Being Numerous*
1969 *Alpine: Poems*

1970 *Communion*
1972 *Seascape: Needle's Eye*
1975 *The Collected Poems of George Oppen*
1978 *Primitive*

OTHER POST-1940 POETS

ANGELOU, Maya
BISHOP, Elizabeth
BRODSKY, Joseph
DUNCAN, Robert
GINSBERG, Allen
HAYDEN, Robert
HEANEY, Seamus
HUGHES, Ted

LOWELL, Robert
PAZ, Octavio
PLATH, Sylvia
SEXTON, Anne
THOMAS, Dylan
WALCOTT, Derek
YEVTUSHENKO, Yevgeny

SEE INDEX FOR FULL LIST

WORLD EVENTS

Age	Contemporary Events
Born 1908	**1908** Henry Ford introduces Model T car **1914–18** World War I **1917** Russian Revolution establishes Communist government **1926** British scientist John Logie Baird demonstrates television **1927** Joseph Stalin becomes dictator of Russia ❶
20 in 1928	**1931** Empire State Building in New York City completed **1933** Nazi Party, led by Adolf Hitler, gains control in Germany **1939–45** World War II: allies, led by U.S. and Great Britain, fight axis powers, led by Germany and Japan **1945** U.S. drops first atomic bombs on Japan ❷
40 in 1948	**1950–53** Korean War: North Korea and China fight South Korea, the U.S., and United Nations troops **1957** Eisenhower sends troops to Little Rock, Arkansas, to ensure school desegregation ❸ **1960** John F. Kennedy elected president **1962** Cuban Missile Crisis erupts after the U.S. discovers Soviet missiles on island **1964–75** Vietnam War: war between communist North Vietnam and U.S. forces supporting South Vietnam ❹ **1967** Arabs and Israelis fight in Six Day War
60 in 1968 Dies 1984 ❺	**1969** American astronaut walks on Moon ❺ **1981** U.S. launches first space shuttle

© DIAGRAM

ORTON, Joe

English playwright
Born Jan. 1, 1933
Died Aug. 9, 1967
Age at death 34

LOOT

by
Joe Orton

Poster advertising one of Orton's comic plays

Joe Orton is remembered for his plays, which capture the changing mood of Britain in the 1960s and which provide cruel yet hilarious attacks on "normal" or conventional society. Often deliberately bad taste, Orton's bizarre and violent comedies shocked many people.

Orton came from a working-class family in the industrial city of Leicester, central England. He was educated privately at Clark's College but did not do well. His family life was not happy, and he dreamed of escaping into an acting career. When Orton was 18, he moved to London to study at the famous Royal Academy of Dramatic Art (RADA). Shortly after his arrival he met Kenneth Halliwell, an older student, and began a homosexual relationship with him.

Orton's acting career failed, and he and Halliwell turned to writing. This was also unsuccessful, and they lived in poverty for several years. When Orton was 29, he was sent to prison for 6 months for defacing library books. Prison was a turning point for Orton; it convinced him that society was rotten and helped to focus his writing. His first play, *The Ruffian on the Stair*, was performed on the radio when Orton was 31. *Entertaining Mr. Sloane* became a success soon afterward. With typical Orton black humor, the play depicts a middle-aged brother and sister who protect their father's killer because they are attracted to him.

As Orton's fame grew, Halliwell became increasingly depressed. He felt neglected and was afraid that Orton was going to leave him. Finally, unable to stand any more, Halliwell murdered Orton and then killed himself.

WORKS INCLUDE

1964 *The Ruffian on the Stair*
1964 *Entertaining Mr. Sloane*
1966 *Loot*
1966 *The Erpingham Camp*

1969 *What the Butler Saw* (published after he died)

OTHER POST-1940 PLAYWRIGHTS

ALBEE, Edward
BECKETT, Samuel
BRECHT, Bertolt
FUGARD, Athol
GENET, Jean
KUSHNER, Tony
MAMET, David
MILLER, Arthur

NORMAN, Marsha
OSBORNE, John
PINTER, Harold
SHEPARD, Sam
SIMON, Neil
SOYINKA, Wole
WILLIAMS, Tennessee

SEE INDEX FOR FULL LIST

WORLD EVENTS

Age	Contemporary Events
Born 1933	**1933** Nazi Party, led by Adolf Hitler, gains control in Germany
	1939–45 World War II: allies, led by U.S. and Great Britain, fight axis powers, led by Germany and Japan
	1941 Germany invades USSR ❶
10 in 1943	**1945** U.S. drops first atomic bombs on Japan
	1945 United Nations (UN), organization working for betterment of humanity, founded ❷
	1945 Cold War begins between USSR and U.S.
	1950–53 Korean War: North Korea and China fight South Korea, the U.S., and United Nations troops
20 in 1953	**1954** British runner Roger Bannister breaks four-minute mile
	1957 Eisenhower sends troops to Little Rock, Arkansas, to ensure school desegregation ❸
	1958 USSR puts first artificial satellite into orbit
	1960 John F. Kennedy elected president
	1961 East Germans build Berlin Wall ❹
	1962 Cuban Missile Crisis erupts after the U.S. discovers Soviet missiles on island ❺
30 in 1963	**1963** Led by Rev. Martin Luther King, Jr., thousands march on Washington DC to press for civil rights for African Americans
	1964–75 Vietnam War: war between communist North Vietnam and U.S. forces supporting South Vietnam
Dies 1967	**1967** Arabs and Israelis fight in Six Day War

© DIAGRAM

179

ORWELL, George

George Orwell was the pen name of Eric Arthur Blair. Two of his books, *Nineteen Eighty-Four* and *Animal Farm* – which contains the memorable phrase "All animals are equal, but some are more equal than others" – have become classics of political **satire**.

Orwell was born in India to English parents and was taken to England as a child. After studying at Eton College, a leading independent school, he served in the Imperial Police in Burma from 1922 to 1927. Returning to Europe, he took a series of poorly paid jobs, while trying to get his writing published. He described this period of his life in his first book, *Down and Out in Paris and London*, published when he was 30. His novel *The Road to Wigan Pier* highlights the grinding poverty of the working classes in Britain at that time.

Orwell fought on the left-wing Republican side in the **Spanish Civil War** and was wounded. Despite his left-wing views, his experiences made him dislike the **communists**, who backed the Republicans, and he attacked them in *Homage to Catalonia*. He was unfit for military service in **World War II** and worked for the British Broadcasting Corporation (BBC). Toward the end of the war he wrote *Animal Farm*. It depicts the betrayal of a revolution. The farm animals overthrow their human rulers, but eventually the pigs take over the former role of the humans. Orwell died from tuberculosis soon after the publication of *Nineteen Eighty-Four*. In this book he describes a nightmare life under the dictatorship of a party leader, known as "Big Brother," whose people are constantly warned: "Big Brother is watching you."

English novelist, poet, and essayist
Born Jun. 23, 1903
Died Jan. 21, 1950
Age at death 46

Illustration of the animal revolutionaries in *Animal Farm*

WORKS INCLUDE

1933 *Down and Out in Paris and London*
1934 *Burmese Days*
1935 *A Clergyman's Daughter*
1936 *Keep the Aspidistra Flying*
1937 *The Road to Wigan Pier*

1938 *Homage to Catalonia*
1939 *Coming up for Air*
1945 *Animal Farm*
1949 *Nineteen Eighty-Four*

OTHER NOVELISTS 1900–40

CONRAD, Joseph
FAULKNER, William
FITZGERALD, F. Scott
FORSTER, E.M.
HEMINGWAY, Ernest
JOYCE, James
KAFKA, Franz
LAWRENCE, D.H.

LONDON, Jack
MANN, Thomas
PROUST, Marcel
STEINBECK, John
WHARTON, Edith
WOOLF, Virginia

SEE INDEX FOR FULL LIST

WORLD EVENTS

Age	Contemporary Events
Born 1903	**1903** American inventors Orville and Wilbur Wright make first airplane flight ❶ **1908** Henry Ford introduces Model T car **1910** George V becomes king of England **1912** Luxury liner *Titanic* sinks
10 in 1913	**1914–18** World War I ❷ **1917** Russian Revolution establishes Communist government **1919** English physicist Ernest Rutherford splits atom
20 in 1923	**1926** British scientist John Logie Baird demonstrates television **1927** Joseph Stalin becomes dictator of Russia ❸ **1929** Stock Market crash ushers in Great Depression **1931** Empire State Building in New York City completed ❹
30 in 1933	**1933** Nazi Party, led by Adolf Hitler, gains control in Germany ❺ **1936–39** Spanish Civil War: conservative forces overthrow government **1939–45** World War II: allies, led by U.S. and Great Britain, fight axis powers, led by Germany and Japan
40 in 1943 **Dies 1950**	**1945** U.S. drops first atomic bombs on Japan **1945** Cold War begins between USSR and U.S. **1948** Apartheid laws, depriving nonwhite people of rights, introduced in South Africa

© DIAGRAM

OSBORNE, John

**English playwright
and novelist**
Born Dec. 12, 1929
Died Dec. 24, 1994
Age at death 65

John Osborne was one of the English writers known in the 1950s as the Angry Young Men. They wrote about ordinary, often working-class characters who feel they do not belong to society.

Osborne was born in London, England, to a family of "misfits" – not working class but not middle class. This gave Osborne a strong sense of not belonging that lasted all his life. Desperately unhappy at school, Osborne left at age 16 and drifted in and out of jobs before becoming an actor and appearing on stage, television, and in films. It is as a playwright, however, that he is remembered.

When he was 27, Osborne wrote the play *Look Back in Anger*, which features the original "angry young man," Jimmy Porter. Working with others, Osborne had already written plays, but these had not been memorable. *Look Back in Anger* caused a sensation, expressing a frustration with society felt by many; great sacrifices had been made during **World War II**, but life for the ordinary person in Britain had changed very little once the war was over.

Osborne's next big success was *The Entertainer* – an **allegory** for the decline of postwar Britain. It follows the fading career of a bitter and frustrated third-rate actor. By the late 1950s Osborne was increasingly working in film and television. Four of his plays were adapted for the movies, and in 1963 he won an Academy Award for best screenplay for *Tom Jones*, based on HENRY FIELDING's novel. In 1991 Osborne published the final volume of his **autobiography**, *Almost a Gentleman*. It reveals an obsession with class and society formed in early life.

Scene from Osborne's famous
play *Look Back in Anger*

WORKS INCLUDE

1956 *Look Back in Anger*
1957 *Epitaph for George Dillon*
1957 *The Entertainer*
1961 *Luther*
1964 *Inadmissible Evidence*

1965 *A Patriot for Me*
1971 *West of Suez*
1972 *A Sense of Detachment*
1981 *A Better Class of Person*
1991 *Almost a Gentleman*

OTHER POST-1940 PLAYWRIGHTS

ALBEE, Edward
BECKETT, Samuel
BRECHT, Bertolt
FUGARD, Athol
GENET, Jean
KUSHNER, Tony
MAMET, David
MILLER, Arthur

NORMAN, Marsha
PINTER, Harold
SHEPARD, Sam
SIMON, Neil
SOYINKA, Wole
WILLIAMS, Tennessee

SEE INDEX FOR FULL LIST

WORLD EVENTS

Age	Contemporary Events
Born 1929 	**1933** Nazi Party, led by Adolf Hitler, gains control in Germany **1939–45** World War II: allies, led by U.S. and Great Britain, fight axis powers, led by Germany and Japan **1945** U.S. drops first atomic bombs on Japan ❶ **1945** Cold War begins between USSR and U.S.
20 in 1949	**1950–53** Korean War: North Korea and China fight South Korea, the U.S., and United Nations troops ❷ **1957** Eisenhower sends troops to Little Rock, Arkansas, to ensure school desegregation **1960** John F. Kennedy elected president **1964–75** Vietnam War: war between communist North Vietnam and U.S. forces supporting South Vietnam **1967** Arabs and Israelis fight in Six Day War
40 in 1969 	**1969** American astronaut walks on Moon ❸ **1980** Ronald Reagan elected president **1981** U.S. launches first space shuttle
60 in 1989  **Dies 1994**	**1989** Communist regimes fall throughout Eastern Europe **1991** Gulf War: UN forces, led by U.S., defeat Iraq and free Kuwait **1992** Bill Clinton elected president **1994** First multiracial elections in South Africa end years of white minority rule. They are won by Nelson Mandela, African National Congress leader ❹

© DIAGRAM

OVID

Roman poet
Born Mar. 20, 43 BC
Died c. 17 AD
Age at death c. 60

The ancient **Roman** poet Ovid is remembered for his witty poems about love and his retelling of ancient myths. He was born in Sulmona, a town in central Italy, into a wealthy, landowning family. His father encouraged him to become a lawyer and sent him to study in Rome, but Ovid found that he loved poetry more than legal argument and soon settled into a life of luxurious living and literature. By age 30 he was the most popular poet in Rome.

Ovid lived during the reign of Augustus, the first emperor of Rome. The old Roman Republic, a system of government that had ruled Rome for centuries, had become corrupt and collapsed after years of bitter civil war. The new emperor was determined to reform Roman society and return it to the old values and strict morals of the early republic. One of Ovid's most popular poems, *the Art of Love*, provoked the anger of Augustus. It was a witty, sophisticated work about how to seduce a lover. Augustus thought the book was immoral and banished Ovid to a desolate town by the Black Sea. He also had all of Ovid's works removed from public libraries.

Before leaving Rome, Ovid had finished his greatest work, the long poem *Metamorphoses*. Its vivid and beautiful retelling of **ancient Greek** and Roman myths remained loved and widely read for centuries after his death. In exile Ovid continued to write. He hated being so far from the life he had enjoyed in Rome and wrote poems begging the emperor to let him return. Augustus, and his successor Tiberius, never relented, and Ovid died far from home.

Statue of the Roman emperor Augustus

WORKS INCLUDE

Between 16 BC and 2 AD
- *Amores*
- *Heroides*
- *The Art of Love*
- *The Cures of Love*

- *Medea*

Between 2 and 17 AD
- *Fasti*
- *Metamorphoses*
- *Tristia*

OTHER ROMAN WRITERS

APULEIUS, Lucius
CATULLUS
CICERO
HORACE
JUVENAL
LUCIAN
LUCRETIUS
PROPERTIUS, Sextus

TERENCE
VIRGIL

WORLD EVENTS

Before his birth

753 City of Rome founded in Italy
509 Rome becomes a republic
272 Rome controls all of Italian peninsula
218 Second Punic War begins: Carthaginian general Hannibal crosses the Alps to attack Rome ❶
215 Chinese build Great Wall
167 Jews, led by Judas Maccabeus, revolt against Syrian-based Seleucid Empire
60 Three military heroes (Caesar, Pompey, and Crassus) form First Triumvirate to rule Rome
49–45 Civil war in Rome between Julius Caesar ❷ and Pompey
44 Julius Caesar assassinated in Rome

During his life ❸

40 Romans appoint Herod king of Judea (modern day Israel)
27 Octavian, given name Augustus, becomes first Roman emperor ❸
BC **4** Probable date of Jesus's birth

After his death

AD **c. 30** Probable date of Jesus's crucifixion ❹
64 Roman Emperor Nero persecutes Christians
70 Romans destroy Jerusalem
117 Roman Empire reaches its greatest extent under Emperor Trajan ❺
164 Plague spreads throughout Roman Empire
405 St. Jerome completes Latin "Vulgate" translation of Bible
455 Vandals, barbarians from central Europe, sack Rome ❻
476 End of western half of Roman Empire
527–65 Byzantine Emperor Justinian conquers much of the old western Roman Empire

© DIAGRAM

OWEN, Wilfred

English poet
Born Mar. 18, 1893
Died Nov. 4, 1918
Age at death 25

The front line in World War I, where Owen fought and died

Wilfred Owen was an English poet who fought and died in **World War I**. One of the most admired of the so-called war poets, he is remembered for his angry poems about the waste and pointlessness of war.

Born in Shropshire, western England, Owen was the son of a railroad station master. After school he began work as a teacher, hoping to study at London University, but there was no money to pay for his courses. He had already begun to write poetry, at first in the style of JOHN KEATS. In 1913 he went to France to teach English. War broke out the following year, and in 1915 he returned to England to enlist in the army, aged 22. He soon became an officer.

In 1917 Owen was invalided home, suffering from concussion and fever. While recovering in a military hospital near Edinburgh in Scotland, he met the older war poet SIEGFRIED SASSOON, who had also been sent home due to ill health. Sassoon encouraged Owen to write about his experiences in the trenches.

Friends tried to find Owen a "safe" post away from the front, but in August 1918 he was sent back to the trenches to command a company. His courage won him a medal, but three months later he was killed – just one week before the end of the war.

Owen wrote most of his famous war poems in the year before he died. Only a few were published in his lifetime. Many of his poems were published by Sassoon two years after Owen's death. Those written after 1917 reflect the horror of life in the war, especially his well-known **sonnet** "Anthem for Doomed Youth."

WORKS INCLUDE

Published after he died
1920 Poems
1931 The Poems of Wilfred Owen
1963 Collected Poems

OTHER POETS 1900–40

AKHMATOVA, Anna
AUDEN, W.H.
DOOLITTLE, Hilda
ELIOT, T.S.
FROST, Robert
GRAVES, Robert
HUGHES, Langston
LOWELL, Amy

MASEFIELD, John
MILLAY, Edna St. Vincent
MOORE, Marianne
POUND, Ezra
SASSOON, Siegfried
TAGORE, Rabindranath
YEATS, W.B.

SEE INDEX FOR FULL LIST

WORLD EVENTS

Age	Contemporary Events
Born 1893 	**1894–95** Following war with China, Japan occupies Korea
	1895 German physicist Wilhelm K. Roentgen discovers X-rays
	1895 Italian physicist Guglielmo Marconi invents radio ❶
	1896 First modern Olympic Games held in Athens, Greece
	1898 French physicists Marie and Pierre Curie discover radioactive element, radium
	1901 Theodore Roosevelt becomes president following assassination of William McKinley
10 in 1903  	**1903** American inventors Orville and Wilbur Wright make first airplane flight ❷
	1905 German-born physicist Albert Einstein publishes theory of relativity
	1906 Earthquake devastates San Francisco
	1908 Henry Ford introduces Model T car ❸
	1909 American explorer Robert Peary reaches North Pole
	1912 Luxury liner *Titanic* sinks ❹
	1912 Woodrow Wilson elected president
20 in 1913 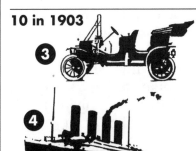 **Dies 1918**	**1914** Panama Canal opens
	1914–18 World War I ❺
	1917 Russian Revolution establishes Communist government
	1917 U.S. enters World War I
	1918 Pres. Woodrow Wilson develops "Fourteen Points" for settling World War I

© DIAGRAM

OYONO, Ferdinand

Cameroonian novelist and short-story writer
Born Sep. 14, 1929

The Old Man and the Medal
Ferdinand Oyono

One of Oyono's novels about life under colonial rule

Ferdinand Oyono is one of the most important African authors writing in French. His novels are considered classics of African literature.

Oyono was born near Ebolowa in southwest Cameroon (West Africa), which was then a French colony. His father was an important chief who had more than one wife. His mother, a Catholic, refused to share her husband and left him while Oyono was still young. She supported herself and her children by working as a seamstress. Oyono helped by working as a priest's personal servant (or "boy"), and later he wrote about this experience in his novel *Boy!*

Oyono went to local schools and then studied law and administration in Paris, France. Lonely and poor in a foreign country, he began to write his first novel, *Boy!*, and then a second, *The Old Man and the Medal*. Like all of Oyono's books, these describe life in Cameroon under French rule. They use humor and **satire** to make fun of the idea that French rule in Africa was of benefit to Africans. *The Old Man and the Medal* is the story of an African given a medal for his loyalty to France. This "loyalty" involves the death of two of his sons in European wars and the loss of his land to a Catholic mission. Oyono's books received little attention at first, though Oyono himself became quite successful as a theater and television actor in Paris.

Cameroon became independent when Oyono was 31. Since then he has worked for his country's government in Europe and Africa, as Cameroon's United Nations delegate, and as minister for foreign affairs.

WORKS INCLUDE

1956 *Boy!*
1956 *The Old Man and the Medal*
1958 *Men without Shoulders*
1960 *The Road to Europe*
1971 *The Big Confusion*

OTHER AFRICAN WRITERS

ACHEBE, Chinua
CLARK-BEKEDEREMO, John Pepper
COETZEE, J.M.
FUGARD, Athol
GORDIMER, Nadine
HEAD, Bessie
MAHFOUZ, Naguib
NETO, Agostinho

NGUGI wa Thiong'o
NWAPA, Flora
OKRI, Ben
PATON, Alan
ROBERT, Shaaban
SENGHOR, Léopold Sédar
SOYINKA, Wole

SEE INDEX FOR FULL LIST

WORLD EVENTS

Age	Contemporary Events
Born 1929 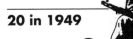	**1931** Empire State Building in New York City completed
	1933 Nazi Party, led by Adolf Hitler, gains control in Germany
	1939–45 World War II: allies, led by U.S. and Great Britain, fight axis powers, led by Germany and Japan
	1945 U.S. drops first atomic bombs on Japan ❶
	1945 Cold War begins between USSR and U.S.
20 in 1949 	**1950–53** Korean War: North Korea and China fight South Korea, the U.S., and United Nations troops ❷
	1960 John F. Kennedy elected president
	1964–75 Vietnam War: war between communist North Vietnam and U.S. forces supporting South Vietnam ❸
	1967 Arabs and Israelis fight in Six Day War
40 in 1969 	**1969** American astronaut walks on Moon ❹
	1980 Ronald Reagan elected president
	1981 U.S. launches first space shuttle
60 in 1989	**1989** Communist regimes fall throughout Eastern Europe
	1991 Gulf War: UN forces, led by U.S., defeat Iraq and free Kuwait ❺
	1992 Bill Clinton elected president
	1994 First multiracial elections in South Africa end years of white minority rule. They are won by Nelson Mandela, African National Congress leader

© DIAGRAM

OZ, Amos

Israeli novelist, short-story writer, and essayist
Born May 4, 1939

Amos Oz is one of Israel's greatest modern writers. He writes about the problems faced by people of Israel today and about the long and complex history of the Jews.

Oz was born Amos Klausner in Jerusalem, Israel, and as a teenager lived for a time on a kibbutz (a communal farm) where he taught in the school. He was educated at the Hebrew University in Jerusalem and at Oxford University in England and was required to serve in the Israeli army during various times of trouble, including the Six Day War of 1967.

Oz belongs to a generation that views the ideals of the founders of modern Israel with suspicion. But unlike many of his contemporaries, he has been content to spend his life on a kibbutz. This attitude, and his perception of the realities of modern Israeli life, is reflected in his work. He expresses the conflicts between the ideals of Israel's founders and the longing of a later generation for a more sophisticated way of life.

Written in the ancient Jewish language Hebrew, Oz's novels have been more widely read than those of any other Israeli writers and have been translated into many languages. They are brilliant works, concerned with guilt, persecution, demonic forces, and the inevitability of fate. In some of his later work there are elements of fantasy. Oz's intelligence and great gifts as a writer always prevent his stories from becoming predictable.

Oz is also noted for his political essays, in which he sometimes expresses highly controversial views.

Book cover for one of Oz's novels about modern Israel

WORKS INCLUDE

1965 *Where the Jackals Howl and Other Stories*
1966 *Elsewhere, Perhaps*
1968 *My Michael*
1973 *Touch the Water, Touch the Wind*

1973 *The Hill of Evil Counsel*
1982 *A Perfect Peace*
1987 *Black Box*
1991 *The Third State*

OTHER ASIAN AND MIDDLE EASTERN WRITERS

BASHO, Matsuo
DESAI, Anita
DING LING
DU FU
HAYASHI Fumiko
KALIDASA
KAWABATA Yasunari
MISHIMA Yukio

MURASAKI Shikibu
NARAYAN, R.K.
SHIMAZAKI Toson
TAGORE, Rabindranath
TANIZAKI Junichiro
WU CHENGEN

SEE INDEX FOR FULL LIST

WORLD EVENTS

Age	Contemporary Events
Born 1939	**1939–45** World War II: allies, led by U.S. and Great Britain, fight axis powers, led by Germany and Japan
	1945 U.S. drops first atomic bombs on Japan
	1950–53 Korean War: North Korea and China fight South Korea, the U.S., and United Nations troops ❶
	1957 Eisenhower sends troops to Little Rock, Arkansas, to ensure school desegregation
20 in 1959	**1960** John F. Kennedy elected president ❷
	1964–75 Vietnam War: war between communist North Vietnam and U.S. forces supporting South Vietnam
	1967 Arabs and Israelis fight in Six Day War
	1969 American astronaut walks on Moon ❸
	1974 Pres. Richard M. Nixon resigns presidency ❹
40 in 1979	**1980** Ronald Reagan elected president
	1981 U.S. launches first space shuttle
	1987 Gorbachev begins reforms in USSR: perestroika (restructuring) and glasnost (openness) ❺
	1989 Communist regimes fall throughout Eastern Europe ❻
	1991 Gulf War: UN forces, led by U.S., defeat Iraq and free Kuwait
	1992 Bill Clinton elected president
	1994 First multiracial elections in South Africa end years of white minority rule. They are won by Nelson Mandela, African National Congress leader

© DIAGRAM

PAGE, P.K.

**English-born
Canadian poet
and novelist
Born** Nov. 23, 1916

P.K. Page
Evening Dance
of the
Grey Flies

Book cover for a collection of
Page's poetry and prose

Although she is best known as a poet, P.K. Page is also an accomplished painter.

Patricia Kathleen Page was born in England but emigrated to Canada with her parents at an early age. After graduating from St. Hilda's School in Calgary, she moved to Montreal, which was at the time the most important center of English-language poetry in Canada. In Montreal she met other poets and artists for the first time; it quickly became apparent that she was a new and important talent. She was 30 when her first volume of poetry, *As Ten as Twenty*, appeared. That same year, while working as a scriptwriter for the National Film Board of Ottawa, she met her future husband, William Irwin.

When Irwin became a diplomat, Page lived abroad with him for ten years; during this time she suffered a writing block that put an end to her poetry. Unable to write, she turned to painting to express herself. As P.K. Irwin she is now a highly respected painter, and her work hangs in Canada's National Gallery. Critics have said that her paintings are so closely related to her poetry that they seem like poems.

Page began writing poetry again when she returned to Canada. Her seventh book, *Evening Dance of the Grey Flies*, was her first entirely new collection of poems for 27 years. From the 1950s Page has kept a daily diary, including the time when she stayed in Brazil from 1957 to 1959. This **autobiographical** work was published as *Brazilian Journal* almost 30 years after it was started. It is a remarkable prose work telling not only of her struggles to complete her poems but of the diplomatic life she and her husband shared.

WORKS INCLUDE

1944 *The Sun and the Moon*
1946 *As Ten as Twenty*
1954 *The Metal and the Flower*
1974 *Poems (1942–73): Selected and New*

1981 *Evening Dance of the Grey Flies*
1984 *The Traveling Musicians*
1985 *The Glass Air*
1987 *Brazilian Journal*
1989 *A Flask of Sea Water*

OTHER POST-1940 POETS

ANGELOU, Maya
BISHOP, Elizabeth
BRODSKY, Joseph
DUNCAN, Robert
GINSBERG, Allen
HAYDEN, Robert
HEANEY, Seamus
HUGHES, Ted

LOWELL, Robert
PAZ, Octavio
PLATH, Sylvia
SEXTON, Anne
THOMAS, Dylan
WALCOTT, Derek
YEVTUSHENKO, Yevgeny

SEE INDEX FOR FULL LIST

WORLD EVENTS

Age	Contemporary Events
Born 1916	**1917** Russian Revolution establishes Communist government
	1927 Joseph Stalin becomes dictator of Russia ❶
	1933 Nazi Party, led by Adolf Hitler, gains control in Germany
20 in 1936	**1939–45** World War II: allies, led by U.S. and Great Britain, fight axis powers, led by Germany and Japan ❷
	1945 U.S. drops first atomic bombs on Japan ❸
	1950–53 Korean War: North Korea and China fight South Korea, the U.S., and United Nations troops
40 in 1956	**1960** John F. Kennedy elected president ❹
	1964–75 Vietnam War: war between communist North Vietnam and U.S. forces supporting South Vietnam
	1967 Arabs and Israelis fight in Six Day War
	1969 American astronaut walks on Moon
60 in 1976	**1981** U.S. launches first space shuttle ❺
	1991 Gulf War: UN forces, led by U.S., defeat Iraq and free Kuwait
	1992 Bill Clinton elected president
	1994 First multiracial elections in South Africa end years of white minority rule. They are won by Nelson Mandela, African National Congress leader
80 in 1996	**1996** Jumbo jet TWA 800 explodes off Long Island in New York

© DIAGRAM

PAINE, Thomas

Thomas Paine was one of the most influential and controversial writers of the **American Revolution**.

Born in Thetford, England, to a very religious family, Paine received a basic but moral education. He grew up influenced by the work of the scientist Isaac Newton and the **philosopher** John Locke, both leading thinkers of the 17th century.

By the age of 36 Paine had married twice and been fired from his job as a customs officer for publishing an argument in favor of higher wages. That year Paine met Benjamin Franklin, who offered to find him a job in America. He also helped him become the editor of *Pennsylvania Magazine*, where Paine wrote about subjects ahead of his time, including women's rights and freedom for slaves.

Paine left the magazine and joined George Washington's army in its retreat across New Jersey in 1776. There he published two series of pamphlets called *Common Sense* and *The American Crisis*, both stirring, patriotic works that made him a leading spokesman for the independence cause.

In 1787 Paine traveled to France, a country in political turmoil just before the **French Revolution**. There he wrote his great defense of revolution, *The Rights of Man*; he also helped draft a constitution for the new republic and was imprisoned for writing against the execution of the French king. His last book was *The Age of Reason*, an analysis of the Bible that caused offense because it seemed to be denying the existence of God. At 65 he returned to America, poor, shunned, and in bad health, and he died seven years later.

English-born American writer
Born Jan. 29, 1737
Died Jun. 8, 1809
Age at death 72

Cartoon of Paine writing a bill of rights for American citizens

WORKS INCLUDE

1776 *Common Sense*
1776–77 *The American Crisis*
1791–92 *The Rights of Man*
1794–95 *The Age of Reason*
1796 *Letter to George Washington*

OTHER 18TH-CENTURY WRITERS

BLAKE, William
BURNS, Robert
DEFOE, Daniel
FIELDING, Henry
GOETHE, Johann Wolfgang von
HOLBERG, Ludvig
JOHNSON, Dr.
POPE, Alexander

ROUSSEAU, Jean Jacques
SCHILLER, Friedrich von
SHERIDAN, Richard Brinsley
STERNE, Laurence
SWIFT, Jonathan
VOLTAIRE

SEE INDEX FOR FULL LIST

WORLD EVENTS

Age	Contemporary Events
Born 1737 	**1740–86** Frederick the Great rules Prussia (now part of Germany) **1749** American statesman and scientist Benjamin Franklin installs a lightning rod in his house
20 in 1757 	**1762–96** Catherine the Great rules Russia **1768–70** During around-the-world trip, English explorer James Cook reaches Australia **1769** Scottish inventor James Watt patents steam engine **1770–1827** Life of German composer Ludwig van Beethoven ❶ **1775–83** American War of Independence: colonies fight Britain for independence ❷
40 in 1777 	**1789** George Washington elected first president of U.S. ❸ **1789–99** French Revolution: French people revolt against monarchy **1793** American inventor Eli Whitney invents cotton gin **1793** King Louis XVI executed; France becomes republic
60 in 1797  **Dies 1809**	**1804** English inventor and engineer Richard Trevithick builds first steam locomotive to run on rails **1804** Merriwether Lewis and William Clark begin exploration of Louisiana Territory ❹ **1807** Robert Fulton launches first successful steamboat in America

© DIAGRAM

PALEY, Grace

American short-story writer and poet
Born Dec. 11, 1922

Book cover for Paley's second collection of short stories

Although she has only published a few collections of short stories, Grace Paley is considered to be one of America's best short-story writers.

Paley was born in New York's Bronx. Her parents were Russian-Jewish immigrants who had both spent time in exile. Paley grew up very aware of politics and the different cultures of New York City. After high school she went to college but did not complete a degree. At the age of 19 she married, and she spent most of the next 20 years raising two children. Since the 1950s Paley has become increasingly active in various political causes. She campaigned against the **Vietnam War**, delivering leaflets and speeches, and has long been an active campaigner for the **women's movement**. Paley has been arrested on several occasions for her activities and has even spent time in jail. On her release she successfully campaigned for improvements in prison conditions.

In the 1950s Paley began writing short stories. After many rejections her first collection, *The Little Disturbances of Man*, was published when she was 37. Paley's political activities meant that she did not get around to finishing her second collection, *Enormous Changes at the Last Minute*, until 15 years later. This book and her more recent collection, *Later the Same Day*, established her fame as a master storyteller. All of Paley's stories are set in New York City and use both sympathy and humor to create believable working-class characters. Her fiction is unusual in that talking rather than plot reveals the characters' personalities, and the stories are often brief. In recent years she has published collections of poetry.

WORKS INCLUDE

1959 *The Little Disturbances of Man*
1974 *Enormous Changes at the Last Minute*
1985 *Leaning Forward*
1985 *Later the Same Day*

1991 *Long Walks and Intimate Stories*
1992 *New and Collected Poems*

BALDWIN, James
BELLOW, Saul
CAMUS, Albert
GARCÍA MÁRQUEZ, Gabriel
GOLDING, William
HELLER, Joseph
IRVING, John
LESSING, Doris

MORRISON, Toni
SALINGER, J.D.
SINGER, Isaac Bashevis
SOLZHENITSYN, Aleksandr
UPDIKE, John
VIDAL, Gore
WALKER, Alice

SEE INDEX FOR FULL LIST

WORLD EVENTS

Age	Contemporary Events
Born 1922 	**1927** Joseph Stalin becomes dictator of Russia **1933** Nazi Party, led by Adolf Hitler, gains control in Germany **1939–45** World War II: allies, led by U.S. and Great Britain, fight axis powers, led by Germany and Japan ❶
20 in 1942  	**1945** U.S. drops first atomic bombs on Japan **1950–53** Korean War: North Korea and China fight South Korea, the U.S., and United Nations troops **1957** Eisenhower sends troops to Little Rock, Arkansas, to ensure school desegregation ❷ **1960** John F. Kennedy elected president **1961** East Germans build Berlin Wall ❸
40 in 1962	**1964–75** Vietnam War: war between communist North Vietnam and U.S. forces supporting South Vietnam ❹ **1967** Arabs and Israelis fight in Six Day War **1969** American astronaut walks on Moon ❺ **1981** U.S. launches first space shuttle
60 in 1982 	**1989** Communist regimes fall throughout Eastern Europe **1991** Gulf War: UN forces, led by U.S., defeat Iraq and free Kuwait **1992** Bill Clinton elected president **1994** First multiracial elections in South Africa end years of white minority rule. They are won by Nelson Mandela, African National Congress leader ❻

© DIAGRAM

PARETSKY, Sara

American crime writer
Born Jun. 8, 1947

Sara Paretsky is one of America's leading **feminist** crime writers.

Paretsky was born in Ames, Iowa. Her father was a scientist and her mother a librarian. She attended the University of Kansas during the 1960s and became involved in the **civil rights movement**. During the 1970s Paretsky earned a Ph.D. in history and a master's degree in business administration. In 1977 she started working at a Chicago-based insurance company where she remained for the next nine years. Her experiences there gave Paretsky the idea of creating a fictional woman heroine battling to hold her own in a man's world. It also gave her background information on how big institutions operate.

Paretsky's first novel, *Indemnity Only*, appeared when she was 35. The book introduced her heroine, private detective V.I. Warshawski – a tough streetwise investigator from Chicago and one of the first female private detectives in crime fiction. A series of V.I. Warshawski books have since followed, and her character's success allowed Paretsky to become a full-time writer at age 38. In 1991 a movie, *V.I. Warshawski*, based on Paretsky's heroine and starring Kathleen Turner, appeared.

V.I. Warshawski is committed to fighting for equality and fairness in society. She champions the rights of women and minorities who come into conflict with large organizations of all kinds – big businesses, unions, the police, the Church, or the medical profession. Unlike most male detectives, Warshawski has a large group of family and friends around her who give her support and help her solve crimes.

Book cover for one of Paretsky's feminist crime novels

WORKS INCLUDE

1982 *Indemnity Only*
1984 *Deadlock*
1985 *Killing Orders*
1987 *Bitter Medicine*
1988 *Blood Shot*

1990 *Burn Marks*
1991 *Guardian Angel*
1994 *Tunnel Vision*

OTHER CRIME AND THRILLER WRITERS

CHANDLER, Raymond
CHRISTIE, Agatha
DOYLE, Arthur Conan
GARDNER, Erle Stanley
GRAFTON, Sue
GRISHAM, John
HAMMETT, Dashiell
HIGHSMITH, Patricia

JAMES, P.D.
Le CARRÉ, John
LEONARD, Elmore
McBAIN, Ed
RENDELL, Ruth
THOMPSON, Jim

SEE INDEX FOR FULL LIST

WORLD EVENTS

Age	Contemporary Events
Born 1947  	**1950–53** Korean War: North Korea and China fight South Korea, the U.S., and United Nations troops **1957** Eisenhower sends troops to Little Rock, Arkansas, to ensure school desegregation ❶ **1963** Led by Rev. Martin Luther King, Jr., thousands march on Washington DC to press for civil rights for African Americans ❷ **1964–75** Vietnam War: war between communist North Vietnam and U.S. forces supporting South Vietnam
20 in 1967  	**1967** Arabs and Israelis fight in Six Day War **1969** American astronaut walks on Moon **1974** Pres. Richard M. Nixon resigns presidency ❸ **1975–79** Communist forces murder hundreds of thousands in Cambodia **1980** Ronald Reagan elected president **1981** U.S. launches first space shuttle ❹
40 in 1987 	**1987** Gorbachev begins reforms in USSR: perestroika (restructuring) and glasnost (openness) ❺ **1989** Communist regimes fall throughout Eastern Europe **1991** Gulf War: UN forces, led by U.S., defeat Iraq and free Kuwait ❻ **1992** Bill Clinton elected president **1994** First multiracial elections in South Africa end years of white minority rule. They are won by Nelson Mandela, African National Congress leader

PARKER, Dorothy

**American critic,
short-story writer,
and poet**
Born Aug. 22, 1893
Died Jun. 7, 1967
Age at death 73

MEN I'M
NOT MARRIED TO

By

DOROTHY
PARKER

DOUBLEDAY, PAGE & COMPANY

Cover for Parker's first book,
Men I'm Not Married To

Dorothy Parker became famous in the 1920s for her cruel humor. Many of the things she said and wrote are still repeated today, including the rhyme "Boys don't make passes / At girls who wear glasses."

Parker was born in New Jersey, and her mother died when she was a baby. Following her education at private schools, Parker moved to New York City. She wrote during the day and earned money at night playing the piano in a dancing school. *Vogue* magazine liked her poems and, when she was 23, gave her a job writing captions for fashion drawings.

Two years later Parker became drama critic for another magazine and began meeting with other writers at the Algonquin Hotel. Their lunches at a special round table soon became famous. Members of this select group – including RING LARDNER and JAMES THURBER – entertained each other by making funny but cruel remarks about people they felt superior to. Parker was usually the only woman in the group, but her humor was often the nastiest, especially when it was directed at other women. During this time she published several collections of poems and short stories. Her stories are characterized by sharp dialogue and detail and by use of **irony**.

After working for the *New Yorker* and other magazines, she moved with her second husband to Hollywood, where they earned a good income writing screenplays for the movie studios.

Parker suffered from depression for most of her life, and as her view of the world became increasingly bleak, humor seemed to desert her. She died alone in the New York hotel that had become her final home.

WORKS INCLUDE

1922 *Men I'm Not Married To*
1926 *Enough Rope*
1928 *Sunset Gun*
1930 *Laments for the Living*
1931 *Death and Taxes*

1933 *After Such Pleasures*
1936 *Not So Deep As a Well*
1939 *Here Lies*
1970 *Constant Reader* (published after
she died)

OTHER WRITERS 1900–40

CONRAD, Joseph
FAULKNER, William
FITZGERALD, F. Scott
FORSTER, E.M.
HEMINGWAY, Ernest
JOYCE, James
KAFKA, Franz
LAWRENCE, D.H.

LONDON, Jack
MANN, Thomas
ORWELL, George
PROUST, Marcel
STEINBECK, John
WHARTON, Edith
WOOLF, Virginia

SEE INDEX FOR FULL LIST

WORLD EVENTS

Age	Contemporary Events
Born 1893 	**1895** Italian physicist Guglielmo Marconi invents radio **1903** American inventors Orville and Wilbur Wright make first airplane flight **1908** Henry Ford introduces Model T car ❶
20 in 1913 	**1914–18** World War I ❷ **1917** Russian Revolution establishes Communist government **1926** British scientist John Logie Baird demonstrates television **1927** Joseph Stalin becomes dictator of Russia **1931** Empire State Building in New York City completed
40 in 1933 	**1933** Nazi Party, led by Adolf Hitler, gains control in Germany **1939–45** World War II: allies, led by U.S. and Great Britain, fight axis powers, led by Germany and Japan **1945** U.S. drops first atomic bombs on Japan **1950–53** Korean War: North Korea and China fight South Korea, the U.S., and United Nations troops ❸
60 in 1953  **Dies 1967**	**1957** Eisenhower sends troops to Little Rock, Arkansas, to ensure school desegregation **1960** John F. Kennedy elected president ❹ **1964–75** Vietnam War: war between communist North Vietnam and U.S. forces supporting South Vietnam **1967** Arabs and Israelis fight in Six Day War

© DIAGRAM

PARKER, Robert B.

American crime writer
Born Sep. 17, 1932

Robert B(rown) Parker is a highly successful crime writer best known for reviving the tradition of private detective stories during the 1970s.

Parker was born in Springfield, Massachusetts, and after graduating from Boston University, he joined the U.S. Army. He then worked in advertising until 1962, when he became a college teacher. At age 41 he published his first novel, *The Godwulf Manuscript*.

In the series of novels that followed, Parker showed his debt to RAYMOND CHANDLER, the great crime writer of the 1930s. Like Chandler, Parker writes in the **hard-boiled** tradition – that is, stories about the tough lives of people on the streets of America's big cities. Parker's hero, Spenser, is in many ways similar to Chandler's hero, Marlowe: on the surface cynical and hard, but essentially a crusader in the cause of justice; streetwise and fond of sarcastic humor, but also well read and intellectual.

Parker also adds a number of features to update the Marlowe model. Instead of being a loner like Marlowe, Spenser has a long-term girlfriend, counselor Susan Silverman. In an attempt to address modern ideas about women's equality, Parker describes the development of the relationship between Spenser and Silverman in depth. He also introduces contemporary social issues, such as drug-taking in the sports world and child abuse.

In 1989 Parker completed an unfinished novel left by Raymond Chandler, *Poodle Springs*. He followed this in 1991 with *Perchance to Dream*, a sequel to Chandler's *The Big Sleep*. His Spenser novels inspired a TV series, *Spenser for Hire*, in the 1980s.

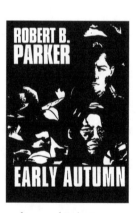

Cover for one of Parker's popular crime novels

WORKS INCLUDE

1973	*The Godwulf Manuscript*	**1984**	*Valediction*
1974	*God Save the Child*	**1989**	*Poodle Springs*
1976	*Promised Land*	**1991**	*Perchance to Dream*
1978	*The Judas Goat*	**1991**	*Pastime*
1981	*Early Autumn*	**1996**	*Chance*

OTHER CRIME AND THRILLER WRITERS

CHANDLER, Raymond
CHRISTIE, Agatha
DOYLE, Arthur Conan
GARDNER, Erle Stanley
GRAFTON, Sue
GRISHAM, John
HAMMETT, Dashiell
HIGHSMITH, Patricia

JAMES, P.D.
Le CARRÉ, John
LEONARD, Elmore
McBAIN, Ed
PARETSKY, Sara
RENDELL, Ruth
THOMPSON, Jim

SEE INDEX FOR FULL LIST

WORLD EVENTS

Age	Contemporary Events
Born 1932	**1933** Nazi Party, led by Adolf Hitler, gains control in Germany
	1939–45 World War II: allies, led by U.S. and Great Britain, fight axis powers, led by Germany and Japan
	1945 U.S. drops first atomic bombs on Japan ❶
	1950–53 Korean War: North Korea and China fight South Korea, the U.S., and United Nations troops ❷
20 in 1952	**1957** Eisenhower sends troops to Little Rock, Arkansas, to ensure school desegregation
	1960 John F. Kennedy elected president ❸
	1964–75 Vietnam War: war between communist North Vietnam and U.S. forces supporting South Vietnam ❹
	1967 Arabs and Israelis fight in Six Day War
	1969 American astronaut walks on Moon ❺
40 in 1972	**1980** Ronald Reagan elected president
	1981 U.S. launches first space shuttle ❻
	1989 Communist regimes fall throughout Eastern Europe
	1991 Gulf War: UN forces, led by U.S., defeat Iraq and free Kuwait
60 in 1992	**1992** Bill Clinton elected president
	1994 First multiracial elections in South Africa end years of white minority rule. They are won by Nelson Mandela, African National Congress leader

© DIAGRAM

203

PASTERNAK, Boris

Boris Pasternak was one of Russia's greatest 20th-century poets, but he is best known for his novel *Doctor Zhivago*.

Pasternak was born in Moscow and grew up in a cultured, artistic home. His mother was a concert pianist, his father a celebrated painter. Pasternak studied music and **philosophy**, and in 1914 aged 24 published a collection of verse, *A Twin in the Clouds*. *My Sister, Life*, his third book, established him as an important new poet.

Pasternak had supported the **Russian Revolution** but was disappointed by the brutality of the new **communist** government. His writings were more concerned with individuals and emotions than political issues, and during the 1930s he fell out of favor with the communist authorities for failing to write about socialist themes. None of his work could be published.

In 1956 Pasternak completed his great masterpiece, *Doctor Zhivago*. The novel describes in moving detail the Russian Revolution and its effects on the lives of Zhivago, a doctor and poet based on Pasternak, and his love Lara, who was modeled on Pasternak's companion, Olga Ivinskaya. The authorities refused publication, seeing the novel as anticommunist, but the manuscript was smuggled into Italy, where it was published in 1957 to worldwide acclaim. In 1958 Pasternak was awarded the **Nobel Prize** for literature. The Russian government was outraged, Ivinskaya was arrested, and Pasternak was forced to refuse the prize. He was persecuted and spent his last years in exile. *Doctor Zhivago* was finally published in Russia in 1988.

Russian poet and novelist
Born Feb. 10, 1890
Died May 30, 1960
Age at death 70

Scene from the film version of
Doctor Zhivago

WORKS INCLUDE

1914 *A Twin in the Clouds*
1917 *Above the Barriers*
1923 *My Sister, Life*
1923 *Themes and Variations*
1926 *The Year 1905*

1927 *Lieutenant Schmidt*
1931 *Spektorsky*
1932 *Second Birth*
1925 *Aerial Ways*
1957 *Doctor Zhivago*

OTHER RUSSIAN WRITERS

AKHMATOVA, Anna
BABEL, Isaac
BULGAKOV, Mikhail
CHEKHOV, Anton
DOSTOEVSKY, Fyodor
GOGOL, Nikolai
GORKY, Maksim
MANDELSTAM, Osip

PUSHKIN, Aleksandr
RATUSHINSKAYA, Irina
SHOLOKHOV, Mikhail
SOLZHENITSYN, Aleksandr
TOLSTOY, Leo
TURGENEV, Ivan

SEE INDEX FOR FULL LIST

WORLD EVENTS

Age	Contemporary Events
Born 1890 	**1895** German physicist Wilhelm K. Roentgen discovers X-rays **1895** Italian physicist Guglielmo Marconi invents radio ❶ **1903** American inventors Orville and Wilbur Wright make first airplane flight **1908** Henry Ford introduces Model T car
20 in 1910 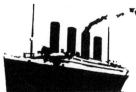	**1912** Luxury liner *Titanic* sinks ❷ **1914–18** World War I **1917** Russian Revolution establishes Communist government **1917** U.S. enters World War I ❸ **1926** British scientist John Logie Baird demonstrates television **1927** Joseph Stalin becomes dictator of Russia
40 in 1930 ❸ ❹	**1931** Empire State Building in New York City completed **1933** Nazi Party, led by Adolf Hitler, gains control in Germany **1939–45** World War II: allies, led by U.S. and Great Britain, fight axis powers, led by Germany and Japan **1945** U.S. drops first atomic bombs on Japan ❹
60 in 1950 ❺ **Dies 1960**	**1950–53** Korean War: North Korea and China fight South Korea, the U.S., and United Nations troops ❺ **1957** Eisenhower sends troops to Little Rock, Arkansas, to ensure school desegregation

© DIAGRAM

PATON, Alan

South African novelist and short-story writer
Born Jan. 11, 1903
Died Apr. 12, 1988
Age at death 85

Paton's famous novel about apartheid in South Africa

Alan Paton was one of South Africa's most important white writers. He is best known for the novel *Cry, the Beloved Country*, which has been made into a film.

Paton was born in Pietermaritzburg in the east of South Africa. Despite the black majority, white South Africans controlled the government and major industries at that time. During Paton's lifetime he witnessed the increase of white power at the expense of the rights of black people. Laws were introduced that dictated where black people could live and what work they could do.

Paton attended the University of Natal and then became a teacher. In 1935 he took over a reform school for African boys near Johannesburg in the northeast. He made many changes that improved the lives of his pupils. Then, aged 43, he wrote *Cry, the Beloved Country* while touring prisons in Europe and the U.S. The book tells of an elderly black minister's grief when he discovers his sister is a prostitute and that his son has killed a white man. It highlights the injustices of the racist **apartheid** system and brought worldwide attention to South Africa.

Following the success of *Cry, the Beloved Country* Paton began writing full time; he also became more active in politics. He campaigned for a nonracial solution to apartheid and was unpopular with the white government. His second novel, *Too Late the Phalarope*, which was banned, is about a white man who is destroyed because of his affair with a black girl. His short stories *Tales from a Troubled Land* and the novel *Ah, But Your Land Is Beautiful* are on the same racial theme.

WORKS INCLUDE

1948 *Cry, the Beloved Country*
1953 *Too Late the Phalarope*
1958 *Hope for South Africa*
1967 *Tales from a Troubled Land*
1967 *The Long View*

1980 *Towards the Mountain*
1981 *Ah, But Your Land Is Beautiful*

OTHER AFRICAN WRITERS

ACHEBE, Chinua
CLARK-BEKEDEREMO, John Pepper
COETZEE, J.M.
FUGARD, Athol
GORDIMER, Nadine
HEAD, Bessie
MAHFOUZ, Naguib
NETO, Agostinho

NGUGI wa Thiong'o
NWAPA, Flora
OKRI, Ben
ROBERT, Shaaban
SENGHOR, Léopold Sédar
SOYINKA, Wole

SEE INDEX FOR FULL LIST

WORLD EVENTS

Age	Contemporary Events
Born 1903 	**1903** American inventors Orville and Wilbur Wright make first airplane flight **1908** Henry Ford introduces Model T car **1914–18** World War I ❶ **1917** Russian Revolution establishes Communist government
20 in 1923 	**1927** Joseph Stalin becomes dictator of Russia **1933** Nazi Party, led by Adolf Hitler, gains control in Germany **1939–45** World War II: allies, led by U.S. and Great Britain, fight axis powers, led by Germany and Japan ❷
40 in 1943 	**1945** U.S. drops first atomic bombs on Japan **1950–53** Korean War: North Korea and China fight South Korea, the U.S., and United Nations troops **1957** Eisenhower sends troops to Little Rock, Arkansas, to ensure school desegregation **1960** John F. Kennedy elected president ❸
60 in 1963 	**1964–75** Vietnam War: war between communist North Vietnam and U.S. forces supporting South Vietnam ❹ **1967** Arabs and Israelis fight in Six Day War **1969** American astronaut walks on Moon ❺ **1981** U.S. launches first space shuttle
80 in 1983 **Dies 1988**	**1987** Gorbachev begins reforms in USSR: perestroika (restructuring) and glasnost (openness)

© DIAGRAM

GLOSSARY

allegory a work in which characters, events, or situations stand for more important spiritual or moral ideas. For example, a story about a fight between an outlaw and a sheriff could be an allegory for the fight between good and evil. **allegorical** – adjective.

American Civil War (1861–65) a war between Northern (Union) states and Southern (Confederate) states. One of the main disputes was over slavery – the South wanted to continue using slaves, while the North believed the practice should be stopped. The North won, and slavery was made illegal throughout the U.S.

American Revolution (1775–83) a war, also called the American War of Independence, between Great Britain and the 13 British colonies in North America. The victorious colonies formed the U.S.

anarchism the belief that there should be no laws or governments and that people should live in voluntarily organized communities. **anarchist** – noun.

ancient Greece the civilization that grew on the islands and mainland of modern-day Greece and Turkey from around 2000 BC to 300 BC. Ancient Greece is often considered the birthplace of Western civilization. **ancient Greek** – adjective.

apartheid a policy of the white minority South African government that kept South Africans strictly separated by race and resulted in great hardship and injustice for the majority of the population. Although in force from 1948 to 1991, racist policies had been in use for many years before 1948.

autobiographical a work that is inspired by the author's own life. For example, a book written by an ex-policeman about a fictional policeman who has experiences very similar to his own is autobiographical.

autobiography a work in which the author tells the story of his or her own life.

ballad a poem that tells a simple story. Ballads are one of the earliest forms of poem. Originally they were sung and usually rhymed (see **poem**, **rhyme**).

beat generation a group of American authors writing in the 1950s who rejected the restrictive conventions of "normal" American society and experimented with drug taking, Asian religions, and sexual freedom. The "beats" or "beatniks," as they came to be called, had a strong influence on the development of youth culture in the 1960s and are admired today for their experimental approach to literature (see **experimental**).

Biafran War (1967–70) civil war in Nigeria, West Africa. The eastern region of the country tried to break away and form an independent state called Biafra. After bitter fighting, Biafra rejoined Nigeria.

biography the story of a person's life written by somebody (the **biographer**) other than that person.

blank verse poetry in which lines do not rhyme with each other (see **rhyme**).

Bloomsbury Group an influential group of British and American writers who met in the Bloomsbury area of London, England, from about 1905 to 1930. They included many leading literary figures of the period who were in revolt against the restrictions of Victorian society (see **experimental**, **Victorian**).

Boer War (1899–1902) a war fought in what is now South Africa between the British and the Boers (or Afrikaners, descendants of Dutch settlers). After a bitter struggle the Boers were forced to surrender and accept British rule.

capitalism a political and economic system based on the belief that individuals and businesses should be free to own and trade the resources used to produce goods and services. These resources include land, natural resources such as oil, and capital – such as buildings, equipment, and money (see **communism**).

chronicle a story that recounts a history of events in the correct date order.

civil rights movement a popular movement to end racist discrimination against African Americans in the U.S. Beginning in the 1800s, it reached its height in the 1950s and '60s, when mass demonstrations and campaigns of civil disobedience forced the government to pass laws ending discrimination. Martin Luther King, Jr., was a leading figure of the movement in the 1960s.

Civil War (see **American Civil War**).

classical from either ancient Greece or Rome (see **ancient Greece**, **Rome**).

Cold War a long period of hostility between groups of communist and noncommunist states from the end of World War II in 1945 until the early 1990s. Russia (then the Soviet Union) led the communist nations, while the United States was the most powerful noncommunist state. Although fighting never actually broke out, both sides built up huge stockpiles of nuclear and other weapons in case of an attack, and there was a constant threat of war. The Cold War ended when many communist governments collapsed in the late 1980s and early 1990s (see **communism**, **World War II**).

comedy of manners a humorous style of drama that makes fun of social customs or manners, most often of the upper and middle classes. Comedies of manners were very popular in late 17th-century England but also appear in the literature of many other periods and cultures.

communism a political, social, and economic system developed from the writings of the German philosopher Karl Marx (1818–83). The goal of communism is to create a world in which everybody has equal wealth and social status. The basic means of production, such as factories and machines, are owned and controlled by the government rather than privately as under capitalism. Communism became an extremely influential idea in the first half of the 20th century, and in many countries revolutionaries overthrew their governments and established communist states. Russia and China were the most powerful communist states. Corruption, poor economic performance, and a lack of personal freedom led to the collapse of many communist governments in the late 1980s and early 1990s (see **capitalism**, **Cold War**, **Russian Revolution**). **communist** – noun, adjective.

conservative opposed to change and in favor of defending traditional values, institutions, and customs.

crime story a work in which criminals or the solving of a crime are the main elements of the plot (see **plot**).

critic a person whose job it is to make judgments on works of literature or drama.

elegy a serious poem with a sad tone, often in memory of a dead person.

English Civil War (1642–51) a war fought in England between supporters of King Charles I (Royalists) and supporters of the English parliament (Parliamentarians) led by Oliver Cromwell. The king was defeated

and executed, and England became a
republic ruled by Cromwell. After
Cromwell's death the monarchy was
restored, in 1660, with Charles II as king.

epic a long work, usually a poem, that
follows the adventures of one or more
heroic figures or that deals with events of
historical or legendary importance. Ancient
epics tell the stories of mythical figures
and often involve gods, monsters, and
impossible feats of strength or skill. Today
an epic may follow a personal journey
through the perils of the modern world.

essay a short prose work in which the
author (the **essayist**) expresses his or her
opinions about a subject (see **prose**).

experimental literature in which
writers have attempted to find new ways
of expressing themselves (see **free
verse**, **magic realism**, **stream-of-
consciousness**, **theater of the absurd**).

fable a short tale that is meant to teach the
reader something about life. Often one or
more of the characters is an animal, plant,
or nonhuman thing that acts and speaks
like a person (see **folklore**, **moral**).

fantasy a work in which characters and
events are not only fictional but are very
unlikely to ever exist in the real world.

fascism an undemocratic form of
government that aims to create a strong,
highly organized, and unified nation.
Fascist governments are usually led by a
powerful dictator and have total control
over all economic, political, and social
institutions. They are often based on the
belief that a particular racial or social
group is superior to others. Property can
be privately owned, but personal freedom
is often restricted. Fascist governments
ruled Italy under Benito Mussolini from
1922 to 1943 and Germany from 1933 to
1945 under Adolf Hitler (see **Nazi**, **World
War II**). **fascist** – noun, adjective.

feminism the belief that women should
have equal opportunities as men in all
economic, political, and social matters.
Also, the movement that aims to achieve
these goals (see **women's movement**).
feminist – noun, adjective.

fiction a work based entirely or mostly on
invented characters and events.

folklore the beliefs, customs, stories,
and traditions passed down through the
generations of a community. Folklore was
the main source of knowledge throughout
much of history before most people could
read and write. Literature often draws on
ideas and stories from folklore.

free verse poetry in which there is no
attempt to rhyme lines with each other or
to stick to a constant rhythm. This style of
poetry first became important in the 19th
century, when writers began to abandon
the traditional rules of poetry writing (see
experimental, **rhyme**, **rhythm**).

French Revolution (1789–99) a violent
popular uprising in which the French king
Louis XVI was overthrown and France
became a republic. The king, other
aristocrats, and many of the revolutionaries
themselves were executed during this
period of instability. The revolution came
to an end in 1799, when the military leader
Napoleon Bonaparte seized power.

genre a style of writing or group of works
that shares the same subject matter, setting,
or ideas (see **crime story**, **fantasy**,
gothic, **magic realism**, **science fiction**).

gothic a style of writing that deals with
spooky and unnatural events, often set in
wild, untamed landscapes or among
ancient ruins. Gothic literature reached
its height in Europe in the 1790s.

Great Depression a worldwide economic
slump in the 1930s. It began in the United
States in 1929, when the Wall Street Crash

wiped out the value of stocks and shares. Banks, factories, and shops closed, leaving millions jobless. The Great Depression affected world trade and brought unemployment, poverty, and starvation to countries all over the world.

hard-boiled a style of crime writing that treats violence, corruption, and the realities of city life without sentimentality.

Harlem Renaissance a flowering of African-American art and literature during the 1920s centered on the Harlem district of New York City. The work of this period promoted pride in black culture and explored the history of the African-American experience.

Holocaust the murder of 6 million Jews and thousands of gypsies, Poles, and Slavs by German Nazis during World War II. The Nazis wanted to wipe out the entire Jewish population of Europe – they rounded up all the Jews and other ethnic groups from areas occupied by the German Army and sent them to concentration camps, where they were executed, starved, or worked to death (see **Nazi**, **World War II**).

humanism an intellectual movement that developed in 14th-century Europe. Inspired by newly discovered ancient Greek and Roman works, humanists celebrated human achievement and took a new interest in understanding the natural world. Humanism emphasizes progress, tolerance, and reason, and it was one of the factors that led to the Renaissance in Europe (see **ancient Greek**, **Renaissance**, **Rome**). **humanist** – noun, adjective.

irony a form of humor in which what occurs is the opposite of what might be expected. An example of irony is when the intended meaning of words used is the exact opposite to their usual meaning; for instance, calling a stupid idea "clever." Irony can also occur in a book or play when what a character thinks is the truth contrasts with what the audience or reader knows to be the truth. **ironic** – adjective.

lay a short story-poem originally meant to be sung. Tales from folklore are often in the form of lays (see **folklore**).

lyric a style of poetry or prose writing mainly expressing the author's emotions and feelings (see **elegy**, **ode**, **poem**, **prose**, **sonnet**). **lyrical** – adjective.

magic realism a style of fiction in which the author includes fantastic or magical events or characters as if they were an everyday part of the real world.

McCarthy Era a period of suspicion and fear in the early 1950s when powerful American senator Joseph McCarthy attempted to show that communists who wanted to destroy the U.S. held important posts in government and other institutions. The investigations led by McCarthy were dubbed witch hunts since they tried to fix guilt on people without any evidence. Many writers who were accused of being communists lost their careers or were imprisoned or forced to leave the country (see **communism**).

Middle Ages the period of European history between about 500 and c. 1450. **medieval** – adjective.

moral a lesson taught in a work of literature, usually about how to live or what is right or wrong (see **fable**, **folklore**).

Napoleonic Wars a series of wars fought by the French military leader Napoleon Bonaparte. Napoleon conquered most of Europe between 1799 and 1812 before being defeated by an alliance of European powers at the Battle of Waterloo in 1815.

Nazi the name of the political party, and any of its members, that was led by Adolf Hitler. The Nazi Party ruled Germany from 1933 until the end of World War II

© DIAGRAM

211

in 1945. The Nazis established a fascist government that emphasized national unity, military strength, and a belief in the superiority of the German people (see **fascism**, **Holocaust**, **World War II**). **Nazism** – noun.

Nobel Prize internationally recognized award for outstanding contributions to many fields, including literature. Founded by the wealthy Swedish inventor Alfred Nobel (1833–96), prizes have been awarded every year since 1901.

novel a long fictional story written in prose. Probably the most popular form of literature today, the novel was developed in Europe in the 18th century. Early novels often took the form of a series of letters written by the characters in which they describe the unfolding events of the story. Traditionally novels have one, long, continuous story, or plot, involving several characters and spanning a specific period of time. In the 20th century many authors began to experiment with new ways of writing novels that ignore these rules (see **experimental**, **plot**, **prose**).

ode a lyrical poem usually in praise of a particular thing or person (see **ancient Greece**, **lyric**).

pastoral a work of literature that has rural life as its main theme is said to be pastoral.

pen name a name used by an author to publish under instead of their real name. Famous pen names include LEWIS CARROLL, GEORGE ELIOT, and MARK TWAIN.

philosophy the study of the most basic ideas that concern humanity. Issues studied by philosophers include what is truth?, what does it mean to exist?, and what is right or wrong? **philosopher** – practitioner. **philosophical** – adjective.

play a work that is supposed to be performed by one or more actors in front of an audience. Usually a play consists almost entirely of dialogue between the characters, although the writer may include specific directions to the actors or instructions about the appearance of the stage or costumes. Plays are one of the oldest forms of literature since they do not rely on the audience being able to read.

plot the unfolding of events that comprise the central story in a work of literature.

poem a work in which the words used are carefully selected and arranged to suggest meanings and associations beyond their literal meanings. Techniques such as rhyme, allegory, and the use of a regular rhythm are common. There are many traditional forms of poems, including ballads and epics, which tend to have particular subject matters or forms. Modern poets have experimented with many new ways of writing poems, such as the use of blank verse, and have extended the range of subject matter to include just about anything (see **allegory**, **ballad**, **blank verse**, **elegy**, **epic**, **free verse**, **lyric**, **ode**, **rhyme**, **rhythm**, **sonnet**, **verse**).

Poet Laureate person appointed to act as the official poet of a state or nation. He or she is expected to write formal poems in honor of special occasions.

prose the ordinary form of written language without the use of deliberate rhyme or rhythm (see **essay**, **novel**, **short story**, **rhyme**, **rhythm**).

psychoanalysis a method of studying and treating the mind founded by the Austrian doctor Sigmund Freud (1856–1939). Freud was the first to theorize that the mind has a hidden, unconscious part that is the source of our desires and fears and which influences our conscious behavior. **psychoanalyst** – practitioner.

Pulitzer Prize annual American award for excellence in several fields, including poetry, drama, and fiction. Founded by Hungarian immigrant and wealthy newspaper publisher Joseph Pulitzer (1847–1911).

pun a "play on words": a humorous use of words that sound the same or similar but have different meanings.

Puritanism a strict form of Christianity that flourished in England during the 16th and 17th centuries. The Puritans wanted to reform the Church of England; after the English Civil War, while the country was ruled by Oliver Cromwell, they were able to realize many of their aims. When the monarchy was restored, however, the Puritans were discriminated against. As a result many traveled to America in search of religious freedom. Many aboard the *Mayflower*, the ship that brought the Pilgrim Fathers to America, were Puritans (see **English Civil War**). **Puritan** – noun, adjective. **puritanical** – adjective.

realism a style of writing that tries to accurately depict characters, events, and settings as they appear in the real world. It became popular in the last half of the 19th century (see **realist**).

realist an author who uses realism in his or her works. Realist writers rejected traditional literature, which tended to concentrate on the stories of exceptional characters such as aristocrats, criminals, or heroes, and wrote instead about the lives of ordinary people (see **realism**).

Renaissance a period of great artistic and scholarly achievement in Europe that marked the end of the Middle Ages and the beginning of the modern period. The Renaissance began in Italy in the 14th century and spread to the rest of Europe, coming to an end in the 17th century. It was sparked by the study of ancient Greek and Roman works that had been unread for centuries (see **ancient Greece**, **humanism**, **Middle Ages**, **Rome**).

Restoration Drama plays written in the period immediately after the restoration of the English monarchy to the throne in 1660. This was a time of great freedom and creativity in the English theater (see **English Civil War**).

rhyme words that end with the same or similar sounds are said to rhyme. Lines of poetry are made to rhyme by having the last word in each line end with the same sound. In some poems every other line rhymes, and many other patterns of rhyming can be used. Lines can even be made to rhyme internally (see **blank verse**, **free verse**).

rhythm the pattern of stressed syllables in a poem – similar to the beat of a piece of music (see **syllable**).

Romanticism an artistic and literary style that emphasizes passion rather than reason, imagination rather than reality, and chaos and action rather than restraint and order. Romanticism became very popular in European literature between about 1770 and 1850. In Romantic literature themes often include strong emotions such as love or revenge, and characters often struggle for freedom. **Romantic** – adjective.

Rome the ancient civilization that began in the Italian city of Rome around 700 BC and had conquered the Mediterranean region and most of western Europe by about 200 AD. The Roman Empire brought order and civilization to Europe for the first time; many Roman institutions and laws form the basis of modern Western civilization. **Roman** – noun, adjective.

Russian Revolution (1917) violent popular uprising in which Czar Nicholas II (the Russian emperor) was overthrown and a communist government established (see **communism**).

saga a story that follows a group of related characters over a long period of time or any long story of adventure or heroic deeds.

© DIAGRAM

satire a work, or the art of writing such works, in which false beliefs, injustices, human behavior, or corruption are pointed out by the use of humor (such as irony), and those guilty of them are made to look foolish. Satire is often used by writers to mock politicians, governments, or whole political systems (see **irony**). **satirical** – adjective. **satirist** – noun. **satirize** – verb.

science fiction a genre of literature in which the author describes great changes brought about by imagined scientific or technological advances (see **genre**).

screenplay the story and dialogue (written by a **screenwriter**) used in the making of a movie or TV program.

short story a short, fictional prose work that tells a complete story or recounts an incident in a simple and direct way, often illustrating an idea or theme (see **prose**).

sonnet a poem with 14 lines and strict rules about the number of syllables per line and the pattern in which the lines rhyme with each other (see **poem**, **rhyme**, **syllable**).

Spanish Civil War (1936–39) a war fought in Spain between fascist forces led by General Francisco Franco and an alliance of communists and other left-wing, antifascist groups. The fascists were supported by Germany and Italy and opposed by International Brigades – units formed by foreign volunteers. Many European and American writers and journalists witnessed or even fought in the war. The fascists' eventual victory led many to fear for the future of Europe (see **fascism**, **Nazi**).

Spanish-American War (1898) a brief war fought between the United States and Spain over the issue of independence for Cuba, then a Spanish colony. Total U.S. victory secured independence for Cuba, while other Spanish colonies, Guam,

Puerto Rico, and the Philippines, became U.S. possessions.

Stalin (1879–1953) communist leader of Russia (then the Soviet Union) from 1929 to 1953. Joseph Stalin was a ruthless and feared dictator; millions of Russians starved because of his harsh economic policies, and millions more were executed or worked to death as enemies of the state. Stalin led Russia to victory in World War II and was the most feared Russian leader of the Cold War (see **Cold War**, **communism**, **World War II**).

stereotype an idea about a person, group, or place that is fixed in the popular imagination. Often a stereotype is negative, incorrect, and insulting. An example is the portrayal of Native Americans as primitives or savages in Western movies.

stream-of-consciousness a style of writing in which the author tries to make it seem to readers that they are sharing in the unspoken thoughts and feelings of the characters.

surrealism a literary and artistic movement that began in Europe in the 1920s and which makes use of dream images and the mentioning or placing of objects in unexpected contexts. **surrealist** – noun. **surrealistic** – adjective.

syllable a word or part of a word that forms one unit of sound when spoken.

theater of the absurd a style of drama that was developed in Europe and America in the 1950s and '60s in which ridiculous or pointless situations are used to express fears about the meaninglessness of human existence.

tragedy a serious work of literature, often a play, in which the downfall of a central character, group, or idea is followed. Tragedy was invented by ancient Greek writers and has been one of the most important forms of theater ever since (see **ancient Greece**). **tragic** – adjective.

trilogy a work in three parts.

verse a general name for poetry or a single, distinct section of a poem (see **blank verse**, **free verse**, **poem**).

Victorian from the period of the reign (1837–1901) of Britain's Queen Victoria. Victoria ruled during a period when Britain was the world's greatest military and industrial power – many important British writers lived during this time.

Vietnam War (1957–75) long-running conflict between the then independent states of North and South Vietnam. The U.S. feared that North Vietnam, a communist state, would overrun South Vietnam and that this would in turn lead to other states in the area becoming communist. U.S. troops began to take an active part in the war from 1965. By the late 1960s American public opinion had turned against the war, eventually forcing a complete withdrawal of U.S. troops in 1973. North Vietnam conquered the South in 1975, and Vietnam became a unified communist state (see **communism**).

Western a story set in the west of the U.S. during the period when white people were first settling there during the 18th and 19th centuries.

women's movement the effort by women, sometimes in highly organized groups, sometimes as loosely connected individuals, to achieve a better social, economic, and political status for all women. The women's movement has achieved many advances, including votes for women and equal rights legislation in many countries. In the 1960s and '70s it was very active in Western countries, challenging narrow views about women's roles and increasing the pressure for change (see **feminism**).

World War I (1914–18) a hugely destructive conflict fought mostly on European soil between the then most powerful nations in the world. It began when the assassination of the heir to the throne of Austria-Hungary drew the major powers into conflict with one another through a system of alliances that had been set up to keep the peace. The Central Powers included Austria-Hungary, Germany, and the Ottoman (Turkish) Empire. They were opposed by the Allies, including the British Empire, France, Russia, and the U.S. Millions of soldiers died as the fighting became bogged down, with neither side able to penetrate the other's defenses. The eventual Allied victory was due to the arrival of U.S. troops in the last year of the war and the collapse of the German economy.

World War II (1939–45) the most terrible and destructive conflict in history. Fought mainly in Europe, East Asia, and North Africa, it involved every major power, cost tens of millions of lives, and caused widespread destruction. The war began in Europe when Nazi Germany and its allies Austria and Italy swept across Europe in an attempt to conquer the entire continent. By 1941 the conflict was global. A surprise attack by Japan (an ally of Germany) on the U.S. naval base at Pearl Harbor brought America into the war in 1941. British, U.S., and other forces invaded occupied Europe in 1944 and pushed the Germans back while Russian forces attacked from the east, eventually forcing a total German defeat. Japan was only defeated after a bloody campaign by U.S. forces in the South Pacific and the first use of atomic weapons on the Japanese cities of Hiroshima and Nagasaki. The end of the war saw Europe in ruins, the U.S. established as the leading world power – opposed only by communist Russia – and Germany divided into two separate countries (communist East Germany and noncommunist West Germany) until 1990 (see **communism**, **Nazi**, **Stalin**).

INDEX

Bold numbers indicate volumes; regular numbers indicate pages within that volume. *Italics* show book titles; smaller works appear in quotes. Authors' names appear not only as separate listings but under headings that indicate region, period, and kind of work: William Shakespeare, for example, appears by name under **S**, by region under **BRITISH AND IRISH WRITERS**, by period under **SIXTEENTH-CENTURY WRITERS**, and by kind of work under both **PLAYWRIGHTS** and **POETS**.

C

F

G

H

© DIAGRAM

N

O

© DIAGRAM

U

V

W

Y

Z

ART & PICTURE CREDITS

PICTURE SOURCES

PUBLISHERS

Abacus; Allison & Busby; Arrow Books; Breyten Breytenbach and J.M. Meulenhoff; Carcanet Press; Century; Chatto & Windus; Chivers Press; Constable and Co.; Deutsch, Andre; Doubleday; Faber and Faber; Fourth Estate; Grove; Hamish Hamilton; HarperCollins Publishers; Heinemann; Hodder and Stoughton; Houghton Mifflin Company; Hutchinson; International Thomson Publishing Services; Jonathan Cape; John Murray; Knopf, Alfred A.; Larousse; Little, Brown and Company; Longman Group; Macmillan; McClelland & Stewart; No Exit Press; Norton and Co., W.W.; Orion Publishing Group, The; Otto Preminger Films; Oxford University Press; Penguin Books; Picador; Puffin Books; Putnam and Grosset Group, The; Random House; Robson Books; Secker & Warburg; St. Martin's Press; Suhrkamp Verlag; Tuttle and Co., Charles E.; Victor Gollancz; Vintage Books; Virago Press; Virgin Publishing; Weidenfeld and Nicolson; Wiley & Sons, John; Women's Press, The; Wylie Agency, The; Zed Books

COVER AND ILLUSTRATION CREDITS

A IS FOR ALIBI by Sue Grafton, Macmillan UK; A LITTLE YELLOW DOG by Walter Mosley, Picador; A PERFECT PEACE by Amos Oz, Chatto & Windus; A TIDEWATER MORNING by William Styron, Jonathan Cape; BABEL TOWER by A.S. Byatt, Chatto & Windus; BULLET PARK by John Cheever, Jonathan Cape; COCKPIT by Jerzy Kosinski, Hutchinson; GOLDFINGER by Ian Fleming, Jonathan Cape; GREEN EGGS AND HAM © Theodor Seuss Geisel 1960; HEART SONGS by E. Annie Proulx, Fourth Estate; KIMAKO'S STORY by June Jordan, Houghton Mifflin Company; LAUGHING BOY by Oliver La Farge, Houghton Mifflin Company; LOWLY WORM'S SCHOOLBAG © Richard Scarry 1987; MARYA, A LIFE by Joyce Carol Oates, Jonathan Cape; MR PALOMAR by Italo Calvino, Martin Secker & Warburg; MY UNCLE SILAS by H.E. Bates, Jonathan Cape; NOW WE ARE SIX by A.A. Milne, illustration by Ernest Shepard, Curtis Brown; OLD POSSUM'S BOOK OF PRACTICAL CATS by T.S. Eliot, illustration by Nicolas Bentley, Faber & Faber; SELECTED POEMS by Galway Kinnell, Houghton Mifflin Company; THE ANASTASIA SYNDROME by Mary Higgins Clark, Century; THE BLUE HAMMER by Ross Macdonald, Allison & Busby; THE COLOR PURPLE by Alice Walker, The Women's Press; THE EMPTY CANVAS by Alberto Moravia, Martin Secker & Warburg; THE FAMISHED ROAD by Ben Okri, Jonathan Cape; THE IPCRESS FILE by Len Deighton, Jonathan Cape; THE PROFESSOR OF DESIRE by Philip Roth, Jonathan Cape; THE RETURN OF THE KING by J.R.R. Tolkien, Houghton Mifflin Company; WHERE THE WILD THINGS ARE © Maurice Sendak 1963; WHIRLIGIG by Ernest Buckler, McClelland & Stewart

Every effort has been made to locate the copyright owners of the examples within this work. Should a publisher recognize a picture they own can they please send proof of ownership, and, should it be required, a full credit will be published in a later edition.

INFORMATION SOURCES

British Library, London; Columbia University; London Public Libraries; Mid-Manhattan Library Picture Collection, New York; Museum of Childhood, London; New York Public Library; Nobel Prize Foundation; Pulitzer Prize Foundation; Schomburg Center for Research in Black Culture; School of Oriental and African Studies, University of London; University of London